Second Edition

Spanish AS and A2

ánimo

Grammar Workbook

Carolyn Burch

OXFORD
UNIVERSITY PRESS

OXFORD
UNIVERSITY PRESS

Great Clarendon Street, Oxford OX2 6DP

Oxford New York

Auckland Bangkok Buenos Aires Cape Town Chennai
Dar es Salaam Delhi Hong Kong Istanbul Karachi Kolkata
Kuala Lumpur Madrid Melbourne Mexico City Mumbai Nairobi
São Paulo Shanghai Taipei Tokyo Toronto

Oxford is a registered trade mark of Oxford University Press
in the UK and certain other countries

British Library Cataloguing in Publication Data

Data available

ISBN 13 978 019 915323 7

10 9 8 7

Typeset by Thomson Digital

Printed by Ashford Colour Press Ltd

The author and publisher would like to thank Victoria Zaragoza (editor)
and Blanca González (language consultant)

Contents

Introduction

This *Ánimo Grammar Workbook* is intended to supplement *Ánimo 1 and 2* in order to strengthen your grasp of the Spanish language and improve your accuracy. Working though the tasks in this book will help you to increase your level of performance in written Spanish and will also boost your fluency in spoken Spanish. By reinforcing your familiarity with Spanish language patterns it should also improve your reading and listening comprehension skills.

As you will see from the contents page, the majority of the book covers points required for AS Spanish. The few points that are additional requirements for A2 only are covered towards the end of the book.

Each section of the book is followed by revision pages, and at the end there is a revision section covering all the major points of the book.

There are various ways in which you could use the tasks in this book:

◆ to assess your strengths in a particular area
◆ to practise a particular grammar point alongside the work you are doing in class on that aspect of the language, especially if you find it is an aspect on which you need to do more work
◆ to revise key language points before a test or examination (for this you may choose to use the revision sections of the book).

On each main grammar point, there is always at least one task in which you are simply required to recognize and understand the meaning of some Spanish which includes examples of that particular point. You then move on to tasks that require you to produce some accurate Spanish.

The answers to the tasks (with a few exceptions in the case of tasks where you have a more open-ended choice of how to respond) are provided in a separate booklet.

Nouns and determiners

Gender

> ### Reminder
> ◆ All nouns in Spanish are either masculine or feminine. The ending of a noun often indicates its likely gender, as shown in the table of typical masculine and feminine endings below.

masculine endings	main exceptions
-o	la mano, la foto(grafía), la moto(cicleta)
-e	la calle, la carne, la clase, la fe, la fiebre, la frase, la fuente, la gente, la leche, la llave, la muerte, la nieve, la noche, la nube, la parte, la sangre, la suerte, la tarde, la torre
-i	la bici(cleta)
-l	la sal, la señal
-r	la flor
-u	la tribu
-y	la ley
feminine endings	**main exceptions**
-a	el día, el mapa, el planeta, and most nouns ending in -ma: el tema, el problema
-ción, -sión and most other nouns ending in -ión	el avión, el camión
-dad, -tad, -tud	
-dez	
-ed	el césped
-ie	el pie
-itis	
-iz	el lápiz
-sis	el análisis, el énfasis, el paréntesis
-umbre	

A Look at the list of noun endings typical for each gender. Add two more examples for each ending. Check the gender in a dictionary to make sure it's not one of the exceptions!

Typical masculine endings

1 -o   el aeropuerto,
el _____, el _____

2 -e   el medio ambiente
el _____, el _____

3 -l   el fútbol,
el _____, el _____

4 -r   el mirador,
el _____, el _____

Typical feminine endings

5 -a   la casa,
la _____, la _____

6 -ción, -sión   la función,
la _____, la _____

> ### Reminder
> ◆ *El* is used instead of *la* in front of feminine nouns beginning with a stressed *a* or *h*, e.g. *el agua*.

B Check the genders of these common nouns in a dictionary and fill in *el* or *la* as appropriate.

1	_____ leche	**7**	_____ cantidad
2	_____ institución	**8**	_____ problema
3	_____ funicular	**9**	_____ víctima
4	_____ gente	**10**	_____ león
5	_____ persona	**11**	_____ costumbre
6	_____ clima	**12**	_____ idioma

> ### Reminder
> ◆ Nouns referring to people (jobs, nationalities, etc.) usually have a masculine and a feminine form.

C Give the feminine form of the following nouns. Not all will change their ending; if in doubt, check the feminine form in a dictionary.

1 maquinista   _____
2 portugués   _____
3 fundador   _____
4 estudiante   _____
5 madrileño   _____
6 profesor   _____
7 joven   _____
8 enfermero   _____
9 americano   _____
10 turista   _____

Singular and plural nouns

Reminder

- Nouns ending in an unstressed vowel or stressed *é*
  or *á* add *-s* to make the plural. Those ending in a
  stressed vowel or a consonant add *-es*. Those with
  an accent on the final syllable lose it in the plural.

A Complete the chart. Check in a dictionary as the list
includes some exceptions.

	singular	plural
1	la mano	
2	el anuncio	
3	el café	
4	el inglés	
5	el sofá	
6	la revolución	
7	el rey	
8	la cabeza	
9	la comunidad	
10	el ordenador	

Reminder

- Nouns ending in *-z* exchange the *-z* for *-ces*.
  Nouns with a final unstressed syllable ending in *-s*
  do not change in the plural.

B Give the plural.
1 la luz   las _____
2 el lunes   los _____
3 la voz   las _____

4 el autobús   los _____
5 el andaluz   los _____

Reminder

- Occasionally Spanish uses a singular noun where
  English uses a plural, or the other way round.

C Use a dictionary to complete the following
sentences.
1 Ha puesto (clothes) _____ en la maleta.
2 Estuve horas esperando para pasar por
   (customs)_____
3 Este año voy de (holiday) _____ a
   Salamanca.
4 Nuestro profesor de alemán siempre nos da
   (homework) _____.

D Complete this paragraph using plural forms of the
nouns in the box.

En mi ciudad, casi todas las (**1**) _____ van
de (**2**) _____ a los (**3**) _____
porque es más fácil y en el parking hay lugar para
(**4**) _____ de (**5**) _____. Pero yo
prefiero los (**6**) _____: me gusta mucho
ver los (**7**) _____ de las (**8**) _____
y de las (**9**) _____, y oír las
(**10**) _____ de los (**11**) _____.

ciento	mercado	color	coche	vendedor
	fruta	supermercado	verdura	
		compra	familia	voz	

Suffixes

Reminder

- Suffixes are endings added to nouns (and occasionally
  adjectives) to put a particular emphasis on their
  meaning.

  Diminutive suffixes (*-ito/-ita, -illo/-illa*) imply 'little'.
  Augmentative suffixes (*-ón/ona, -azo/aza, -ote/ota*)
  imply 'big'.
  Pejorative suffixes (*-ucho/ucha, -acho/-acha, -uzo/
  -uza, -uco/-aca, -(z)uelo/-(z)uela*) imply 'worse'.
  Some suffixed nouns have come to have a meaning
  of their own, e.g. *palabrota* (swear word).

A Match the nouns on the left with their meanings on
the right, drawing a linking line between each pair.
1 hombretón   a little while
2 gripazo   a huge door
3 chiquilla   a short little chap
4 perrito   a little bell
5 ratito   a nasty bout of the flu
6 campanilla   a hefty bloke
7 bajito   a very small girl
8 portón   a little dog

Definite and indefinite articles

A Decide whether the definite or the indefinite article makes sense in these sentences and fill in the correct word each time (*el, la, los, las, un, una, unos* or *unas*).

1 En ____ centro de Madrid hay demasiado tráfico.

2 Tengo ____ amigos en España.

3 En mi ciudad hay ____ tiendas y ____ campo de fútbol, pero no hay ____ piscina.

4 Sevilla es ____ ciudad muy histórica con ____ monumentos fantásticos.

5 Tengo ____ tío en Málaga, y tengo ____ primos en ____ Islas Canarias: ¡es ideal para ____ vacaciones!

6 Sierra Nevada está en ____ sur de España, y ____ Picos de Europa están en ____ noroeste.

7 En Andalucía ____ toreros son tan famosos como ____ futbolistas.

8 En ____ Pirineos se pueden ver ____ aves magníficas.

9 A ____ turistas alemanes les gustan ____ playas españolas.

10 Ayer por ____ tarde tuvo lugar ____ accidente de tráfico en ____ centro de Santiago, enfrente de ____ catedral. ____ motociclista que estaba doblando a ____ izquierda chocó contra ____ autocar que estaba dejando ____ peregrinos irlandeses. ____ peregrinos no resultaron heridos, pero ____ motociclista sufrió ____ fracturas en ____ mano y en ____ rodilla.

B Translate into Spanish.

1 Pablo is a dentist.

2 Conchita hopes to become a teacher.

3 My brother is an engineer and my sister is a student.

4 I'd like to be a translator.

5 His dream is to be a tennis player.

C Underline the articles in these sentences, then translate the sentences into good English.

1 Los zapatos de Manolo Blahnik son muy caros.

2 La vida en Madrid es muy interesante.

3 ¿Cuál es tu opinión – es importante mantener las costumbres regionales, o no?

4 El vino español es menos caro que el vino francés.

5 Me gustan mucho las tapas y la cerveza española.

D Translate these sentences into Spanish, paying particular attention to whether or not you need to include articles.

1 Venezuela is a beautiful country.

2 Chilean enchiladas are delicious.

3 I'd like to become a journalist, but probably I'll become a secretary!

4 German cars are popular in all of Europe, but Spanish cars are less expensive.

5 Most traditional Andalucian houses are white.

6 He likes sports, especially basketball and pelota.

7 My father is a plumber and my brother is a nurse.

8 He has hurt his head and his hand – he's in a bad mood!

9 I don't like big cities very much but I do love pretty little towns.

10 She is allergic to mussels so she doesn't eat paella.

Nouns and determiners

Reminder
- *Lo* is used with an adjective to form an abstract noun.

E Translate the following sentences into English.

1 Lo bueno es que en nuestra región tenemos un clima excepcional. Lo malo es que en verano, ¡hay demasiada gente!

_____

_____

2 Lo bueno es que la construcción da mucho empleo. Lo malo es que ahora tenemos muchos apartamentos de vacaciones que no se venden.

_____

3 Lo bueno es que por aquí hay campos de golf muy bonitos. Lo malo es que para mantener los hermosos, se necesitan cantidades enormes de agua.

_____

Reminder
- *De + el* contracts to *del*, and *a + el* contracts to *al*.

F Complete the following phrases using *al* or *del*.

1 Voy [a] el cine. _____
2 el director [de] el colegio _____
3 el bar [de] el teatro _____
4 Han ido [a] el supermercado. _____
5 el pronóstico [de] el tiempo _____

G Translate the following sentences into Spanish.

1 The head [*la directora*] of the marketing department is ill.

_____

2 She saw a bull in the middle of the field.

_____

3 Ana is going to send an e-mail to the bank.

_____

4 He gave the horse a carrot.

_____

5 I've taken 100 euros from the cashpoint and now I'm going to the market.

_____

_____

6 I'm going to ring the hospital.

_____

Possessive adjectives

Reminder
- Possessive adjectives (*mi, tu, su, nuestro, vuestro, su*) must agree (masculine/feminine, singular/plural) with the noun that follows them. Only *nuestro* and *vuestro* change their ending from -o to -a for the feminine, but all of them add an -s for the plural.

A Translate the following phrases into Spanish.

1 my brothers _____
2 our grandparents _____
3 your (*tú*) homework _____
4 their jeans _____
5 his books _____
6 your (*Vd.*) car _____
7 our sisters _____
8 your (*vosotros*) house _____

B Complete the passage with the correct form of the appropriate possessive adjective each time.

Muchos jóvenes dicen que (**1**) _____ padres no están de acuerdo con (**2**) _____ opiniones. Por ejemplo, Luisa dice que a (**3**) _____ padre no le gusta (**4**) _____ amigos. 'Pero tengo derecho a elegir a (**5**) _____ amigos, sin pedirle (**6**) _____ opinión,' dice Luisa. El problema de Xavier es que a

(**7**) _____ madre no le gusta (**8**) _____ ropa, sobre todo (**9**) _____ camisetas con eslóganes. 'Me pregunta siempre: ¿Por qué nunca llevas (**10**) _____ camisa verde que te han comprado (**11**) _____ abuelos? O: ¿Dónde están (**12**) _____ zapatos?'.

Reminder
- There is also a 'long' or 'strong' form of possessive adjectives: *mío, tuyo, suyo, nuestro, vuestro, suyo*. This is used in comparisons, or after the verb *ser*. It is also used in phrases equivalent to English 'of mine', e.g. *una idea mía* 'an idea of mine'.

- Sometimes *de* + a subject pronoun is needed instead of *suyo* etc. to avoid ambiguity.

C Translate the following sentences into English.

1 Tu novio es más guapo que el mío.

_____

2 Estas llaves son nuestras, no son vuestras.

_____

3 El bocadillo de jamón es tuyo; el de queso es mío.

_____

Adjectives and adverbs

Agreement of adjectives; shortened adjectives

Reminder

♦ In Spanish, adjectives have different endings depending on whether the words they describe are masculine or feminine, singular or plural.

A In each of these sentences, underline the adjective(s) and circle the ending(s). Circle the noun each adjective describes. Note at the end of the sentence whether the noun is masculine or feminine, singular or plural.

1 Para mí Salamanca es una ciudad universitaria perfecta. _____
2 Tiene un centro antiguo muy hermoso. _____
3 Me gusta también la parte moderna y comercial de la ciudad. _____
4 La vida universitaria es animada e interesante. _____
5 Hay estudiantes españoles, extranjeros, jóvenes y mayores. _____

B Circle the correct adjective(s) in each sentence.

1 León no es una ciudad especialmente turístico/turística.
2 Sin embargo, tiene un centro históricos/histórico muy bonito/bonita.
3 Pero principalmente es un lugar moderno/moderna y prósperos/próspero.
4 Mi monumento preferido/preferida de León es la catedral gótica/gótico.

C Complete the following passage with the correct forms of the adjectives in the box.

El norte de España es menos (**1**) _____ por los turistas (**2**) _____ que el sur, lo que no es muy (**3**) _____ porque el norte está mucho más (**4**) _____. La costa del sur es, naturalmente, muy (**5**) _____ con sus playas (**6**) _____, sus hoteles y apartmentos (**7**) _____, y su clima (**8**) _____. Pero si en el futuro, el clima del sur se vuelve demasiado (**9**) _____, el norte podría volverse la destinación (**10**) _____ de los turistas que buscan una semana de descanso.

| famosas | lógico | cálida | británicos | mediterraneo |
| preferida | caluroso | conocido | cercano | innumerables |

Reminder

♦ Most adjectives simply exchange the final -o for an -a for the feminine form, while those ending in -e change only to add an -s for the plural.

Adjectives ending in -án, -ín, -ón, -or, ol and -és add a final -a for the feminine form, -es for the masculine plural form and -as for their feminine plural. Watch out for disappearing accents when these adjectives add endings.

D Complete the list with the feminine forms of the adjectives.

1 un monumento interesante – una catedral _____
2 un centro encantador – una plaza _____
3 un bar barcelonés – una playa _____
4 un vestido verde – una falda _____
5 un turista holgazán – una camarera _____
6 un avion inglés – una guía _____

Reminder

♦ Some Spanish adjectives shorten when placed in front of masculine singular nouns.

E Complete the following passage, choosing a suitable adjective from the box for each gap, adding agreements as necessary and using the appropriate shortened forms.

La semana pasada fui a la costa con un (**1**) _____ amigo. No lo pasamos muy bien. El (**2**) _____ día, hacía muy (**3**) _____ tiempo. Teníamos hambre, pero ¡no había (**4**) _____ restaurante (**5**) _____! El (**6**) _____ día visitamos la casa de un (**7**) _____ escritor, pero no me gustó – fue muy (**8**) _____. Y el (**9**) _____ día, tuvimos que volver a casa. ¡Qué desastre!

| aburrido | tercero | primero | abierto |
| bueno | segundo | grande | malo | ninguno |

Position of adjectives

> ### Reminder
> ◆ Most adjectives in Spanish go **after** the noun that they describe.

A Underline the adjectives and translate the phrases into English.
1 una persona famosa _____
2 un actor serio _____
3 una entrevista interesante _____
4 unas preguntas personales _____
5 una situacion difícil _____

B Translate the following into Spanish.
1 a pleasant day _____
2 a happy family _____
3 the intelligent students _____
4 some important exams _____
5 classical music _____
6 a wonderful present _____
7 a stupid answer _____
8 the shy children _____
9 my French friends _____
10 a permanent crisis _____

> ### Reminder
> ◆ A number of common adjectives can be placed before or after the noun.

C Translate the following into English on a separate sheet.

Mañana, el pobre Antonio va a pasar un mal día. Es el día de los grandes premios de teatro y, un joven director va a recibir el primer premio que Antonio soñaba con ganar.

> ### Reminder
> ◆ Some adjectives change their meaning according to whether they are placed before or after the noun.

D Look at the adjectives in the following sentences and decide which of the alternative meanings (given at the end of each sentence) is correct.
1 Mi vieja amiga tiene dos hijos grandes.
[old (long-time)/old (aged); big/grand]
2 Este político es un gran hombre – siempre ha comprendido la situación de los agricultores pobres. [great/big; poor (pitiful)/poor (financially)]

3 ¿Has comprado la nueva película de Antonio Banderas?
Sí, y ¡hoy tarde voy a verla en mi pantalla nueva¡
[new (different)/brand new]

> ### Reminder
> ◆ Only a very few adjectives always come **before** the noun in Spanish. These include possessive adjectives and adjectives of quantity.

E Translate the following sentences into English.
1 ¿No has comprado bastante aceitunas?
_____
2 Bueno sí –¡he comprado demasiado aceitunas!
_____
3 En mi ciudad hay muchos bares y algunos restaurantes, pero no tenemos ningún cocinero importante.
_____
4 En la biblioteca no vi a ningún estudiante, pero sí vi a otras personas – por ejemplo, algunos viejos dormidos.
_____
_____

(See page 9 for a reminder about the shortening of some adjectives when placed before a noun.)

> ### Reminder
> ◆ When there is more than one adjective describing a noun, you have a choice: if they are of equal importance, you place them after the noun and join them with *y*; otherwise, the adjective that is less closely connected to the noun is placed before it.

F Translate the following sentences into Spanish.
1 The actress was driving a small black car.
_____
2 She was wearing a fabulous white dress.
_____
3 She is staying in a beautiful private villa.
_____
4 There were some good photos in the regional paper.
_____
_____

Comparative and superlative adjectives

Reminder

◆ To compare two things, use *más … que, menos … que,* or *tan … como.*

A Fill in the most appropriate words: *más, menos* or *tan,* and *que* or *como.*

1 España es _____ montañosa _____ Argentina.
2 Argentina es _____ pobre _____ Bolivia.
3 El clima del norte de Chile es _____ seco _____ el del sur, pero no es [_____ seco _____ el de Bolivia.
4 El Salvador no es _____ largo _____ Chile.
5 Perú es _____ turístico_____ El Salvador.

Reminder

◆ The adjective in a comparative sentence agrees with the noun it relates to.

B In exercise A above, circle the endings on the adjectives. Then write a sentence following the same pattern for each of the following groups of words.

1 Nicaragua, Guatemala, montanañosa.

_____

2 Chile, Méjico, pobre.

_____

3 El clima Argentina, el de Ecuador, el de Uruguay seco.

_____

4 Panama, Perú, largo.

_____

5 Chile, Colombia, turístico.

_____

Reminder

◆ A few comparative forms are irregular:

bueno > mejor; malo > peor; grande > mayor; pequeño > menor
They are usually placed before the noun.
Note that to compare physical size, *más/menos grande/pequeño* are used, while *mayor* and *menor* are used to compare age, degrees of importance and abstract size, e.g. *la mayor parte.*

C Underline the appropriate word to complete these sentences.

1 La mejor/peor solución es la educación.
2 Para unas vacaciones en la playa, Costa Rica es mejor/peor que Bolivia.

3 Mi hermano menor/mejor me gusta menos que mi hermana mayor/más grande.
4 Las casas del campo son mayores/más grandes que las de la ciudad.

Reminder

◆ To say 'the most' or 'the least' use *el, la, los, las* or *lo* with *más* or *menos* and the adjective.

D Complete these sentences with *el, la, los, las* or *lo* and *más* or *menos* to form the superlative of the adjective. Then translate the sentences into English.

1 Yo creo que Salamanca es _____ ciudad _____ hermosa de España.

_____

2 En muchos países, el SIDA es uno de _____ problemas _____ serios para los médicos.

_____

3 No puedo decir cual es _____ país _____ interesante, Méjico o Chile, los dos son fascinantes.

_____

4 No me gustaría vivir en Bogotá; es una de _____ ciudades _____ peligrosas del mundo.

_____

5 Las comedias mejicanas están entre _____ películas _____ populares.

_____

Reminder

◆ The adjective agrees with the noun that comes immediately before it.

E Underline the correct form of the adjective in each of these phrases.

1 las drogas más peligroso/peligrosas
2 las calles más sucias/sucios
3 la sierra más alto/alta
4 las economías menos ricos/ricas
5 los problemas climáticos/climáticas más grave/graves.

Reminder

◆ Spanish adjectives have an absolute superlative (extremely, absolutely, the most, etc.) which is formed by replacing the final vowel with *-ísimo(s)/ísima(s).*

F Change the adjectives in the following sentences into absolute superlatives.

1 Buenos Aires es una ciudad animada, me encanta. _____

2 Acabo de visitar, el viaje era difícil pero el lugar esmuy bello.

More determiners: demonstrative and indefinite adjectives

Reminder

◆ Use *este, esta, estos, estas* to say 'this' and 'these'.

◆ Use *ese, esa, esos, esas* to say 'that' and 'those' referring to objects far from the speaker but near the listener(s).

◆ Use *aquel, aquella, aquellos, aquellas* to refer to objects far away from both the speaker and the listener(s).

A Translate into Spanish.

1 that diet _____
2 these substances _____
3 this discovery _____
4 those foods _____
5 these children _____

B Choose the appropriate demonstrative to complete each sentence.

1 ¿Ves este/aquel/esa mercado al final de la calle?
2 Por favor, dame ese / esta/ esa botella de aceite de oliva.
3 Voy a comprar dos kilos de aquellos / estas / estos manzanas — mm, ¡son deliciosas!
4 No me gustan esas / aquellas / esos dulces, son demasiados azucardos.
5 Los adultos tienen que aceptar parte de la responsabilidad de aquella / este / estos / problema.

C Translate into English.

1 Estas zapatillas de deporte son más caras que esas.
_____

2 ¿Qué son aquellos árboles?
Aquellos son manzanos, pero estos son perales.
_____
_____

3 ¿Qué bocadillo prefieres? ¿Este de jamón o ese de queso?
_____

4 ¿Cuál es tu mochila? ¿Esta o esa?
_____

5 Necesito comprar algunas postales, pero no me gustan estas.
_____

6 ¿Cuál jersey vas a comprar? ¿Ese azul o este rojo?
_____

7 Me gustan los dos, pero hay que elegir – me llevo este.
_____

8 Niños, ¿veis aquellos caballos? Allí, delante de aquella casa.
_____

9 Estos vaqueros son demasiado pequeños. ¿Me puedo probar esos?
_____

10 ¿Ves a aquel hombre? Es él que me dio esas flores.
_____

Reminder

◆ The Spanish word for 'all' is *todo*. It works as an adjective, so must agree with the noun to which it refers.

D For each of the following sentences, underline the form of *todo* used, and circle the noun it refers to. Underline the appropriate abbreviation to indicate whether it is masculine or feminine, singular or plural.

1 Voy a estar a dieta toda esta semana. m/f/sing/pl
2 Voy a dejar todos mis pasteles favoritos. m/f/sing/pl
3 Voy a comer fruta con todas las comidas. m/f/sing/pl
4 Voy a perder los 5 kilos que engordé durante las vacaciones. m/f/sing/pl
5 Pero, primero, ¡voy a comer todo lo que queda en el frigo! m/f/sing/pl

E Complete these sentences with the correct form of *todo*.

1 En Semana Santa, _____ la familia vino a visitarnos.
2 _____ mis primos vinieron de Chile.
3 _____ el mundo lo pasó bomba, comiendo, cantando, bebiendo y riendo
4 _____ las chicas bailaron, pero algunos chicos no quisieron bailar.

(See page 29 for more information and practice on indefinite adjectives such as *mucho, otro, cada,* etc.)

Interrogatives and exclamations

Reminder

◆ Question words (interrogatives) always have an accent in Spanish: ¿Dónde? ¿Cuándo? ¿Cómo? ¿Por qué? ¿Cuánto? etc.

◆ ¿Cuánto? is an interrogative adjective so if it refers to a noun it must agree with that noun, e.g. ¿Cuánta gente hay?

◆ ¿Qué? is used before a noun to ask 'which?' or 'what?' – it does not change its form. It is also used with verbs to ask more general questions, e.g. ¿Qué vamos a hacer?

A Complete the questions in the following dialogue with the most logical interrogative, remembering to include an accent.

Luisa, dime, ¿_____ están mis llaves? ¿Las has visto?

¿_____? ¿_____ dices? ¿_____ veces has perdido esas llaves? ¿_____ es posible?

¿_____ no las pones cerca de la puerta como te lo he sugerido mil veces?

No sé, querida, me he olvidado, pero ahora me faltan y tengo mucha prisa. ¿_____ hora es?
¿_____ tiempo tengo?

Son las ocho menos diez. ¿_____ sale tu tren?

A las ocho y veinte. Lo voy a perder.

Mira, ¡aquí están tus llaves! ¡En el baño! Dios mío, ¿_____ voy a hacer contigo?

Reminder

◆ ¿Cuál? also means 'which?' or 'what?' but is used to ask for more specific information, implying a choice between options, e.g. ¿Cuál es la capital de Bolivia? ¿Cuál? does not change for the feminine but it has a plural form ¿Cuáles?.

◆ ¿Quién? means 'who?'. It does not change for the feminine but it has a plural form ¿Quiénes?.

B Translate the following questions into Spanish.

1 What is the capital of Venezuela?

_____

2 Who is the president of Argentina?

_____

3 What solution do you suggest?

_____

4 Who are those men?

_____

5 What is the difference between Castilian Spanish and, for example, Colombian Spanish?

_____

_____

6 Who has phoned today?

_____

7 With whom are you going to the conference, Señor Ramón?

_____

_____

8 What were the causes of the Civil War?

_____

9 Who became President of Spain after the death of Franco?

_____

_____

10 What's your opinion? Who is going to win the election?

_____

_____

Reminder

◆ Words introducing exclamations always have an accent in Spanish.

C On a separate sheet of paper, translate the following phone conversation into English.

Escucha, Mercedes, tengo una noticia sorprendente sobre Miguel y Ana...

¿Qué noticia? ¿Van a divorciarse? ¡Qué lástima!

No, pero Miguel la ha dejado finalmente.

¿Cómo? ¿Miguel ha dejado a Ana? Pero ¡qué sorpresa! Yo habría pensado que Ana iba a dejar a Miguel. Bueno, ¡qué noticia!

Sí, qué hombre tan simpático, y ella, bueno, no quiero darte mi opinión sobre ella...

Sí, ¡qué escándalo!

Adverbs, intensifiers and quantifiers

Reminder

♦ Adverbs are used to describe a verb, an adjective or another adverb. English adverbs usually end in -ly. Spanish adverbs are formed by adding -*mente* to the feminine form of the adjective, although the adjective can sometimes be used as it is, e.g. *rápido* instead of *rápidamente*. The only common irregular adverbs are *bien* (well) and *mal* (badly).

A Write the adverb corresponding to each of these adjectives, and give its English meaning in brackets.

1 frecuente _____
(_____)

2 fácil _____
(_____)

3 triste _____
(_____)

4 malo _____
(_____)

5 tranquilo _____
(_____)

6 bueno _____
(_____)

Reminder

♦ Adverbs form their comparative in the same way as adjectives, by the addition of *más* or *menos*. For the superlative, include *lo* before *más/menos*. Use *que* to say 'than'.

The only common irregular comparative adverbs are *mejor* (better) and *peor* (worse).

B Complete the following sentences, choosing a comparative or superlative expression from the box.

1 Nuestro equipo jugó mal, pero el otro equipo jugó _____.

2 ¿Podría explicarme el problema _____?

3 Durmió mal el sábado, pero ayer durmió _____.

4 Voy al cine _____ al teatro.

5 El alpinismo se aprende _____ el fútbol.

6 Javier corre _____ su hermano.

7 Tengo que hablar _____ con él para resolver el problema.

más frecuentemente que	más claramente
menos fácilmente que	mucho mejor
más seriamente	peor	menos rápido que

Reminder

♦ It is common in Spanish for an adjective or an adverbial expression to be used instead of an adverb, because adverbs ending in -*mente* can be long and clumsy.

C In each sentence, underline the word or expression that is used adverbially. Translate the sentences into English.

1 Mi entrenador me habló de una manera muy franca.

_____

2 En este pais se puede esquiar bastante barato.

_____

3 Por fin llegamos al estadio.

_____

4 Federico se entrena de un modo bastante independiente

_____

5 Los miembros del equipo trabajan juntos muy contentos.

Reminder

♦ Words known as intensifiers and quantifiers can be placed before adverbs (or adjectives) to extend the meaning. The most common ones are *muy, bastante, mucho* and *poco*, but there are several other useful ones.

D In the following phrases, circle the **main** adverb or adjective, then translate into English the remaining words. These are the quantifiers or intensifiers.

1 muy felizmente _____
2 completamente imposible _____
3 bastante fácil
4 demasiado caro _____
5 mucho más importante _____
6 cada vez más rápido _____
7 especialmente difícil _____
8 sumamente complicado _____
9 aún menos frecuente _____
10 totalmente ridículo _____
11 poco prudente _____
12 realmente fantástico _____

E Choose any suitable phrase from those in exercise D to complete each of the following sentences. Remember to add agreements if necessary.

1 Este problema es _____

2 Tienen unas ideas _____

3 El precio de los pisos aumenta

_____

4 Para mí, la solución que propones es

_____

5 ¿Te has dado cuenta que Carmen me habla

_____?

F Write sentences in Spanish to include six other expressions from exercise D.

_____

_____

_____

_____

_____

_____

G Translate the following paragraph into Spanish.

Robberies are happening more and more often. Everyone is very concerned. The police say that crime detection is extremely complicated and too expensive but I think that excuse is totally ridiculous. They are completely obsessed with arresting motorists who drive with little care; obviously, that problem's very important but in my opinion robberies are much more serious.

_____

_____

_____

_____

_____

_____

_____

_____

Revision: nouns, determiners, adjectives, adverbs

A Underline the noun in each list that has a different gender to the others.

1 libertad sistema idea concepción sala
2 ambiente resultado análisis frase coche
3 avión historia cantidad gente investigación
4 crimen robo descubrimiento proceso pena
5 droga adicción problema pobreza relación

B Complete this paragraph using singular or plural forms of the nouns in the box as appropriate.

En nuestro (**1**) ——————— de (**2**) ———————, tenemos mucha (**3**) ———————. Hay seis (**4**) ——————— nuevos, con muchos (**5**) ——————— útiles. Siempre trabajamos en (**6**) ——————— para hacer (**7**) ——————— por Internet – por ejemplo, cuando tenemos (**8**) ——————— que escribir y necesitamos (**9**) —— u otros (**10**) ——————— sobre la (**11**) ——————— en España. Tenemos también muchos (**12**) ——————— como CDs y (**13**) ———————. Con respecto a los (**14**) ———————, hay una pequeña (**15**) ——————— con los (**16**) ———————, otras (**17**) ——————— de (**18**) ———————, y muchos (**19**) ——————— de los (**20**) ——————— hispanohablantes .

> estadística par obra proyecto país vídeo
> departamento biblioteca programa dato
> ordenador vida referencia suerte mapa
> investigación lengua libro diccionario material

C Complete these sentences with *un, una, el, la, unos, unas, los, las, lo* or no article, as appropriate. In two instances you will need *al* or *del*.

1 Después de acabar ——— colegio, quiero trabajar como ——— guía turística, antes de ir a ——— universidad.
2 Si es posible, me gustaría encontrar ——— puesto en ——— sur de España, porque ya conozco ——— poco Andalucía.
3 He comprado ——— libros sobre ——— región – me interesa no sólo ——— paisaje y ——— atracciones turísticas, sino ——— historia también.
4 ——— Moros construyeron ——— palacios fantásticos en esta parte ——— país: por ejemplo, ——— Alhambra de Granada, donde hay también ——— jardín magnífico.
5 Fui ——— palacio ——— verano pasado. Me gustaron mucho ——— fuentes y ———

estanques. ——— interesante es que en ——— época de ——— Moros, ——— agua representaba ——— riqueza. Hoy en día ——— agua es todavía muy preciada en ——— Andalucía.

D Translate these phrases into Spanish.

1 her boss and his enormous salary
_____
2 our area and its traffic problems
_____
3 my life and my future plans
_____
4 His friends live near ours.
_____
5 That is your opinion but it's not mine.
_____
6 I've parked my car next to theirs.
_____

E Rewrite the following sentences including the adjectives given in brackets after each one. Think carefully about the position and agreement of the adjectives.

1 Mis amigos quieren un piso con un balcón y vistas.
(portugués nuevo grande bonito)
_____
_____
2 No estoy de acuerdo con sus ideas, pero es un amigo y un colega.
(todo político bueno simpático)
_____
_____
3 ¡La hermana de mi amiga va a casarse con un torero!
(mayor madrileño grande colombiano)
_____
_____

F Translate the following sentences into Spanish.

1 His family is larger than mine but more united.
_____
_____
2 The majority of Spanish universities are smaller than British ones.
_____
_____
3 Vegetarianism is not as popular in Spain as it is in the UK.

4 Organic food is not always more expensive, but it is more common in markets than in supermarkets.

_____

_____

_____

5 Vegetables and fruit are cheaper than cheese and meat, and healthier too!

_____

6 He drives less carefully than his wife, but she drives faster.

_____

_____

7 He writes much better than she does, but much more slowly.

_____

_____

4 Why are you getting up? What time is it? Oh no, what a pain – I'm going to be late for work!

_____

5 What are the differences between life in Spain and life in Chile?

_____

What a question! How much time have you got?

_____

G Circle the most appropriate demonstrative adjective to complete each sentence.
1 ¿Ves estas/esos/aquellas montañas en la distancia? Son los Pirineos.
2 Ven aquí y mira – en ese/este/aquella mapa podemos ver la ruta completa.
3 Siempre he vivido en este/ese/aquel pueblo, nunca he visitado Madrid, tampoco Granada; me gustaría mucho ver esas/aquellos/estas ciudades.
4 Por favor, dame ese/este/aquel CD – voy a cambiar de música porque detesto a esa/esta/aquella cantante.

H Translate the following sentences into Spanish.
1 What a catastrophe! How will she react?

_____

2 Has she gone? What a shame! When did she leave?

_____

_____

3 What is the capital of Costa Rica? And who is the leader of the country?

_____

_____

Prepositions, conjunctions and pronouns

Prepositions

Reminder

◆ Prepositions often tell you about the position of something.
(Check page 8 for a reminder about *al* and *del*.)

A Choose a suitable preposition from the box below to complete each gap in the following sentences.

1 La oficina está _____ la iglesia, _____ una pastelería y una librería. (opposite, between)
2 Es difícil aparcar _____ la calle. (in)
3 Pero hay un parking _____ la plaza, _____ el hotel Mirador. (behind, next to)
4 No se puede fumar _____ la oficina. (inside)
5 Si me llamas, te encontraré _____ el edificio. (in front of)
6 Si no estoy en la oficina, deje las cartas _____ la mesa, o _____ la silla _____ la ventana. (on, on, under).

> sobre al lado de en detrás de enfrente de debajo
> de entre dentro de delante de

Reminder

◆ Some prepositions tell you when something happens.

B Choose a suitable preposition from the box below to complete each gap in the following paragraph.

Tengo trabajo en este garaje (1) _____ el verano, (2) _____ ir a la universidad. Pero si tengo bastante dinero, voy a ir de vacaciones (3) _____ dejar mi empleo. El horario no es malo: hay que llegar (4) _____ las ocho (5) _____ la mañana, y tenemos dos horas libres (6) _____ la una (7) _____ las tres. Generalmente salgo (8) _____ las cuatro.

> hacia después de a desde
> antes de durante hasta por

C Translate these sentences into Spanish.

1 We were dancing from 10 p.m. to 2 a.m.
_____

2 I'll arrive around eight o'clock and will wait for you in front of the cinema – it's opposite the cathedral.
_____
_____

3 Give me that book – look, it's on the floor, under the newspaper, between the sofa and the chair.
_____
_____

4 If we leave in the evening, after the rush hour, we'll be there in two hours.
_____
_____

Reminder

◆ In Spanish you do not always use the same prepositions as in English.

D Study the following sentences and translate the bold phrases into English.

1 No llegó **a tiempo**; llegó **al día siguiente.**
_____

2 Vivo a **50 km de** Madrid.
_____

3 Telefonea a su madre **dos veces a la semana**; ¡siempre hablan **sobre el tiempo**!
_____

4 ¿Prefieres estar **al sol** o **a la sombra**?
_____

5 Tienen un hijo **de nueve años**.
_____

6 Le gusta **ir de compras** con su hermana.
_____

7 Voy al trabajo **en bici**, pero cuando llueve voy **en autobús**.
_____

8 Mi libro estaba **en la mesa**, pero se cayó **al suelo.**
_____

9 El tren salió finalmente **hacia las dos**.
_____

Reminder

◆ Prepositions often need careful attention as it is often not the most obvious translation that is appropriate and it will vary from context to context.

E In the following sentences, underline the prepositions and the nouns to which they relate. Write in the space at the end of each an appropriate translation of the words you have circled. Think about the contextual meaning of the sentence as a whole and check possible meanings in a dictionary – don't assume it's the most obvious one.

1 Según nuestros cálculos, esta ciudad tiene sobre sesenta mil habitantes.

_____   _____

2 Esos criminales van a comparecer ante el tribunal mañana; a mi ver, Martínez es el peor de todos.

_____   _____   _____

3 Por fin llegaron, pero estuve horas esperándoles – estuve bajo la lluvia desde las once.

_____   _____   _____

4 Pero ¡mi padre se cayó por la escalera! Ante esa situación, no pude irme con prisa.

_____   _____   _____

F Translate the following into Spanish using prepositions from exercise E.

1 According to my father, delinquents like that should appear before a judge.

_____

_____

2 Faced with these problems, the government should take some decisions – and in a hurry!

_____

_____

3 Of all the bars in Madrid, this is the largest – in my view, there are around 500 people in here.

_____

_____

Reminder

◆ The prepositions *para* and *por* need special attention; they can both be translated as 'for' but each also has other meanings.
Para usually relates to purpose, destination or use.
Por often has the meaning 'along', 'by' or 'through'.

G Choose *por* or *para* in each of the following sentences and underline the one you have chosen.

1 ¿Qué haces por/para relajarte?
2 ¿Tienes las entradas por / para el partido?
3 Voy a la oficina en el autobús por / para no tener que aparcar.
4 Siempre vuelvo por / para el parque por / para relajarme al fin del día.
5 ¡Darte prisa! ¡El tren está por/para salir!
6 Es demasiado tarde – el tren es por/para salir.
7 Dormir 8 horas cada noche es clave por / para vivir sano.
8 Me llama 10 veces por / para hora por / para decirme lo que hace.

H Now translate the following into Spanish, using *por* or *para* as appropriate.

1 The marathon passes through the centre of the city during the afternoon.

_____

_____

2 At first she bought an exercise bike to get fit, but now she runs along the riverside every day in the evening.

_____

_____

3 We're looking for a cashpoint – is there one near here?

_____

Yes, take the street on the right and cross the bridge – there's a cashpoint on the corner.

_____

4 I was walking around the market looking for a present for my mother.

_____

_____

Reminder

◆ The preposition *de* has many uses, and does not necessarily correspond to the English 'of'.

I Underline the construction with *de* in each sentence and write a translation of the sentence in the space below.

1 Llevaba una camisa de seda.

Prepositions, conjunctions and pronouns

2 No estoy de acuerdo contigo.

3 El rojo no está de moda.

4 Aquel edificio de ocho pisos data del siglo XX.

5 El señor de Madrid hablaba de sus negocios.

6 De vez en cuando voy de compras con mi madre.

7 Mi hermana tiene un hijo de dos años. ¿Ah, de veras?

8 El camión de Juan ya estaba lleno de madera.

J On a separate sheet, use each of the eight constructions you have identified in exercise I to write a sentence in Spanish.

Reminder

◆ The preposition *a* has many uses, and does not necessarily correspond to the English 'at' or 'to'.

K Use a dictionary as necessary to find the Spanish expressions equivalent to the following English ones.

1 at the end of the year

2 on the next day

3 on the left

4 on time

5 at 10 euros a kilo

6 in the shade

7 five times a month

8 at the age of eighty

9 20 km from my house

10 at times

L Now translate the following sentences into Spanish.

1 At times you can buy apples in the market at two euros a kilo.

2 Take that road on the right and we'll be able to park in the shade.

3 At the age of sixty she was still swimming three times a week.

4 On the next day there was a bad accident only a few metres from my mother's house.

5 At the end of the year I'm taking my holiday.

6 You will not finish in time, I'm sure.

Reminder

◆ When a person or animal is the direct object of a verb, the preposition *a* must be placed in front of the noun. When used in this way it is called the 'personal *a*'. Remember that *a* will combine with *el* to form *al*.

M Choose a verb from the box for the gap in each sentence, using each verb only once. Put the verb into an appropriate form for the context and insert the personal *a* at the appropriate point.

1 El niño _____ su hermano porque había cogido su juguete.

2 _____ su profesora de inglés.

3 La bala _____ la víctima.

4 _____ su marido durante tres años.

5 _____ camarero que se diera prisa.

6 _____ su amigo.

| odiar | matar | echar de menos |
| golpear | pedir | engañar |

Conjunctions

Reminder

◆ Conjunctions are linking words.

A Choose a suitable ending for each sentence, underline the conjunction used in each case and write the English meaning of the conjunction in the brackets afterwards.

1 Es un pueblo turístico, ☐
2 Estudia para sus exámenes, ☐
3 Los estudiantes se quejan ☐
4 He comprado dos teléfonos móviles, ☐
5 Mis padres me critican ☐
6 Salió de la casa ☐
7 ¿Te gustaría jugar al tenis ☐
8 Vivo todavía con mis padres ☐

a después espera ir a la universidad. (_____)
b cuando llego a casa demasiado tarde. (_____)
c o prefieres ir al cine? (_____)
d así que hay muchos hoteles. (_____)
e y voy a dar uno de ellos a cada una de mis hijas. (_____)
f pero me gustaría más vivir solo. (_____)
g porque los profesores no escuchan. (_____)
h sin cerrar la puerta. (_____)

Reminder

◆ Certain conjunctions require the following verb to be in the subjunctive. (There is more detail and practice on this on page 72.)

B Check the meanings of the conjunctions in the box then choose a suitable one to complete each of the following sentences.

1 Iremos al parque _____ puedan ver las fuentes.
2 Hágalo _____ llamarle.
3 _____ haga buen tiempo, no vale la pena salir.
4 _____ vayas a Madrid, no te olvides de escribirme.
5 _____ compres los regalos, ven a verme.

6 No podemos comprar este coche _____ te toque la lotería.
7 ¿Cómo puedo leer _____ tocas la guitarra?

> para que   sin que   cuando   a menos que
> después que   mientras   antes de

C Rewrite the following pairs as single sentences choosing a conjunction from those you have used in exercises A and B. You may need to change the form of the verb in the second sentence.

1 Antonio no fuma. Hace mucho deporte.
_____
_____

2 Bebe vino de vez en cuando. Nunca ha bebido demasiado.
_____
_____

3 Come mucha fruta. Trata de mantenerse en forma.
_____
_____

4 Corre cada mañana. Toma el desayuno.
_____
_____

5 Hace buen tiempo. Va al trabajo en bici.
_____
_____

6 Hace ejercicios. Ve la televisión.
_____
_____

D Translate the following sentences into Spanish, on a separate sheet of paper.

1 I would like to become a translator but I know it's difficult.
2 When he was younger he smoked much more.
3 While her friends were at the cinema she was working.
4 Many people are vegetarians because they think vegetables are healthier than meat.
5 You can't earn lots of money without working hard.
6 I'm going to have a shower before I go out.
7 Do you want to go to a bar after eating or do you prefer to go home?

Personal and reflexive pronouns

Reminder

♦ The subject pronouns are *yo, tú, él, ella, usted* (Vd.), *nosotros/as, vosotros/as, ellos/as, ustedes* (Vds.) but they are not used unless required for emphasis, or when the verb ending is not sufficient to make the subject clear. *Vd.* and *Vds.* are often included for politeness. Latin American speakers use *ustedes* rather than *vosotros*. Note the accents on *tú* and *él* to distinguish them from the possessive pronoun *tu* and the definite article *el*.

A In each of the following sentences the subject pronouns have been included. Give the reason in each case.

1 Yo soy médico y ella es enfermera.

_____

2 Ella trabaja en Granada pero él vive en Málaga.

_____

3 Ellos son vegetarianos, pero ellas comen mucha carne.

_____

4 ¿Qué desean Vds.?

_____

5 Usted recibirá su carta mañana, y ella recibirá la suya el miércoles.

_____

Reminder

♦ *Tú* and its plural *vosotros* are the informal words for 'you'; *usted* (Vd.) and its plural *ustedes* (Vds.) are the formal words used for adults you do not know well. These decisions determine which form of the verb you use.

B Write beside each of these people which pronouns and verb forms you would use in addressing them: *tú, vosotros, usted* or *ustedes*.

1 tus abuelos _____
2 el nuevo jefe _____
3 el hermano menor de tu amiga _____
4 dos clientes en la tienda donde trabajas

_____
5 un grupo de niños _____
6 el perro de tu vecino _____

Reminder

♦ Reflexive pronouns are used to form reflexive verbs.

me	myself	*nos*	ourselves
te	yourself	*vos*	yourselves
se	himself/herself/ yourself (Vd.)	*se*	themselves/ yourselves (Vds.)

Remember that in the infinitive form the reflexive pronoun is attached to the end of the verb – *llamarse, darse prisa*.

C Fill in the reflexive pronouns in Maribel's description of her working day.

1 Ahora _____ he acostumbrado a mi trabajo en el hospital.
2 _____ levantamos muy temprano, y hay que duchar _____ y vestir _____ muy rápido. _____ pongo mi uniforme de enfermera.
3 Los otros enfermeros _____ quejan de la rutina dura.
4 Yo prefiero callar _____, pero debo confesar que _____ siento cansada todo el tiempo.
5 Durante el día, _____ ocupamos de nuestro trabajo, y no tenemos tiempo para preocupar _____ de otras cosas.
6 En esta profesión, ¡uno no _____ aburre nunca!
7 Por la tarde, mis amigos y yo _____ encontramos en el bar.
8 Tomamos una copa y _____ divertimos, pero tengo que acostar _____ bastante temprano.

Reminder

♦ Reflexive pronouns are also used to convey 'each other'.

D Translate the following phrases into Spanish.
1 They love each other.

_____

2 They call each other on the phone every day.

_____

3 They meet in the square every evening.

_____

4 They often give each other little presents.

_____

5 Everyone's wondering when they are going to get married.

_____

Direct object pronouns

Reminder

◆ A direct object pronoun replaces a noun that is the object of a verb. The Spanish direct object pronouns are: *me, te, lo, la, nos, os, los, las. Le* and *les* are sometimes used instead of *lo* and *los* to refer to male people.

A Underline the direct object pronoun in each sentence, then translate the sentences into English.

1 Odio la música anticuada, no la escucho nunca.

2 Sin embargo, me gusta mucho la música clásica, siempre la escucho cuando estudio.

3 Me encanta también los programas de jazz en la radio, los escucho para relejarme.

4 ¿Tienes estos CDs? No, los he perdido.

5 Compraste aquellas entradas para el concierto? No, no las compré, eran demasiado caras.

Reminder

◆ Direct object pronouns go in front of the verb, as seen in the exercise above. However, when the verb is in the **infinitive**, **present continuous** or the **imperative**, they are attached to the end of the verb.

B Underline the direct object pronoun in each sentence, then translate the sentences into English.

1 ¡Están escuchándola! _____

2 Me encanta ese CD: voy a comprarlo.

3 Esa música está demasiado fuerte. ¡Bájala por favor!

4 ¿Su nuevo CD? Está escuchándolo.

5 A todos les encanta la música de Shakira, pero a mí no: ¡la odio!

6 Tienen sus entradas, señoras? ¡Necesito verlas, por favor!

7 No tengo el último CD de David Bisbal, pero creo que voy a recibirlo de mi hermana por mi cumpleaños.

8 ¿Dónde está el mando? No sé, estoy buscándolo.

Reminder

◆ When you use a negative, *no* goes in front of the object pronoun.

C Write negative answers in Spanish, using direct object pronouns to avoid repeating the words in bold.

1 ¿Tienes **los billetes**?
No, _____

2 ¿Esperas **a tu novio**?
No, _____

3 ¿Descargas **esta canción**?
No, _____

4 ¿Grabamos **este concierto**?
No, _____

Reminder

◆ In the perfect tense, the direct object pronoun goes in front of *haber*.
In the future tense with *ir*, the pronoun may either be placed in front of the form of *ir* or joined to the infinitive.

D A cook is demonstrating a recipe. Underline all the direct object pronouns, then translate the passage into English on a separate sheet.

Bueno, hoy hacemos una ensalada de frutas, con naranjas, un melón, y uvas. Vamos a sazonarla con jengibre y menta. Bueno, aquí tengo las naranjas – las he pelado y las voy a cortar en rodajas ... y las uvas, lo mejor es pelarlas, pero si no hay tiempo de hacerlo, no importa. Lo importante es cortarlas en dos y quitarles las pepitas. Yo las he pelado, como ven Vds. ... también el melón, lo he cortado en pedazos. Bueno, ahora tomo todas las frutas y las mezclo en este bol. Es buena idea rociarlas con jugo de limón, para que no se descoloren ... Ahora, el jengibre ... tenemos que pelarlo y cortarlo en pedazos muy pequeños ... voy a añadirlos a la ensalada. Para acabar, la menta. Tengo unas doce hojas, y las voy a cortar. Lo mejor es hacerlo en el último momento, para mantenerlas frescas. Y aquí tenemos una ensalada riquísima de frutas – ¡aun más rica cuando la coman con nata montada!

E Translate the following sentences into Spanish, taking care with the position of the direct object pronoun.

1 I don't like classical music very much so I don't listen to it.

2 Can you explain these instructions? I can't understand them!

3 Daniel's lost his MP3 player again; have you seen it?

4 I'm looking for Felicia and Xavier. Have you seen them?

5 Where's that vase – has she broken it?

6 I bought some cakes – are we going to eat them?

7 I love music and I'm going to study it at university.

8 I couldn't resist those boots – I had to buy them!

Indirect object pronouns

Reminder

◆ An indirect object pronoun replaces a noun (usually a person) that is linked to the verb by a preposition, usually *a* (to), e.g.
Les mando un regalo. I'm sending them a present.
The Spanish indirect object pronouns are *me* 'to me', *te* 'to you', *le* 'to him', 'to her', 'to you (Vd.)', *nos* 'to us', *os* 'to you', *les* 'to them', 'to you (Vds.)'.

A Underline the indirect object pronouns in the following sentences. Translate the phrases in bold into English on a separate piece of paper.

En Navidad siempre hay regalos. Este año, **mis padres me regalaron entradas** para un concierto de mi grupo preferido, y **yo les di unos DVDs**. Mi hermano es muy musical así que **mis padres le regalaron una guitarra nueva. Mi abuela nos envió dinero; me voy a comprar un nuevo MP3**, ya lo he visto en Ebay. Mi viejo reproductor tiene solo 500 MB, y no es suficiente para toda **la música que tengo**. Mi hermanita no tien e MP3, **le daré el viejo. Siempre me estaba pidiendo** que se lo prestase, pero siempre **le contestaba que no.**

B Using the sentences in exercise A, complete the list of common verbs followed by an indirect object in Spanish.

1	to give (as a present)	regalar
2	to give	
3	to send	
4	to buy yourself	
5	to be needed	
6	to ask (for something)	
7	to lend	
8	to reply	

C Translate these sentences into Spanish.

1 I talked to them yesterday.

2 We asked him why he had left.

3 My friend lent me some money.

4 They phoned us last week.

5 You've given her a present.

6 I've told you the truth.

7 She's going to write to them on Monday.

8 I'm going to give her the cheque tomorrow.

Reminder

◆ Indirect object pronouns are needed to refer to parts of the body.

D Translate the following into English.

1 Me duelen los oídos.

2 Se ha roto la pierna.

3 Le duelen los ojos.

4 Ven aquí, Manuelito – voy a lavarte las manos.

5 ¿Por qué tomas esa aspirina? ¿Te duele la cabeza?

Reminder

◆ Some verbs conveying a wish, request or instruction are followed by an indirect object and *que* + subjunctive.

E Rewrite the following sentences, replacing the noun in bold with an indirect object pronoun.

1 Alberto pidió **a Felipe** que le prestara su nuevo CD.

_____

2 El médico aconsejó **al pianista** que jugara menos frecuentemente.

_____

3 Siempre estoy pidiendo **a mis vecinos** que bajen la televisión.

_____

4 Mi padre ha prohibido **a mis hermanas** que vayan a bailar a ese club.

_____

5 Su amigo le dijo **a Enrique** que escuchara ese CD de salsa, pero no le gustó nada.

_____

6 La profesora ha permitido **a nosotros** que estudiemos en la biblioteca.

_____

7 Mis padres no permiten **a mi hermana** que aprenda a tocar la batería.

_____

Reminder

◆ As you saw in exercise E, the personal *a* is needed with a noun representing a person or animal when the noun is the indirect object.

F Translate the following sentences into Spanish.

1 I asked Enrique to teach me to play the guitar, but he said it was impossible.

_____

2 She invited my friend to go to a concert but he told her to leave him in peace.

_____

3 He doesn't allow his dog to come into the room when he's playing the piano.

_____

Order of pronouns

Reminder

◆ When there are several pronouns in the same sentence, they go in the following order:

reflexive	indirect object	direct object	
me	me	me	[verb]
te	te	te	[verb]
se	le	lo/le/la	[verb]
nos	nos	nos	[verb]
os	os	os	[verb]
se	les	los/les/las	[verb]

The same order applies when the pronouns are joined to the end of an infinitive, imperative or present participle.

A In the following sentences, underline the **indirect object pronouns**. Then translate the sentences into English.

1 ¿Estos CDs? Me los dio ayer.

_____

2 ¿Esas canciones? Ya te las hemos enviado.

3 Te lo han dicho pero no me lo han dicho a mí.

_____

4 Me lo has dicho mil veces – ¡no me lo digas otra vez!

5 Conchita, ¿qué haces con mis cascos? ¡Dámelos, por favor!

6 Esas entradas deben llegar mañana. Mándemelas hoy por la tarde, por favor.

Reminder

◆ When two third person object pronouns are used together, the first one always changes to *se* to make the phrase easier to pronounce.

Prepositions, conjunctions and pronouns

B Translate the bold phrases into English.

1 Cuando recibo cosas que no me gustan, **siempre se las doy.** _____

2 Ella le da el dinero, y **él se lo da a ellos.**

_____

3 **Se lo he dicho** pero siempre se olvida.

_____

4 Siempre lleva ese anillo. **María se lo dio** hace muchos años. _____

5 He comprado unos guantes para Nina y **voy a regalárselos** para su cumpleaños.

_____

6 He averiguado los precios y **voy a decírselos** cuando lo vea. _____

Pronouns after prepositions

Reminder

◆ As in question 2 of exercise B above, sometimes *a él, a ella, a ellos, a Vd.* etc. need to be added (usually after the verb) for clarity or emphasis.

A Choose the correct pronoun from the box to complete the translations below.

1 I sent it to her but she gave it to him.
Yo se lo mandé _____, pero ella se lo dio _____.

2 My new painting? Well, I wanted to show it to you first, but those girls wanted to see it so I showed it to them.
¿Mi nuevo cuadro? Bueno, quería mostrárselo _____ primero, pero esas chicas querían verlo así que se lo mostré _____.

| a él | a ella | a ellas | a Vd. |

Reminder

◆ The sentences in exercise A are examples of the use of pronouns after prepositions in Spanish. Pronouns used in this way are the same as the subject pronouns, except for *mí* and *ti*. (The accent on *mí* distinguishes it from the possessive pronoun *mi*.) With *con*, there is a special form for the first, second and third persons: *conmigo, contigo, consigo*.

B Translate the following into Spanish.

1 Pablo, do you want to go on holiday with us?

_____

2 This letter is for you, madam.

_____

3 He sent the message via her.

_____

4 I can't go without you. Come with me!

_____

5 I can't see because he's in front of me.

_____

Relative pronouns

Reminder

◆ The relative pronoun ('who', 'which', 'that', 'whom') that you will need most often is *que*. Remember that the relative pronoun cannot be left out in Spanish as it can in English.

A Underline the relative pronoun, and the noun and the verb it relates to, in the following sentences. Then translate the underlined phrases into English.

1 La revista que prefiero de todas es ¡Hola!

_____

2 ¡El grupo que ha ganado es mi grupo favorito!

_____

3 ¿Has encontrado los detalles biográficos que buscabas?

_____

4 He enmarcado el autógrafo que me dio.

5 Prefiero los cantantes que escriben sus propias canciones.

_____

_____

B Translate the following sentences into Spanish, being careful to include a relative pronoun where it is needed, even if there is none in the English.

1 The man who has just arrived is the actor's father.

_____

2 The people who criticise her don't understand the situation.

_____

3 The person I'd love to meet is Christina Aguilera.

_____

4 The group I like best is El sueño de Morfeo.

_____

5 The magazine I bought yesterday has some great photos of the royal family.

_____

Reminder

◆ Sometimes the relative pronoun is preceded by a preposition, most often *a, de, con* or *en*. In such cases you need to use *a que/de que* for things, and *a quien(es)/de quien(es)* for people.

C Choose a suitable relative pronoun and a suitable preposition from the box to fill the gaps in these sentences.
1 Esos son los amigos _____ estudiaba en Salamanca.
2 He olvidado el nombre de la mujer _____ hablábamos.
3 ¿Tienes una amiga _____ te gustaría venir a la fiesta?
4 El problema _____ se refiere es muy grave.
5 El cantautor _____ discutía ese artículo me parece muy interesante.
6 Aquella actriz _____ mandé una carta no ha respondido.

a	de	con	en
que	quien	quienes	

Reminder

◆ After other prepositions, *el cual, la cual, los cuales, las cuales* are used (note that although *cual* alters for the plural, it does not alter for the feminine).

D Translate the following sentences into English.
1 Es un concurso en el que los concursantes tienen que actuar para el público, el cual elige a tres finalistas.

2 Aquel concursante a favor del cual habías votado, no ganó.

3 ¡La estantería sobre la cual he puesto mis libros se ha caído!

4 Al lado de la puerta hay una maceta, dentro de la cual encontrarán las llaves.

5 La ruta por la cual viajasteis es muy bonita.

Reminder

◆ When a relative pronoun is separated from the word to which it refers, it is replaced by *el cual* or *el que*. *El papagayo de mi tío, **el que** es verde, no habla nunca.* If *que* were used here, the uncle rather than the parrot would be green. The definite article must agree with the word referred to.

E Read these sentences and answer the question following each one.
1 La casa de mi amigo, la cual está en Madrid, es bastante pequeña.
Who/what is quite small – the house or the friend? _____
2 El gato de Enrique, el cual tiene catorce años, está enfermo.
Who is ill – Enrique or the cat? _____
3 Los amigos españoles de mis padres, los que han telefoneado, van a visitarnos.
Who is going to visit – the friends or the parents? _____

Reminder

◆ *Donde* also functions as a relative pronoun.

F Translate the following into Spanish.
1 This is the place where we have to turn left.

2 I'm visiting friends in the town where I was born.

3 This is the square where we used to have a beer.

Reminder

◆ To say 'whose' you use *cuyo* (whether for people or things); *cuyo* must agree with the **noun** it refers to, not with the owner. It may help to think of it as an adjective rather than a pronoun.

G Complete the sentences with *cuyo, cuya, cuyos* or *cuyas*.
1 La amiga _____ coche he pedido prestado, vive en Navarra.
2 Tengo que hablar con ese hombre _____ perros están siempre corriendo en mi jardín.
3 El pobre hombre _____ hijas están enfermas ya ha perdido su empleo.

Possessive and demonstrative pronouns

Reminder

◆ Possessive pronouns in English are 'mine', 'yours', 'ours' 'theirs'. In Spanish, possessive pronouns take the same form as the strong possessive adjectives (see page 8). Remember that which one you use depends on who owns the object, but that their agreement must match the noun they describe.

	singular		plural	
	masculine	feminine	masculine	feminine
mine	el mío	la mía	los míos	las mías
yours	el tuyo	la tuya	los tuyos	las tuyas
his/hers/ yours (Vd.)	el suyo	la suya	los suyos	las suyas
ours	el nuestro	la nuestra	los nuestros	las nuestras
yours	el vuestro	la vuestra	los vuestros	las vuestras
theirs/ yours (Vds.)	el suyo	la suya	los suyos	las suyas

A Choose the correct possessive pronoun in each sentence and underline it.

1 Veo a mis abuelos muy rara vez; con qué frecuencia ves a los tuyos / las tuyas?

2 Mi madre es muy nerviosa pero la vuestra / el tuyo parece mucho más relajada.

3 Nuestra generación comprende mejor la tecnología que la suya / el vuestro.

4 Su solución a este problema no va a resultar – la nuestra/el nuestro sería mejor.

5 ¿Mis padres? Están muy bien, gracias – ¿y los tuyos/las tuyas? Están más viejos que el mío/los míos, ¿verdad?

6 Vamos en tu coche; es mucho más cómodo que el nuestro/los nuestros.

7 Dices que nuestro piso es pequeño, pero ¿has visto la suya/el suyo?

B Complete the answers to the questions with a possessive pronoun.

1 ¿Este es el móvil de tu marido? Sí, es

_____

2 Mi hermano no puede ayudarme con mis deberes, porque está haciendo _____.

3 Mamá, ¿por qué la casa de Pepe es más grande que _____? ¡Yo quiero una casa como _____!

4 Sabes, Lisa, tu marido es muy simpático – ¡no es como _____!

5 Cuando compres tus bocadillos, ¿podrías comprar _____ al mismo tiempo?

Reminder

◆ Demonstrative pronouns in English are used to say 'those who', 'the one(s) which' or 'this one/that one'. The demonstrative pronouns in Spanish are as follows. Note that the neuter forms don't take an accent.

	masc. sing.	fem. sing.	neuter sing.		masc. plural	fem. plural
this	este	esta	esto	these	estos	estas
that	ese	esa	eso	those	esos	esas
that	aquel	aquella	aquello	those	aquellos	aquellas

Reminder

◆ Remember that they are used only when there is no noun in place, and that they must agree with the noun that they replace.

C Complete the sentences by writing in a phrase from the box.

1 Prefiero este restaurante, pero es más caro _____.

2 No tenemos que comprar bocadillos, podemos _____.

3 Las mejores frutas _____.

4 No hay mucha diferencia entre este supermercado _____.

5 ¡Rosa! ¿Has visto _____?

6 _____ mi amiga.

es aquella   aquello   son aquellas   que ese
esto   y aquel   comer estos   esa es

Indefinite pronouns and adjectives

Reminder

◆ The most common indefinite pronouns in Spanish (they also serve as indefinite adjectives) are *algo* (something), *alguien* (someone) and *alguno* (some, a few). *Algo* and *alguien* do not change their form, but the indefinite adjective *alguno* must agree with the noun it describes. Like *ninguno* it shortens, becoming *algún* before a masculine singular noun.

A *Algo* or *alguien*? Fill in the gaps with the appropriate indefinite pronoun.

1 Tengo _____ que decirte.
2 _____ llamó pero no sé quién era.
3 _____ le ha pasado a Felipe. Anda muy deprimido – debería hablar con _____.
4 ¿Tiene _____ que declarar, señor?
5 ¿Tienes ganas de beber _____?
6 _____ te ha mandado un texto.
7 Hay mucha gente en la plaza – _____ ha ocurrido.

B Choose a word from the box to fill each gap.

1 _____ cosas me preocupan – por ejemplo mi examen de inglés.
2 ¿Tienes _____ noticia para mí?
3 Me llamarán _____ día.
4 Ha comprado _____ cosas para ti.
5 No sé qué libros voy a llevar, pero llevaré _____.

> algún alguno alguna algunas algunas

Reminder

◆ *Algo* can be used with an adjective, for example *algo interesante*. It can also be used with *de* + infinitive, for example *algo de comer*.

C On a separate sheet, translate the following conversation into English.

¿Quieres algo de comer?
Bueno, no sé ... no tengo mucha hambre ... ¿tomamos algo ligero?
Sí, sin duda hay algo apetitoso en el frigorífico ... ¿prefieres algo dulce?
No, gracias, preferería algo salado. ¿Tenemos espaguetis, por ejemplo?
¿Espaguetis? Pero ¡has dicho que querías algo ligero!

Reminder

◆ *Mucho*, *poco*, *tanto* and *todo* are also used as indefinite pronouns and adjectives. They must agree with the noun they represent or describe.

D Choose *mucho*, *poco*, *tanto* or *todo* (you must use each of them at least once) to fill the gaps in these sentences, remembering to make them agree as necessary.

1 ¿Hay fuentes en los jardines de la Alhambra? Sí, hay _____.
2 Ha escrito _____ artículos, pero nunca ha escrito una novela.
3 Mi vecino canta _____ el día – ¡me vuelve loca!
4 ¿Has comido algo? Muy _____ porque no me siento bien.
5 Me gusta la vida sencilla – no necesito _____.
6 Tengo _____ problemas, no sé qué voy a hacer.

Reminder

◆ *Varios*, *cualquier(a)*, *otro*, and *cada* (*uno*) are also used as indefinite pronouns and adjectives.

E Translate the following sentences into English.

1 Necesitamos identificar otra solución.
_____

2 Tengo que elegir – ¿esta camisa o la otra?
_____

3 Podéis coger cualquiera de los libros.
_____

4 Les dio un regalo a cada uno.
_____

5 Cada estudiante tiene varios libros que leer.
_____

Reminder

◆ Interrogative pronouns *qué* and *cuál/cuáles* have an accent like all interrogatives. *Qué* does not change its form. *Cuál* does not alter in the feminine, but adds -*es* in the plural

F Choose *qué*, *cuál* or *cuáles* to fill the gaps in the following sentences.

1 ¿_____ vaqueros prefieres?
2 ¿_____ haces? Nada.
3 ¿_____ de estas rutas es la mejor?
4 ¿_____ de estos CDs vas a llevar cuando te vayas de vacaciones?
5 ¿_____ te ha afectado a ti?

Revision: prepositions, conjunctions and pronouns

A Translate the prepositions in brackets to complete this passage.

[1 *To*] _____ encontrar la casa, siga estas instrucciones. Estamos [2 *near*] _____ Santa Felicia, [3 *20 km from*] _____ San Miguel. Primero, vaya [4 *to/as far as*] _____ el centro de San Miguel y siga el camino que le lleva [5 *towards*] _____ Santa Felicia. Cuando salga de Santa Felicia, [6 *before*] _____ cruzar el puente, doble [7 *to*] _____ la izquierda, [8 *opposite*] _____ el colegio. Hay una carnicería [9 *on*] _____ la esquina. Continúe [10 *as far as*] _____ un lago que verá [11 *on*] _____ la derecha. [12 *After*] _____ el lago, busque un pequeño camino [13 *next to*] _____ una cruz. Tómelo, y continúe [14 *along*] _____ este camino. [15 *After*] _____ unos dos kilómetros, encontrará nuestra casa [16 *in front of*] _____ usted. Si sale a las diez, debería llegar [17 *around*] _____ las diez y media.

B Choose *a* or *de*, *al*, *del* or *en* to fill each gap in the following sentences.
1. Tienen un hijo _____ veintitrés años – va a casarse _____ finales de año.
2. No estoy _____ acuerdo con todas sus opiniones, pero le respeto _____ él.
3. _____ veces está muy cansado, pero _____ los noventa años, eso no es sorprendente.
4. Nunca le ha pegado _____ su mujer, pero siempre está dándole patadas _____ pobre gato.
5. Llenó el bol _____ frutas frescas.
6. ¿Piensas _____ mí _____ vez en cuando?

C Choose a conjunction to complete the following sentences; use any that makes good sense but use each one in the box at least once. Then, on a separate sheet, translate the completed sentences into English.
1. Siempre charla durante una hora _____ la llamo a ella, _____ _____ ella me llama a mí, ¡hablamos durante sólo cinco minutos!
2. Es difícil comprenderlo _____ habla muy rápido _____ ha perdido los dientes.
3. No puedo decidir _____ hablar contigo.
4. El viaje es muy largo _____ hace mucho calor _____ tendré que ducharme _____ llegar.
5. _____ estudies en Madrid, vas a hacer nuevos amigos, _____ ¡no te olvides de nosotros!

cuando	pero	porque	despuues
de	y	antes	de	asi	que

D Underline the direct object pronouns and circle the indirect object pronouns in the following sentences. Then translate the sentences into English on a separate sheet of paper.
1. Se lo he explicado dos veces, pero no me escuchan.
2. Corta el limón y añádelo a la sangría. La sangría está lista para tus invitados – sírvesela inmediatamente.
3. Cariño, ¿tienes las llaves del coche? Dáselas a mi madre, por favor, porque le he prometido prestárselo para el fin de semana.
Pero ¿qué me dices? ¡Yo lo necesito para ir al aeropuerto! ¡Me vas a volver loco!

E Translate the following sentences into Spanish.
1. Where are my sunglasses? Nadia, have you borrowed them again? Give them to me, please!
2. Ana wants to speak to you. She's asking for that map. What? She's lost it already? But I gave it to her yesterday!
3. The history teacher's always asking me difficult questions – I don't understand them and I don't like him.
4. Do you remember that CD José mentioned? Well, he's finally bought it and he's listening to it now. Would you like to hear it?
5. I'd love to go out with you, but my boyfriend wouldn't like it. He's very possessive about me. Sorry!

F Fill the gaps in the following sentences with *que*, *quien*, *quienes* or *donde*.
1. El hombre con _____ hablaba vive en la ciudad _____ nací.

2 La chica _____ te gusta es la misma de _____ te hablé.

3 La tienda _____ compré estos vaqueros no es la misma _____ me recomendaste.

4 La empresa a _____ he enviado mi solicitud, me ha dado una cita para una entrevista. Es la empresa _____ trabaja ese chico con _____ salí la semana pasada.

G Translate the following into English.

1 Ese vaso es mío, ¿no?
Sí, es el tuyo y éste es el mío.

_____

_____

2 Su madre es programadora y su hermano es ingeniero. ¡Y su prima trabaja para mi padre!

_____

3 Una amiga mía quiere salir con aquel hombre.
¿Aquél, el gordito vestido de negro?
No, no, ése, el alto que lleva vaqueros.
Ah, aquél.

_____

_____

_____

_____

4 ¿Dónde está el libro que estaba leyendo?
Está allí, debajo del mío. Pero ese libro no es muy bueno – deberías leer este otro, es mucho mejor.

_____

_____

_____

5 ¿Vuestro padre vive todavía en esa misma casa?
No, esa casa era demasiado grande para él y ahora vive en la ciudad, muy cerca de una de mis hermanas Esperaba vivir en su piso con ella, pero su marido ha dicho que no ¡porque la madre de él ya vive allí!

_____

_____

_____

_____

_____

6 Estamos invitando a todos nuestros amigos a una fiesta. ¿Quieres venir con tu novio?
Mi novio me ha dejado por una amiga mía. Pero podría pedirle a una amiga que venga conmigo ...

_____

_____

_____

_____

H Fill each gap with one of the indefinite pronouns or adjectives from the box.

1 Hay _____ turistas en la playa.

2 Hay _____ que hacer cuando llueve.
¿Ponen _____ interesante en la televisión esta tarde?

3 _____ de ellos son bastante inteligentes, pero no _____. La inteligencia es _____ raro en los hámsters.

4 ¡_____ día encontraré a _____ interesante que no esté casado!

5 Hay _____ al teléfono que quiere hablar contigo.
¿Quién es?
No sé. _____ inglés. Tú y tus novios, yo no los conozco a _____ .

6 Puedo prestarte _____ de los periódicos – los he leído _____ .

| algún alguno/a/os/as alguien algo |
| poco todo/a/os/as cualquier/a/as |

The main tenses of verbs

> The present tense: regular verbs; the present continuous, the present participle

Regular verbs

Reminder

◆ The present tense is used to describe what is happening now or what usually happens. It can also refer to what you are about to do in the immediate future, and to make a polite request.

A In the numbered sentences below, either a or b has a verb in the present tense. Find it and underline it.

1 a ¿Vas de compras el sábado?
  b ¿Fuiste de compras el sábado?

2 a Sí, compré ropa y vino.
  b Sí, voy al mercado cada semana.

3 a ¿Vas en bici?
  b Normalmente sí, pero esta semana fui en autobús.

4 a ¿Y tu hermana te acompañó?
  b No, juega al tenis los sábados.

5 a ¿Gastaste mucho dinero?
  b No, en el mercado todo es bastante barato.

6 a ¿Vas a tomar otro café?
  b No, gracias, he quedado con mi hermana dentro de diez minutos.

7 a Bueno, ¡salúdale de mi parte!
  b No lo olvidaré. ¿Me das mi chaqueta, por favor?

B Match the six sentences to the reasons for using the present tense.

1 Mando un texto a mi amigo madrileño. ☐
2 Nos enviamos textos una vez a la semana. ☐
3 La visito el domingo. ☐
4 Vive en un piso muy moderno. ☐
5 En Madrid, todo el mundo sale por la tarde para tomar una copa. ☐
6 Nos conocemos desde 1990. ☐

The present tense is being used to describe ...

a something that will happen in the near future
b something which happens regularly
c something which began in the past and is continuing
d something that is happening at the moment
e someone's current situation
f something that is a 'universal' or general fact

Reminder

◆ The endings for a regular -ar verb in the present tense are: hablo, hablas, habla, hablamos, habláis, hablan.

C Complete the verbs and translate the phrases into English.

1 (Yo) _____ (charlar) _____
2 (Tú) _____ (cantar) _____
3 Pablo _____ (bailar) _____
4 (Vd.) _____ (visitar) _____
5 (Nosotros) _____ (tomar) _____
6 Marisol y yo _____ (viajar) _____
7 (Vosotros) _____ (gastar) _____
8 (Ellos) _____ (pasar) _____

Reminder

◆ The endings for a regular -er verb are: como, comes, come, comemos, coméis, comen.

D Choose a verb from the box for each gap, put it into the correct form, and translate the sentences into English.

1 [Nosotros] Siempre _____ en un restaurante los viernes.
_____

2 [Tú] No _____ fumar tanto.
_____

3 En nuestro mercado se _____ frutas riquísimas.
_____

4 ¿_____ Vds. cuándo llega el tren de Madrid?
_____

> vender   deber   saber   comer

Reminder

◆ The endings for a regular -ir verb are: vivo, vives, vive, vivimos, vivís, viven

E Use a suitable verb chosen from the box to translate the sentences into Spanish.

1 The shops open at three.
_____

2 My boyfriend writes poetry for me.
_____

3 My father lives 10 km from our house.
_____

4 In his article he describes the scenery of Navarra.
_____

> vivir   abrir   describir   escribir

The present continuous, the present participle

◆ The present continuous (appropriate part of *estar* + present participle) is used (as it is in English) to describe a process that is going on at the present moment.

To form the present participle, replace the infinitive ending as follows: *-ar – ando*; *-er/-ir – iendo*. Note that some *-ir* verbs change their spelling from *e* to *i* or *o* to *u* in the present participle, e.g. *durmiendo, prefiriendo*.

A Underline the form of *estar* and circle the whole present continuous verb in the sentences below. Write the English translation of the circled phrase in the space at the end of each sentence.

1 Están preparando pasteles para la fiesta.

2 ¡Entrad! Estamos viendo un DVD.

3 Cuando la visito, siempre está trabajando.

4 ¡León! ¡Oye! ¿Estás durmiendo?

5 He pelado las naranjas para la sangría, y ahora estoy cortándolas.

6 ¡Hola, Alejandro! Un momentito ... ¡estamos bañando al perro! Ah, lo siento, se está sacudiendo ... No, Brutus, ¡basta ya! ¡Estás salpicando a Alejandro!

B Translate the following sentences into Spanish.

1 Please talk more quietly, children – I'm listening to this music!

2 Miguel's been in the bath since 8 o'clock. He always says he's reading El País but in my opinion he's sleeping.

3 Where are the boys? They're watching the Barça match with the neighbours.

4 Could you call back in half an hour? We're just getting up.

Reminder

◆ The present participle is also used in the following constructions:
– after *seguir* it means to continue doing something
– after *ir* it also means to keep doing something
– after *llevar* it means to spend a certain amount of time doing something

C Choose an appropriate expression from the box to complete the following sentences.

1 Manuela _____ *Don Quixote.*
2 _____ en la Universidad de Salamanca.
3 Isabel y Enrique _____ al tenis cada tarde.
4 _____ el precio de la gasolina.
5 _____ aquí hasta el mes entrante.
6 ¿Por qué _____ estas flores ridículas?

> seguiré trabajando   va subiendo
> siguen jugando   llevan dos años estudiando
> sigues enviándome   sigue leyendo

Reminder

◆ There is another form of present participle, used as an adjective. The ending is *-ante* for *-ar* verbs and *-iente* for *-er* and *-ir* verbs. Remember that these present participles must agree, so although they do not change their form for the feminine, they do add an *-s* in the plural.

D Complete the table with the English for the following expressions.

1	el día siguiente	
2	agua corriente	
3	la semana entrante	
4	plantas vivientes	
5	una idea sorprendente	

The main tenses of verbs

Reflexive verbs

Reminder

- ◆ Reflexive verbs work in the same way as non-reflexives but with the addition of the reflexive pronoun (see page 22 for the pronouns).

A Translate the following sentences into English.

1 Nico, ¿estás levantándote? ¡Son las once!

_____

2 Mi hermano lleva un año construyéndose una casa.

_____

3 Se llama Xavier, como su padre y su abuelo, pero sus hijos se llaman Antonio y Ramón.

_____
_____

4 Vamos, niños, hay que darse prisa para llegar a tiempo.

_____

5 ¿Os divertís en Madrid?
Sí, mucho. Nos estamos permitiendo el lujo y nos alojamos en un buen hotel. Salimos todas las noches ¡y nos acostamos hacia las dos de la madrugada!

_____
_____
_____

B Translate the verbs in brackets to complete the text.

Durante las vacaciones, [we get up] _____ hacia las diez; generalmente [I have a bath] _____ y Maribel [has a shower] _____. [We get dressed] _____ antes de las once, porque a las once y media nuestros amigos a menudo nos visitan para tomar café. Siempre [we enjoy ourselves] _____ con ellos, contando historias y charlando sobre cualquier tema. Por la tarde, [we go off to] _____ todos a nuestro bar preferido. Es muy popular y [it fills up] _____ hacia las nueve. [We never take] _____ el coche, porque normalmente [we treat ourselves] _____ de bebernos una botella de Rioja. ¡Por supuesto, [we go to bed] _____ bastante tarde! Sí, durante las vacaciones [we don't rush] _____ y [we feel] _____ más relajados.

Reminder

- ◆ See page 63 on using reflexive forms to avoid the passive.

Spelling change verbs and common irregular verbs

Reminder

- ◆ Many verbs in Spanish have a spelling change in several of their present tense forms. The most common changes are as follows (remember that the *nosotros* and *vosotros* forms are not affected):

e > ie	o > ue	e > i	u > ue
querer	poder	pedir	jugar
entender	encontrar	corregir	costar
pensar	dormir	seguir	contar
cerrar	volver	elegir	encontrar
preferir	llover		
sentir	mostrar		
quiero	puedo	pido	juego
quieres	puedes	pides	juegas
quiere	puede	pide	juega
queremos	podemos	pedimos	jugamos
queréis	podéis	pedís	jugáis
quieren	pueden	piden	juegan

A On a separate sheet, translate the first paragraph into Spanish and the second into English. In the second one, the present tense is used for dramatic effect and you could do the same in English.

1 My team is playing very badly. We're all playing very badly – don't we want to win? Except for Diego, of course. Hey, Diego, you're playing really well!

2 ¡Qué día! Voy de compras a las doce menos cuarto y no encuentro a nadie. La tienda cierra a las once y media hoy porque el comerciante juega en un equipo de fútbol. Vuelvo a casa, pero no puedo entrar porque mis llaves están en la cocina. Llueve mucho, y pienso que voy a acabar empapado. Finalmente, le pido al vecino que me permita entrar por su balcón. Me siento muy cansado.

Reminder

- ◆ Here are some additional spelling changes that affect the first person only in some common irregular verbs.

conocer/conozco	hacer/hago	salir/salgo
dar/doy	poner/pongo	tener/tengo
estar/estoy	saber/sé	ver/veo

B Choose an appropriate verb from the box above to complete each sentence.

1 No _____ nunca los domingos. _____ las tareas domésticas y _____ la televisión.

2 Siempre le _____ un regalo para su cumpleaños, pero este año no _____ qué comprar.

3 Mi jefe me ha invitado a cenar con su familia. No los _____ muy bien, así que me _____ algo bastante elegante.

4 _____ muy cansada, pero _____ que terminar este trabajo.

C Translate the following into Spanish.
– I never do my homework because I go out every night.
– I know that – I know you pretty well!
– Alright, I'll give you my notes, but this is the last time!

_____

_____

_____

Reminder

◆ Watch out also for the spellings of the following irregular verbs:

decir: digo, dices, dice, decimos, decís, dicen
ir: voy, vas, va, vamos, vais, van
oír: oigo, oyes, oye, oímos, oís, oyen
tener: tengo, tienes, tiene, tenemos, tenéis, tienen
venir: vengo, vienes, viene, venimos, venís, vienen

D Identify the most appropriate verb from the box above, and select the correct form to fill each gap in the following passage.

Los políticos siempre nos (1) _____ que (2) _____ a cambiar todo. (3) _____ los discursos cada año y no (4) _____ mucha confianza en ellos. Señoras, señores, Vds. (5) _____ que comprender que mis amigos y yo (6) _____ de un país donde los políticos son poco fiables. Les (7) _____ que, si queremos cambiar el mundo, (8) _____ que hacerlo nosotros mismos.

Ser and estar

Reminder

◆ In Spanish there are two verbs meaning 'to be': *ser* and *estar*.

Ser is used before nouns, pronouns and adjectives when something is being defined or a long-term or intrinsic characteristic is being described. It is also used in expressions of time and in stating amounts or measurements, for example *son las dos*.

Estar is used before adjectives when a temporary state or condition is being described, and often with prepositions to state location.

Both verbs are irregular, but *ser* is more so. Here is the present tense of each:

Soy, eres, es, somos, sois, son
Estoy, estás, está, estamos, estáis, están.

A Underline the examples of *ser* and circle the examples of *estar* in this paragraph. On a separate sheet of paper, make a list of the phrases containing the verbs you have identified and next to each one, explain why each verb is used in each case. (For example: *Su casa es grande* – *ser* because it's a permanent characteristic.)

Su casa es grande, su mujer es una modelo guapa, y sus dos hijos son inteligentes. Pero su mujer está en Brasil con otro hombre, su madre está enferma, su padre está un poco deprimido, su hermano está en la cárcel, y su hija es heroinómana. ¡Qué vida!

B Underline the correct verb form from among the options given to complete these sentences.

1 Los viernes por la tarde Antonio y Marco no son/está/están/es nunca en casa.

2 Yo estoy/soy/son/está muy enfadada con mi marido porque están/es/eres/está una persona muy difícil.

3 Estas ideas estoy/es/son/están nuevas.

4 Mi novio eres/está/son/es fontanero, así que están/estamos/somos/eres bastante ricos.

5 El presidente soy/están/son/está de vacaciones y la economía estoy/está/somos/están en crisis.

6 ¿De dónde son/está/es/están Vds.? Y ¿dónde está/eres/están/son los otros miembros de su familia?

7 Andrés es/eres/está/estamos muy nervioso antes de su examen, pero no soy/es/son/está necesario porque están/es/esto/está muy inteligente.

The main tenses of verbs

Modes of address; *gustar*

Reminder

◆ There are two levels of formality for saying 'you' in Spanish. Which you use depends on how well you know the person and their age or position in relation to you. Each has both singular and plural forms.

	Singular	Plural
Less formal	*tú*	*vosotros, vosotras*
More formal	*Vd.* (*usted*)	*Vds.* (*ustedes*)

The choice governs not only the pronoun (when needed) but of course the verb form. For example:

	Singular	Plural
Less formal	*hablas*	*habláis*
More formal	*habla*	*hablan*

A Write down which form you would use in each of the following contexts: *tú, vosotros, vosotras, Vd.* or *Vds.*

Para hablar con ...

1 otra estudiante en la clase _____
2 un cliente en el bar donde trabajas _____
3 dos de tus amigas _____
4 tres turistas que preguntan el camino _____
5 algunos niños que juegan en la calle _____

6 un perro que ha entrado en tu jardín _____
7 la hija de tu hermana _____
8 la directora de tu instituto _____
9 los miembros de tu equipo de vóleibol _____
10 un hombre que ha venido a la casa para reparar la televisión _____

Reminder

◆ The verb *gustar* must agree with its subject, not with the person who 'likes' or 'dislikes'.

B Fill the gaps with the correct form of *gustar*, and then translate the sentences into English on a separate sheet.

1 Me _____ la idea del programa, pero no me _____ los presentadores.
2 ¿Te _____ los programas reality ?- Sí, me _____ algunos, pero prefiero los programas sobre la casa, la decoración, no me _____ Supervivientes.
3 Me _____ los anuncios, pero aparte de eso, no me _____ mucho la televisión.
4 Les _____ ver películas y las noticias, pero no les _____ ni las series ni los realitys.

Negatives

Reminder

◆ To make a statement negative, place *no* between the subject and the verb.
If there are object pronouns in front of the verb, *no* is placed in front of them instead of next to the verb.

A Make the following sentences negative.

1 Según este artículo, es demasiado tarde para salvar el medio ambiente.

_____

2 Debemos vivir sin preocuparnos del futuro.

_____

3 Mi coche, por ejemplo, consume mucha gasolina.

_____

4 En mi familia nos gusta comprar productos con mucho envoltorio de plástico.

_____

5 A los niños les interesa este problema.

_____

6 Tiran basura por la calle y olvidan la importancia del reciclaje.

_____

Reminder

◆ To add a negative 'checker' to a statement or question (as in English 'don't I?', 'isn't it?'), simply add *¿no?* in Spanish.
To translate simple negative constructions about hoping, thinking etc., such as 'I hope not' and 'I don't believe so', you need to use *que no* after the verb in Spanish. *Que sí* is used similarly for positive reactions.

B Translate the following exchanges into English.

1 Has visto esta entrevista, ¿no? – Creo que no. No he visto el periódico.

_____

2 ¿No te gusta leer los periódicos? – Claro que sí, pero ¡no tengo tiempo!

_____

3 Pero ves la tele, ¿no? – Claro que no, tengo demasiado trabajo.

_____

4 Pero ¿no te interesan las noticias, lo que pasa en el mundo? – Supongo que sí, pero mis amigos me ponen al día!

Reminder

◆ Spanish uses double negatives, that is, *no* plus a second negative word such as *nada, nadie, nunca, jamás, ninguno, tampoco, ni … ni, ni siquiera, más, más que*. Among these words only *ninguno* agrees with the noun; it shortens to *ningún* in front of a masculine singular noun.
When double negative words are used with *no*, *no* must go before the verb (and any object pronouns). The second negative word comes after the verb. You can use two or more negative words in the same sentence.

C Choose an appropriate negative word or expression to fill each gap.
1 Los periodistas esperaron tres horas cerca de la casa, pero no vieron a _____.
2 No me interesa _____ la política _____ el deporte.
3 No me gusta _____ de esos diarios.
4 Fuimos al quiosco pero no compramos _____.
5 Aquel periódico no es serio, no hace _____ análisis.
6 ¡_____ había _____ una sola foto!
7 El actor no leyó la revista, su mujer _____.
8 ¿El Mundo? No lo leo _____.
9 Hoy no he visto _____ los titulares.
10 No tiene sentido hablar con él, no le interesa ni nada ni _____.

Reminder

◆ *Nadie, nada* and *ninguno* can be used with *que* and an infinitive.

D Use *nadie que, nada que* or *ninguno que* to complete the sentences.
1 En el aeropuerto, los turistas no tenían _____ _____ declarar.
2 Una mañana libre – no tengo _____ _____ hacer; ¡no lo creo! No tengo _____ trabajo _____ hacer, y no tengo _____ clientes _____ llamar.

Reminder

◆ Except for *más* and *más que*, the negative words listed above may be used without *no* and placed before the verb.
They may also be used on their own as a short negative response.

E Translate sentences 1–4 into English, and sentences 5–8 into Spanish.
1 Ni siquiera nos saludaron.
   _____
2 ¿Nadie me ha dejado un mensaje? – Nadie.
   _____
3 Nunca encontrarán la solución a este problema.
   _____
4 Ni mi padre ni mi madre están contentos. Yo tampoco.
   _____
5 Nothing has changed.
   _____
6 He didn't even open his e-mails.
   _____
7 I know you will forget me. – No, never.
   _____
8 Neither the teacher nor your friends understand you. Neither can I.
   _____

Reminder

◆ Other useful negative expressions are *aún … no* (still … not), *todavía … no* (not yet) and *sin* (without).
To translate 'without anything' or 'without anyone', you must use the negative word, not the positive one, in Spanish, e.g. *sin **nada**, sin **nadie***.
Sin can also be used with an infinitive, but see page 57 for a reminder on using *sin que* with a verb in the subjunctive.

F Translate the following sentences into English.
1 A mi abuelo no le gusta Internet, prefiere el periódico.
   _____
2 ¿Has comprado mi periódico? No, todavía no.
   _____
3 Se marchó sin ella, y sin decirle adiós.
   _____
4 Llegaremos antes de las once sin problema.
   _____

37

The perfect tense

Reminder

◆ The perfect tense is used as it is in English to refer to actions which have recently been completed. It usually translates directly into the English perfect tense, so *has comido* would be 'you have eaten'.

A Underline the perfect tense verb in each sentence and translate the sentences into English on a separate sheet.

1 Rosa y Jaime han llegado, pero Carlos ha llamado para decirnos que tiene un problema con su coche – va a llegar a las diez.
2 ¿Han visto este artículo sobre el turismo en Chile?
3 No hemos visitado la Catedral Vieja, pero hemos estado en casi todos los otros sitios principales y ahora vamos a beber algo fresco.
4 ¿Has visto esta guía? – Sí, pero no voy a comprarla porque ya he comprado otra, con mapa.

Reminder

◆ The perfect tense is formed with the appropriate form of *haber* plus a past participle. The forms of *haber* are: he, has, ha, hemos, habéis, han. Remember that in all other contexts you should use *tener*, not *haber*, to mean 'have'.

B Fill each gap with the correct form of *haber*.

1 Todos los miembros de la Sociedad Cervantes se _____ apuntado para la excursión a Valladolid
2 _____ terminado, señores?
3 Chicas ¿ _____ estado en Sevilla alguna vez?
4 Niños, ¿os _____ lavado las manos?
5 Mi hermano y yo vivimos aquí en Zaragoza pero ¡nunca _____ visitado el palacio morisco!

Reminder

◆ Regular verbs form their past participles like this:
hablar – habl**ado**   comer – com**ido**   vivir – viv**ido**

C Fill the gaps with the past participle of the appropriate verb from the box.

1 Mis amigos me han _____ a pasar una semana con ellos en Buenos Aires.
2 Blanca ha _____ un nuevo piso cerca de la Plaza Mayor, ¡qué suerte!

3 ¿Nunca has _____ en el restaurante 'Alhambra'? Vamos allí el sábado.
4 ¿Ese chico catalán? Últimamente no he _____ con él.

| hablar   comer   comprar   invitar |

Reminder

◆ A few common verbs have irregular past participles. (Check the verb tables on pages 86–91.)

D Translate the sentences into Spanish on a separate sheet using the verbs suggested.

1 Have you told Manuel the result of the match? (*decir*)
2 I've lost my bag – have you (*tú*) seen it? (*perder*, *ver*)
3 I don't know what I've done but they refuse to call me. (*hacer*)
4 We've put the luggage in the car and now we're waiting for our friend. (*poner*)

Reminder

◆ When using the perfect tense, the two parts of the verb must stay together. Don't be tempted to put pronouns or negative words between *haber* and the past participle.

E Underline the perfect tense verb in each sentence. Then translate the sentences into English.

1 No he entendido nunca la física.
_____
2 Nunca se lo ha dicho a nadie, pero no trabaja.
_____
3 ¿Aún no te han mandado ese dinero?
_____
4 No hemos recibido ninguna información sobre ellos.
_____

Reminder

◆ To say someone has just done something, you use the present tense of *acabar de* + infinitive.

F Put *acabar de* into the appropriate form in the following sentences. Then translate into English the expression using *acabar de*.

The preterite tense

Reminder

◆ This tense is used to refer to events or actions which took place in the past. They are not usually as recent as events described by the perfect tense, and there is not the same sense of them having just been completed. However, in Latin American Spanish you are more likely to find the preterite used for recent events.

A Decide whether you would use the perfect tense or the preterite tense to translate the verbs in the following sentences into Spanish. Underline those you would translate using the <u>preterite</u>.

1   I wrote an email to that programme but I haven't had a reply.
2   The new series of Gran Hermano started last week but I haven't seen it.
3   The president has decided to take part in a TV debate; last year he refused to appear.
4   Yesterday I watched a programme on global warming. Parts of southern Europe have suffered serious floods recently and the programme explained how this is related to climate change.
5   On Friday Julio received an invitation to take part in a TV competition; he's never appeared on TV so he got very excited.
6   Esteban and Mercedes bumped into that TV personality last week – they haven't stopped talking about it!
7   I don't believe it, I've missed a whole episode of my favourite soap! My granny rang up and talked for 40 minutes.
8   Last month Antonio saw a programme about heart problems and he decided to eat more healthily. But look – he's just ordered a banana split! He lost some weight at the start but now I think it's his motivation that has gone.

Reminder

◆ The preterite tense is formed as follows:

hablar	comer	vivir
hablé	comí	viví
hablaste	comiste	viviste
habló	comió	vivió
hablamos	comimos	vivimos
hablasteis	comisteis	vivisteis
hablaron	comieron	vivieron

B Using the prompts, write out in full on a separate sheet these passages about what people did at the weekend.

Roberto
1   [hablar] con Isabel por teléfono
2   [invitar] a ir con él a la playa
3   [descubrir] que a Isabel no le gusta el mar
4   [llamar] a Susana
5   [dejar] un mensaje con el padre de Susana
6   no [recibir] ninguna respuesta de Susana
7   [salir] solo y [comer] muchas patatas fritas

Vosotros
1   [cenar] con la familia
2   [leer] los periódicos
3   [comprar] algunas cosas para la casa
4   [lavar] el coche
5   [escribir] algunos correos electrónicos

Yo … / pero ellos …
1   [perder] mi empleo / [ganar] diez mil euros
2   [tomar] una cerveza / [beber] tres botellas de Rioja
3   [vender] mi bici / [comprar] un coche
4   [comer] en casa / [salir] con sus amigos a un restaurante
5   [decidir] no ir de vacaciones / [reservar] un hotel

C On a separate sheet, translate all the following into Spanish.

Yesterday Señor Martín arrived at the company at 8 a.m. He went into his office, took off his jacket and sat down. He had a coffee and took out his papers.

He worked for two hours, preparing for an important meeting. At 10 o'clock his visitors arrived. He offered them coffee and everybody gathered in the meeting room. They spent three hours discussing rights and fees. Finally they all signed a contract.

Afterwards they all went out and had a good lunch. Señor Martín did not return to the office in the afternoon.

Reminder

◆ Some of the most common verbs – *dar, decir, estar, haber, hacer, ir, poder, poner, querer, saber, ser, tener, traer, venir* – are irregular in the preterite. Check their forms in the table on pages 86–93. Note that the verb *saber* in the preterite means 'to find out' rather than 'to know'.

The main tenses of verbs

D Choose the appropriate verb from those listed above, and use it in its correct form to complete the following sentences. Use a different verb in each sentence.

1 ¿Qué _____ Vds. el fin de semana pasado? _____ a Barcelona y ¡lo pasamos bomba!

2 Enrique _____ un regalo a sus hijos – ¡dos gorras rojas! Se las _____ inmediatamente.

3 Anoche llamé a José. Cuando _____ que estaba enfermo, le _____ que debería ir al médico.

4 Nuestros amigos _____ a cenar a las nueve; _____ flores para Maribel.

Reminder

◆ Certain groups of verbs have spelling changes in the preterite.

The following -ir verbs change the middle e to i in the third person singular and plural, e.g. advirtió, advirtieron, prefirió, prefirieron.

advertir, conseguir, corregir, divertir(se), elegir, mentir, preferir, referir, reírse, repetir, seguir, sentir(se), vestir(se)

Verbs ending in -car change their c to qu in the first person singular, e.g. busqué.

Verbs ending in -gar change their g to gu in the first person singular, e.g. pagué.

Verbs ending in -zar change their z to c in the first person singular, e.g. crucé.

Verbs ending in -ducir change their c to j in the preterite, e.g. conduje, condujiste, etc.

Verbs ending in -eer need an accent on the stressed i; unstressed i changes to y, e.g. leí, leíste, leyó, leímos, leísteis, leyeron.

In verbs ending in -ñer or -ñir, the unstressed i is dropped after ñ in the third person singular and plural, e.g. gruñó, gruñeron.

E Translate the following sentences into Spanish.

1 I looked for *Guía TV* but couldn't find it.

2 They preferred the more expensive screen but they chose the cheaper one.

3 Yesterday Margarita enjoyed herself – she drove to the beach, and read a whole novel.

4 I paid for our dinner because Esteban's credit card didn't work; he felt very uncomfortable because the waiter laughed.

F Read this account of an exchange visit and fill the gaps with the prompted verbs in the preterite tense (most, though not all, are irregular and/or require a spelling change).

El junio pasado _____ [yo] (1 ir) a España por primera vez. _____ (2 Alojarse) con mi amiga Ángela y su familia. El primer día sus padres _____ (3 estar) muy simpáticos: _____ [yo] (4 tener) muchos errores, pero no _____ [ellos] (5 reírse). Me _____ (6 corregir) con una sonrisa. Un día _____ (7 visitar) a la abuela de Ángela. No la _____ (8 entender), así que _____ (9 repetir) las palabras más lentamente. Me _____ (10 gustar) mucho mis vacaciones. _____ (11 hacer) muchas cosas interesantes. Por ejemplo, _____ (12 ir) a Salamanca. ¡El hermano de Ángela _____ (13 conducir) muy rápido y me _____ (14 dar) miedo!

En Salamanca _____ (15 buscar) un regalo para la madre de Ángela y _____ (16 encontrar) un florero azul. El último día de mi visita, _____ (17 poner) algunas flores en el florero y se lo _____ (18 regalar) a ella. Me _____ (19 decir) que le gustaba mucho.

The imperfect tense

A Underline the verbs in the imperfect and translate the sentences into English.

Teenagers quiz their grandparents about how things used to be.

1 ¿Dónde vivíais?

2 ¿Cuántos hijos teníais?

3 ¿Trabajabais los dos?

4 ¿Cuánto ganaba un trabajador típico en aquellos tiempos?

5 ¿Adónde ibais de vacaciones?

6 ¿Qué hacíais para relajaros?

7 ¿Comíais las mismas cosas que hoy en día?

8 ¿Erais felices?

B Fill in the gaps in the chart and translate the *yo* phrases into English, as done for <u>trabajar</u>.

C Match up the sentence halves. Then underline all the verbs in the imperfect tense.

Era un día típico en el hotel. **¿Que hacían los clientes?**

1 La señora González leía ☐
2 Los jóvenes desayunaban ☐
3 El coronel jugaba ☐
4 La señora Martínez y su hermana se daban ☐
5 Roberto se peleaba ☐
6 El señor Ricardo esperaba ☐
7 La familia Domingo hacía sus maletas ☐
8 Clara hablaba por teléfono ☐
9 La señorita Pascual tomaba ☐
10 Los negociantes tomaban ☐

a con su hermano.
b una copa en el bar.
c un paseo en el jardín.
d una novela romántica.
e con todas sus amigas.
f antes de salir.
g al golf.
h a un amigo en la recepción.
i una ducha.
j en el comedor.

	trabajar	trabajábamos	(yo) trabajaba	I worked (was working, used to work)
1	comprar			
2	jugar			
3	lavar			
4	beber			
5	ver			
6	traer			
7	conducir			
8	escribir			
9	salir			

D Fill the gaps with the appropriate imperfect form.

1 Lorca _____ sólo tragedias sino también poesías. (*escribir*)

2 ¿ _____ en la universidad cuando empezaste a leer su poesía? (*estudiar*)

3 La Guerra Civil terminó con muchas vidas que _____ tanto. (*prometer*)

4 En aquella época muchos escritores, poetas y pintores _____ juntos. (*trabajar*)

5 No _____ la literatura y las otras artes como totalmente distintas. (*ver*)

6 Siempre _____ un café a las nueve. (*ellos/tomar*)

Reminder

◆ The only irregular imperfects in Spanish are *ir* and *ser*:

ir	ser
iba	era
ibas	eras
iba	era
íbamos	éramos
ibais	erais
iban	eran

E Fill each gap with the correct form of *ir* or *ser*.

1 En aquellos días (*nosotros*) _____ al colegio a pie.

2 ¿Qué le pasó a Miguel? _____ deportista, pero hoy en día ¡está muy gordo!

3 El señor Alfonso _____ a Madrid en tren todos los fines de semana.

4 _____ rico pero he perdido todo.

5 ¿Te acuerdas de Enrique? _____ muy guapo.

6 Cuando (*vosotros*) _____ jóvenes, ¿adónde _____ de vacaciones?

F Fill in the gaps, using the verbs from the box, to explain how Enrique spent his time when he was a student.

1 _____ Literatura española en la Universidad de Salamanca.

2 _____ incondicional del teatro.

3 _____ al teatro y al cine varias veces por semana.

4 _____ mucho tiempo leyendo obras de teatro.

5 _____ representaciones con otros estudiantes.

6 _____ sobre revistas películas y obras de teatro.

7 _____ con convertirse er un gran escritor de tragedias.

8 _____ la campeona de natación de su colegio.

escribir	pasar	soñar	ser
organizar	estudiar	ir	

G Fill each gap with an appropriate verb in the imperfect tense, choosing from those in the box below each text.

Los viejos tiempos

1 **La abuela habla**

Ah sí, cuando yo era joven la gente _____ en forma. _____ a todas partes a pie – nadie _____ coche en aquellos días – y, sabes, todos _____ duro. Las mujeres _____ toda la ropa a mano y _____ la casa todas las mañanas. También _____ tres veces al día.

lavar	trabajar	estar	limpiar	tener	cocinar	ir

2 **Los padres hablan**

A los veinte años, _____ deportistas. _____ al bádminton todos los días, _____ paseos por la montaña y _____ un jardín grande donde _____ mucho trabajo. Sí, _____ una copa por la tarde y _____ de vez en cuando a comer a un restaurante, pero generalmente _____ sano y no _____ muchas cosas dulces.

hacer	comer	jugar	tomar	ser
salir	dar	tener	vivir	

3 **El joven habla**

He dejado mis malas costumbres. Antes, _____ pasteles y patatas fritas todo el tiempo. No me _____ ni comer frutas ni tomar vitaminas. _____ horas viendo la televisión, _____ muy tarde, _____ cuatro veces por semana a los bares con mis amigos y _____ mucho. También _____ diez cigarrillos por día. _____ demasiado gordo y _____ estresado.

interesar	sentirse	estar	pasar
fumar	comer	ir	acostarse	beber

The imperfect continuous

Reminder

◆ The imperfect continuous tense is used to refer to an action that was going on at a precise moment when something else happened. It often implies a contrast between the situation as it was, and the new event. It is formed by using the imperfect tense of *estar*, with the present participle; in other words, it's the imperfect form of the present continuous (see page 33).
Estaba leyendo *cuando sonó el teléfono.*

A Use the imperfect continuous form of a verb from the box to fill each gap.

¿Qué estaban haciendo los jugadores cuando el entrenador entró?

1 Jorge _____ unos plátanos.
2 Guillermo _____ su MP3.
3 Alberto _____ flexiones.
4 Mateo y Diego _____ al árbitro.
5 Enrico _____ su gol a Julio.
6 Felipe _____ fotos de Enrico en su móvil.
7 Mani _____ un agua mineral.
8 Ahmed y Esteban _____ a sus novias.
9 Lisa _____ un cigarrillo.
10 Pero Luis y yo _____ .

> describir telefonear comer hacer beber criticar sacar escuchar

B Complete the following sentences in Spanish using the imperfect continuous of the verbs given.

1 [Yo / trabajar] _____ demasiado en aquella época.
2 [Yo / pasar] _____ casi todo el tiempo en la oficina.
3 [Yo / dormir] _____ solamente seis horas.
4 Mi marido siempre [decir] _____ que [yo / perjudicar] mi salud.
5 [Yo / estresarse] _____ pero no lo [tomar] en serio.
6 Lo peor era que [yo / beber] demasiado y no comía bien.
7 En realidad, [yo / ignorar] _____ a mi marido y mi propia salud.
8 [Yo/hacer] _____ mis deberes cuando recibí tu correo.

Reminder

◆ With reflexive verbs in compound tenses, the two parts of the verb must stay together and the reflexive pronoun usually goes at the end of the present participle. Note that the verb takes an accent in this case. Occasionally the pronoun is placed before both parts of the verb.

C Translate sentences 1–4 into English and sentences 5–8 into Spanish.

1 Estaba despertándose cuando empezó a llover.
_____
2 Estaba bañándose cuando la tormenta empezó.
_____
3 Estaba afeitándose cuando los rayos empezaron.
_____
4 Una hora más tarde, el viento se estaba quitando cuando salió de la casa.
_____
5 I was getting up when the phone rang.
_____
6 I was having a shower when you arrived.
_____
7 I was getting dressed when the phone rang again.
_____
8 I was getting furious but you answered it.
_____

D Write sentences in the past tense to explain Raimundo's alibis for the times when the various crimes were committed.
Example: *el ladrón entra / Raimundo duerme*
Cuando el ladrón entró, Raimundo estaba durmiendo.

1 Alguien rompe la ventana / Raimundo juega al vóleibol.
_____
2 Alguien se lleva mi bici / Raimundo pasea al perro en el parque.
_____
3 El matón atraca a una señora / Raimundo ve la televisión con su novia.
_____
4 El ladrón entra en la tienda de ordenadores / Raimundo bebe una cerveza en el bar.
_____
5 Alguien se lleva la radio de mi coche / Raimundo hace las compras en el supermercado.
_____

Using contrasting past tenses

Reminder

- You use the **perfect** tense to refer to something that has just recently happened.
- You use the **preterite** tense to refer to actions or events that took place and were completed at a certain point in the past.
- You use the **imperfect** tense to refer to actions, events or states that were taking place for some time, that used to take place, or that took place regularly over a period of time.
- You use the **imperfect continuous** tense to refer to something that was going on when another event occurred.

A Decide whether you would use the imperfect or the preterite to translate the verbs in the following sentences. Write I or P in the boxes.

1 He drove to the studio every day. ☐
2 The concert lasted for four hours. ☐
3 The new group were not very happy together. ☐
4 You used to play in a band, didn't you? ☐
5 She appeared in a talent show last year. ☐
6 The group played every Thursday in local bars. ☐
7 They played the barman's favourites for his birthday. ☐

B Underline the correct version of the verb in each sentence.

La juventud de mi abuela

1 Nació/nacía el 18 de marzo de 1944.
2 Su padre se murió/muría dos meses después de su nacimiento.
3 Vivió/vivía con su madre en una pequeña casa.
4 Empezó/Empezaba el colegio a la edad de cinco años.
5 Le gustó/gustaba mucho el colegio.
6 Pero cuando cambió/cambiaba de colegio, encontró/encontraba problemas.
7 Los profesores fueron/eran mucho más estrictos.
8 Ella no estuvo/estaba contenta, y terminó/terminaba el colegio cuando tuvo/tenía catorce años.
9 Dejó/dejaba su pueblo y fue/iba a Bilbao.
10 Empezó/empezaba su primer trabajo en 1958.
11 Trabajó/trabajaba como maquinista en una fábrica.
12 Vivió/Estaba viviendo en Bilbao cuando conoció/conocía a Basilio.
13 Basilio fue/era un joven andaluz que trabajó/trabajaba en Bilbao.
14 Basilio fue/era alto y bastante guapo; a mi abuela le gustó/gustaba inmediatamente.
15 Después de poco, Basilio y mi abuela salieron/salían todos los fines de semana.
16 Fueron/iban a los bares de Bilbao, dieron/daban paseos cerca del mar, bailaron/bailaban y fueron/iban al cine.
17 Se casaron/se casaban en 1961.
18 Durante cinco años vivieron/vivían en Bilbao.
19 En 1966 decidieron/decidían mudarse a Sevilla, porque el padre de Basilio estuvo/estaba muy enfermo.
20 Después de mudarse a Sevilla, tuvieron/tenían dos hijas. Estuvieron/Estaban muy contentos en Sevilla.

C Translate these sentences into Spanish.

1 Have you seen my book about Joaquín Rodrigo? I was reading it when you came in.

_____

2 Rodrigo was already studying piano and violin and giving concerts when he decided to go to Paris.

_____

3 Carmen called again. Have you sent her those tickets? No, sorry, I haven't sent them. I was getting them ready when a visitor arrived, and then I forgot.

_____

_____

4 The singer was singing with his eyes closed when he fell off the stage. He fell onto a spectator who was dancing in the front row. The singer is fine but the spectator has a broken wrist and is receiving treatment for shock.

_____

_____

_____

5 While I was driving from Casares to Estepona my car broke down. I called the garage but it was closed. It was very hot, so I went to sleep. When I woke up it was 3 o'clock. I rang the garage again and a lorry arrived after half an hour. The driver gave me a drink because I was very thirsty and didn't have any water.

_____

_____

_____

_____

_____

The pluperfect tense

Reminder

◆ This is the tense you use to refer to what 'had' been done, i.e. one stage further back in the past than events in the perfect tense that 'have' been done. Like the perfect tense, it combines the verb *haber* and the past participle, but you use the imperfect tense of *haber* instead of the present. For example, with *mirar*:

perfect tense	pluperfect tense
he mirado	**había** mirado
has mirado	**habías** mirado
ha mirado	**había** mirado
hemos mirado	**habíamos** mirado
habéis mirado	**habíais** mirado
han mirado	**habían** mirado

A Match up the phrases that go together.
1 Luisa no aprobó su examen, porque ☐
2 Escribió una buena redacción, porque ☐
3 Tenía mucho frío, porque ☐
4 Llegó tarde, porque ☐
5 No participó en la clase de educación física, porque ☐
6 La señora Ramona la regañó, porque ☐
7 Se peleó con Carla, porque ☐
a Había olvidado sus zapatillas de deporte.
b Había perdido el bus.
c No había terminado sus deberes.
d Había aprendido mucho vocabulario.
e No se había puesto el abrigo.
f Carla no la había telefoneado como prometió.
g No había repasado.

B Write out what each sentence you created in exercise A means in English. Underline each example of the pluperfect tense.

Reminder

◆ As with the perfect tense, when writing the pluperfect you need to remember that certain common verbs have irregular past participles.

C Translate the following account into Spanish.
Before we left ... Michaela had taken the dog to her mother's house; Julia had given the neighbours our mobile phone number; Selina and Michaela had done the packing; I had seen the doctor because I needed some tablets; and Marco had bought some sandwiches for the journey.

D Rewrite each of these pairs of sentences as a single one using *porque* and the pluperfect to explain cause and effect.
Example:
El jefe no durmió bien el domingo por la noche. El lunes, estaba de mal humor.
El lunes, el jefe estaba de mal humor porque no había durmido bien el domingo por la noche.

1 Esta mañana Francisca perdió unos documentos importantes. El jefe le gritó.

_____

_____

2 Los ingenieros no hicieron su trabajo durante el fin de semana. El lunes, los ordenadores estaban estropeados.

_____

_____

3 La semana pasada al jefe de marketing se le olvidó el pudieron teléfono móvil en el tren. Durante toda la semana los clientes no pudieron contactarle.

_____

_____

_____

4 El señor Ramírez se durmió en su oficina. No participó en la reunión.

5 El micrófono se rompió. No podían oír lo que decía el jefe.

_____

Reminder

◆ As with the perfect tense, in the pluperfect the two parts of the verb must never be separated by pronouns or negatives.

E Translate the following sentences into Spanish on a separate sheet.
1 Before the success of the Concierto de Aranjuez in 1939, Rodrigo had encountered many difficulties in life.
2 As a child he had contracted diphtheria.
3 As a result of this disease he had been left blind.
4 He had learned braille in order to be able to study piano and violin.
5 He had gone to Paris to work with other composers.
6 He had lived in poverty.

Direct and indirect speech

Reminder

◆ Direct speech is used for quoting word for word what someone else said.
Dijo: 'No me gustan los churros'.
◆ Indirect speech is used to explain what the person said without quoting them directly.
Dijo que no le gustaban los churros.

A Here is an account of how a man describes to his friend what he can see from the window as he observes an incident at the building opposite. What were his original words?
Example: *Dice que algo pasa en la calle.*
'Algo pasa en la calle.'

1 Dice que la policía ha llegado.

2 Dice que entran en la casa.

3 Dice que ahora salen con un hombre.

4 Dice que hay también una mujer.

5 Dice que la mujer parece muy nerviosa.

6 Dice que el hombre parece totalmente loco – grita y gesticula.

7 Dice que la policía se ha llevado al hombre y a la mujer y que todo el mundo vuelve a su casa.

Reminder

◆ Changing a passage like this, where all the descriptions relate to a third party, is relatively straightforward. However, when you change between direct and indirect speech, you will almost always need to change not only the verb in every sentence, but also other words that relate to the speakers, especially pronouns. For example:
Dice: 'Necesito mis ocho horas de sueño y no me levanto nunca antes de las siete.'
Dice que necesita sus ocho horas de sueño y que no se levanta nunca antes de las siete.

B Manuel is relaying a phone message from someone who is coming to visit. Change the visitor's statements to indirect speech, altering the text shown in bold.
Example:
'Voy a traer a mi perro conmigo.'
Dice que va a traer a su perro consigo.

1 'He hecho mis maletas y voy a salir.'

2 'Tengo dos maletas enormes.'

3 'Voy a llamar un taxi para ir a la estación.'

4 'Pienso comprarme un bocadillo en el tren ...'

5 '... no es necesario darme nada de comer.'

6 'Espero llegar a las dos.'

7 'Tengo mi móvil conmigo – voy a darte el número ...'

C The visitor asks Manuel some questions. Change them to indirect speech, as Manuel would relay them to the rest of the family. You may need to use *si, dónde, cuánto* as link words, remembering that they need their accents because they are being used in a question even though it is indirect. Note also that you need *que* after *preguntar*, just as you do after *decir*.
Example:
'¿Puedes ayudarme con mis maletas?'
Me pregunta que si puedo ayudarle con sus maletas.

1 ¿Dónde está vuestra casa?

2 ¿Estáis lejos de la estación?

3 ¿Puedes venir a buscarme a la estación?

4 ¿Qué tipo de coche tienes?

5 ¿Puedes llamarme si hay algún problema?

D A friend is watching a TV programme in the next room while you are cooking, and he/she is telling you what is being said. For each description in indirect speech, write the original direct speech.
Example: *Dice que va a dejar a su mujer.*
          'Voy a dejar a mi mujer.'

1 Dice que no quiere verla más.
_____

2 Dice que nunca va a volver.
_____

3 Dice que su vida comienza de nuevo.
_____

4 Pregunta que si esta noticia le interesa.
_____

5 Su mujer contesta que sale con su amigo Federico desde el año pasado, así que no le importa mucho.
_____
_____

E Two women explain how they chose whether or not to continue working after they had started a family. Turn Alicia's statements into indirect speech, starting each sentence with *Dice que*. Then turn Bárbara's account into direct speech.

Alicia

1 'Decidí dejar mi trabajo.'
_____

2 'Quería pasar más tiempo con mi hijo.'
_____

3 'También prefería tener un programa menos rígido.'
_____

4 'Alejandro y yo estábamos preocupados porque el niño no estaba muy robusto.'
_____

5 'Estoy muy contenta con mi decisión.'
_____

Bárbara

6 Dice que tuvo que volver al trabajo por razones económicas.
_____

7 Dice que encontró a una muy buena niñera.
_____

8 Dice que volvió al trabajo seis meses después del nacimiento de su hijo.
_____

9 Dice que no quería quedarse en casa.
_____

10 Dice que no se arrepiente de haber mantenido su independencia.
_____

Reminder

◆ If you are writing indirect speech using past tenses (perfect or preterite) you will often need to make use of the pluperfect. For example:
   Dijo: '**Llegué** a las once y **salí** a las dos.'
   Dijo que **había llegado** a las once y que **había salido** a las dos.
   Dijo: '¡He terminado mis deberes!'
   Dijo que **había terminado** sus deberes.

F Read the account of last year's business trip and rewrite it, changing each verb into the pluperfect and the third person. The rewrite has been started for you.

Llegamos a Gerona el lunes e hicimos algunas visitas. El jefe de la empresa nos invitó a hacer una visita a la fábrica, lo cual hicimos el jueves. Hablamos con algunos empleados. También hemos participado en algunas reuniones y firmamos un contrato. Por la tarde salimos con el jefe y su mujer – fuimos al teatro y después comimos en un restaurante.

Habían llegado a Gerona el lunes y habían hecho algunas visitas ...

G When Elena got back from Barcelona last week she was asked how things had gone. Complete the sentences to report what she said. The first one is done for you as an example.

1 Dijo que (she had enjoyed the visit)
   ... le había gustado la visita.

2 ... nunca ... (she had never been to Barcelona)
_____

3 ... siempre ... (she had always wanted to see the city)
_____

4 ... la gente ... (the people had been very friendly)
_____

5 ... había ... (she had visited the Sagrada Familia twice)
_____

6 ... siempre ... (she had always admired Gaudí's work)
_____

The main tenses of verbs

The immediate future

Reminder

◆ To talk about the immediate future use *ir a* + an infinitive: *Voy a comprar este libro.*

A Complete the following sentences to explain what plans people have for a fitter lifestyle. Use the immediate future.

1 [Yo] / hacerse socio de un centro deportivo.

   _____

2 Guillermo / jugar al fútbol con sus hijos.

   _____

3 Lorenzo / comprar una bici de ejercicio.

   _____

4 Luisa / hacer una hora de natación cada mañana.

   _____

5 Consuelo y Mercedes / renunciar al queso y al chocolate.

   _____

6 [Nosotros] / dar paseos en bici. ¿[Vosotros] / apuntarse?

   _____

7 ¿[Tú] hacer algo, Paco?

   _____

B Translate the following sentences into Spanish.

1 Tomás says he is going to go to the gym with his brother.

   _____

2 That's not going to last, in my opinion.

   _____

3 I don't know – he says he's going to become a member.

   _____

4 A waste of money! He's never going to become a sportsman, he doesn't like sport.

   _____

5 Maybe, but he says he's going to go once a week, and he's going to lose 10 kg.

   _____

6 If he's going to lose 10kg, he's not going to be there once a week, but once a day!

   _____

The future tense

Reminder

◆ The future tense is used to describe a less definite, more remote future.
The future tense of regular verbs is formed by taking the infinitive of the verb and adding the endings shown below. The stress is always on the ending, and the endings are the same for all verbs.
hablar**é**, hablar**ás**, hablar**á**, hablar**emos**, hablar**éis**, hablar**án**

A In these sentences people are talking about their long-term plans. Complete the sentences using the verbs given.

1 Yo _____ un BMW y una casa cerca del mar. (comprar)

2 Ricardo es muy trabajador – _____ mucho dinero. (ganar)

3 Teresa _____ francés y negocios y _____ como traductora. (estudiar, trabajar)

4 ¿[Tú] _____ en Madrid? Sí, y _____ empleo en una editorial. (vivir, encontrar)

5 ¿David y Felicia _____ algún día? (casarse)

6 ¿[Vosotros] _____ a Argentina u _____ en España? (volver, quedarse)

Reminder

◆ Several common verbs are irregular in the future tense. However, although they have an irregular stem, the endings follow the regular pattern.
dar, daré; decir, diré; haber, habré; hacer, haré; poder, podré; querer, querré; saber, sabré; salir, saldré; tener, tendré; venir, vendré

B Translate the following sentences into Spanish.

1 They will give their manager a new contract.

   _____

2 He will leave after another two years.

   _____

3 I'm sure we will be able to win the cup next year.

   _____

4 Will you come to watch the final with us as usual?

   _____

5 Afterwards we'll go out for dinner and have a party!

_____

6 The only problem is, Manolo won't want to celebrate, because he's not with our team.

_____

7 It's simple: he will have to change teams!

_____

C Fill the gaps in the horoscopes, putting all the verbs into the future. The passages address the reader as _Vd._ Then write your own predictions for the two missing signs (_Sagitario_ and _Capricornio_)!

Acuario

_____ (recibir) una sorpresa magnífica. _____ (encontrar) a una vieja amiga que le _____ (dar) unas noticias muy interesantes.

Piscis

No _____ (tener) mucha suerte. _____ (Coger) una enfermedad misteriosa y no _____ (poder) salir. _____ (Necesitar) el apoyo de sus amigos.

Aries

Un nuevo contacto le _____ (traer) la oportunidad de un nuevo empleo, o su jefe le _____ (conocer) un ascenso. _____ (Tener) que tomar una decisión importante.

Tauro

Un viaje interesante _____ (ser) posible. _____ (Ver) lugares sorprendentes, _____ conocer a personas fascinantes, y _____ (gastar) mucho dinero.

Géminis

_____ (Deber) prestar atención a su salud. _____ (Sentirse) cansado y le _____ (faltar) energía. _____ (Ver) a un médico que le _____ (decir) que descanse más.

Cáncer

Un amigo le _____ (dejar) y _____ (sentirse) triste. _____ (Intentar) algunas veces ponerse en contacto con él, pero no _____ (contestar) a sus mensajes.

Leo

Su futuro le _____ (preocupar) esta semana. Se _____ (hacer) muchas preguntas pero no _____ (saber) las respuestas. _____ (Pensar) mucho y el fin de semana _____ (tomar) una decisión importante.

Virgo

Un niño _____ (ser) muy importante en su vida. Le _____ (mostrar) a Vd. lo importante en la vida y _____ (comenzar) a cambiar sus opiniones. _____ (Hacer) dos descubrimientos importantes.

Libra

Su vida _____ (estar) llena de problemas y dificultades emocionales. Pero su familia le _____ (comprender) y le _____ (ayudar), y al final _____ (descubrir) el valor de su amor.

Escorpio

Problemas económicos le _____ (preocupar). No _____ (ganar) mucho pero _____ (gastar) demasiado. _____ (Terminar) la semana con dificultad, y ¡la próxima semana _____ (deber) ahorrar dinero!

Sagitario

_____
_____
_____
_____
_____

Capricornio

_____
_____
_____
_____
_____

Revision: the main tenses of verbs

A Revise the rules on spelling changes in the present tense, then fill in the missing forms from memory.

1 [ellas] _____ (jugar)
2 [tú] _____ (dormir)
3 [yo] _____ (pensar)
4 [nosotros] _____ (pedir)
5 [ellos] _____ (querer)
6 [vosotros] _____ (corregir)
7 [yo] _____ (jugar)
8 [ellas] _____ (poder)
9 [Vd.] _____ (volver)
10 [él] _____ (entender)
11 [tú] _____ (encontrar)
12 [–] _____ (llover)
13 [Vds.] _____ (sentir)
14 [yo] _____ (preferir)
15 [ella] _____ (mostrar)

B Revise the present tense of irregular verbs, then fill in the missing forms from memory.

1 [yo] _____ (saber)
2 [tú] _____ (decir)
3 [yo] _____ (salir)
4 [nosotros] _____ (ir)
5 [yo] _____ (estar)
6 [Vd.] _____ (oír)
7 [yo] _____ (poner)
8 [ellas] _____ (tener)
9 [Vd.] _____ (venir)
10 [él] _____ (decir)
11 [tú] _____ (ir)
12 [yo] _____ (tener)
13 [Vds.] _____ (ser)
14 [yo] _____ (hacer)
15 [ella] _____ (ser)

C Fill each gap with the appropriate form of *ser* or *estar*, using the present tense in sentences 1–5 and past tenses in sentences 6–10.

1 Me gustan mis nuevos vecinos – _____ andaluces.
2 Su pueblo _____ al norte de Granada.
3 _____ simpáticos, pero su hija _____ muy tímida.
4 Me gustaría presentárselos pero no _____ en casa.
5 _____ importante _____ amigos con sus vecinos.

6 Cuando vi a Maribel la semana pasada, ella _____ sola en el parque.
7 _____ un poco triste, y muy cansada.
8 Su padre _____ enfermo y, ya sabes, _____ su cumpleaños.
9 Su novio no _____ en Madrid y _____ una situación complicada.
10 Los últimos meses _____ bastante difíciles para ella.

D Translate the following negative sentences into Spanish.

1 I have never visited London.

_____

2 No-one has left you a message.

_____

3 I didn't see anyone in the bar.

_____

4 They don't like any of those people.

_____

5 He never calls his mother – he didn't even call on her birthday!

_____

6 I have nothing to say to them.

_____

E Complete the gaps in the following sentences using the perfect tense of the verbs given; then translate the sentences into English. Watch out for irregular past participles.

1 Enrique no la _____ _____ hoy. (*ver*)

_____

2 Niñas, ¿no os _____ _____ todavía? (*levantarse*)

_____

3 [Ellos] Me _____ _____ la noticia, pero yo no se la _____ _____ a ella. (*decir* x2)

_____

4 [Yo] _____ _____ las maletas y Pablo las _____ _____ en el coche. (*hacer, poner*)

_____

5 ¿Por qué [tú] _____ _____ tan temprano? [Yo] _____ _____ _____ pero no _____ _____ _____ . (*venir, ducharse, vestirse*)

_____

F Revise the preterite forms, especially of the irregular verbs, and then translate the following into Spanish on a separate sheet using the preterite tense. The infinitives of the verbs you need are in the box below.

1 What did they give you?
2 I couldn't open the door, so I rang the bell.
3 He read the paper and told her the news.
4 I lost my glasses yesterday. I looked for them everywhere and finally found them on the television.
5 We went to the Picos de Europa in May. We drove from San Sebastián.
6 Isabel came to see us last week. She brought four suitcases!

> encontrar ir tocar dar conducir perder poder
> venir buscar traer leer abrir decir

G Complete the following sentences with either the imperfect or the imperfect continuous form of the verb given.

1 _____ cuando entré. (*leer*)
2 _____ mucho cuando _____ en la cárcel. (*leer, estar*)
3 Cuando [yo] _____ en la ciudad, _____ a la piscina todas las mañanas. (*trabajar, ir*)
4 _____ muy rápido cuando atropelló al gato, que _____ en el centro de la calle. (*conducir, dormir*)
5 A mis abuelos les _____ mucho escuchar música. Cuando [nosotros] les _____, siempre _____ música. (*gustar, visitar, escuchar*)

H Translate the following sentences into Spanish, using the pluperfect where appropriate.

1 Last week she went on holiday; she had packed at the weekend.

2 She said she had told me the dates of her holiday.

3 In fact, she had decided to go without telling me!

4 When he got to the house, he couldn't get in – he had left his keys at the restaurant.

5 He found that he had also forgotten his credit card.

6 He phoned the restaurant – luckily, they had found his things and had kept them for him.

I Read the following extract from *Leyendas* by Gustavo Adolfo Béquer. Draw up a table like the one below. Complete it for all the verbs in the extract. Use a dictionary as necessary but think about the best way to translate the verbs in context.

verb	tense	translation into English

LA CRUZ DEL DIABLO

El crepúsculo comenzaba a extender sus ligeras alas de vapor sobre las pintorescas orillas del Segre, cuando, después de una fatigosa jornada, llegamos a Bellver, término de nuestro viaje.

Bellver es una pequeña población situada a la falda de una colina, por detrás de la cual se ven elevarse, como las gradas de un colosal anfiteatro de granito, las empinadas y nebulosas crestas de los Pirineos.

Los blancos caseríos que los rodean, salpicados aquí y allá sobre una ondulante sábana de verdura, parecen a lo lejos un bando de palomas que han abatido su vuelo para apagar su sed en las aguas de la ribera …

A la derecha del tortuoso sendero que conduce a este punto, remontando la corriente del río y siguiendo sus curvas y frondosas márgenes, se encuentra una cruz.

El asta y los brazos son de hierro; la redonda base en que se apoya, de mármol, y la escalinata que a ella conduce, de oscuros y mal unidos fragmentos de sillería.

La destructora acción de los años, que ha cubierto de orín el metal, ha roto y carcomido la piedra de este monumento, entre cuyas hendiduras crecen algunas plantas trepadoras que suben enredándose hasta coronarlo, mientras una vieja y corpulenta encina le sirve de dosel.

Yo había adelantado algunos minutos a mis compañeros de viaje y, deteniendo mi escuálida cabalgadura, contemplaba en silencio aquella cruz, muda y sencilla expresión de las creencias y la piedad de otros siglos.

Un mundo de ideas se agolpó en mi imaginación en aquel instante. Ideas ligerísimas sin forma determinada, que unían entre sí, como un invisible hilo de luz, la profunda soledad de aquellos lugares, el alto silencio de la naciente noche y la vaga melancolía de mi espíritu.

More verb forms

The conditional

Reminder

- The conditional is used to express 'should/ought to', and 'would': *Debería cambiar de empleo*. She should change her job.
  Nos gustaría ir de vacaciones. We would like to go on holiday.
  Note: You do not need the conditional simply to ask whether someone 'would like' something. You can simply use *querer*, e.g. *¿Quieres ir al cine?*

A Underline the conditional verbs and translate the sentences into English.

1 Deberían dejar de fumar.

   _____

2 No gustaría hacer un curso de tenis.

   _____

3 Ayer me dijo que me vería en la piscina a las diez.

   _____

4 Yo, en tu lugar, compraría un nueva bicicleta de ejercicio.

   _____

5 ¿Podrías traer un litro de leche? No tengo tiempo para salir.

   _____

6 Raquel me dijo que nunca viviría en la ciudad.

   _____

7 Yo que tú hablaría con ella para explicarle todo.

   _____

8 Por favor, ¿podríais decirnos dónde está el centro deportivo?

   _____

Reminder

- To form the conditional, take the infinitive and add the endings shown in bold below. As in the future tense, some verbs are irregular (see page 48).

hablar	decir
hablar**ía**	dir**ía**
hablar**ías**	dir**ías**
hablar**ía**	dir**ía**
hablar**íamos**	dir**íamos**
hablar**íais**	dir**íais**
hablar**ían**	dir**ían**

B Translate the following into Spanish.

1 you (*tú*) would eat _____

2 I would go _____

3 they would choose _____

4 you (*vosotros*) would drink _____

5 you (*Vd.*) would sell _____

6 he would know _____

7 I would go out _____

8 you (*vosotros*) would come _____

9 we ought to _____

10 they would make _____

11 she would be able to _____

12 they would put _____

13 you (*Vds.*) would see _____

14 we could ask Pilar _____

15 I should answer _____

C Choose a suitable verb from the box and put it in the conditional to fill each gap.

¿Qué haría un atleta serio?

1 Se _____ cada día.

2 _____ muchas frutas y verduras.

3 _____ con un entrenador.

4 _____ la actuación de otros atletas.

5 _____ muy pocas bebidas alcohólicas.

6 _____ bien su salud.

7 _____ una variedad de actividades.

8 _____ una dieta tan sana como fuera posible.

9 _____ en competiciones.

10 Se _____ temprano.

> hacer entrenarse cuidar beber acostarse
> estudiar comer participar trabajar tener

D Translate this paragraph into Spanish on a separate sheet.

In a cleaner environment … we would all be healthier. Traffic problems would disappear, fewer children would suffer from asthma, and the streets would be less dirty. We'd also be able to save endangered species.

Reminder

- In sentences with *si* and the conditional, you often need to use the subjunctive in the *si* part of the sentence. See page 58 for guidance and practice on these constructions.

The forms and uses of the subjunctive (present, imperfect, perfect, pluperfect)

Reminder

◆ The subjunctive is rare in English (the only really common usage is 'If I **were** you') but it is very frequently needed in Spanish. Its use often shows that there is something not quite definite about the event or action referred to; it can imply wishful thinking, something that could have happened, or something hypothetical that is not proved or hasn't happened yet and may not.

A Underline the subjunctive verbs in the following sentences. Then match them with the translations that follow: write the letters in the boxes.
1 Quiero que vengas conmigo.
2 Les voy a pedir que me ayuden.
3 Me dijeron que esperara aquí.
4 Prefiero que tú conduzcas.
5 Siento que su perro haya muerto.
6 Mi amigo me aconsejó que tomara estas pastillas.
7 Me gustaría que me llamaras.
8 Espero que hayan recibido mi mensaje.
9 Felipe nos pidió que le diéramos dinero.
10 No es verdad que lo haya hecho.

a I'd like you to call me.
b I'd prefer you to drive.
c It's not true that he did it.
d I'm sorry your dog has died.
e I want you to come with me.
f I hope they have received my message.
g My friend advised me to take these pills.
h They told me to wait here.
i I'm going to ask them to help me.
j Felipe asked us to give him some money.

B Identify whether the verb is present subjunctive, perfect subjunctive or imperfect subjunctive in each sentence in exercise A. Write Pr.S., Perf.S. or Imp.S. for each sentence.

Reminder

◆ To form the present subjunctive, take the *yo* form of the present tense. Remove the *-o* (or *-oy*) ending.To *-ar* verbs, add the present tense endings of *-er* verbs. To *-er* and *-ir* verbs, add the present tense endings of *-ar* verbs.

hablar	comer	vivir
hable	coma	viva
hables	comas	vivas
hable	coma	viva
hablemos	comamos	vivamos
habléis	comáis	viváis
hablen	coman	vivan

C Translate the following examples into English on a separate sheet.
1 Pilar, necesito que me hagas un favor. Quiero que vayas al supermercado para hacer las compras.
2 Tienes que apagar tu cigarrillo – el jefe no nos permite que fumemos en la oficina.
3 Prefiero que llegues el viernes, porque el jueves tengo que trabajar.
4 ¿Quiere que le ayude, señor?
5 El médico ha aconsejado a mi hermana que no trabaje.
6 Dígale que me envíe un e-mail.
7 Voy a pedirles que hagan menos ruido.
8 Es una lástima que no puedas venir.
9 Me sorprende que no te guste Mónica.
10 Dudo que esté divirtiéndose en Madrid – odia las ciudades.
11 Necesito alguien que sepa conducir.
12 Iremos a Barcelona para que puedas ver la Sagrada Familia.
13 A menos que haga demasiado frío, vamos a dar un paseo por la playa.
14 Quiero que hagas tus deberes antes de que salgamos.
15 Sin que me lo digas, no puedo saber cuál es el problema.

Reminder

◆ Remember that verbs which have a spelling change or irregular form in the first person singular in the present tense will have the same change in the present subjunctive.

More verb forms

D Use one of the following common irregular verbs to translate each of these sentences into Spanish.

decir	telefonear	ir	oír	poner	querer
saber	salir	tener	enviar	venir	ver

1 I'm surprised that he goes to their house.

_____

2 I need you to lend me your laptop because my modem has broken.

_____

3 I don't think he wants to invite her – I don't believe he sees her these days.

_____

_____

4 I want you (*tú*) to know that I'm not happy that you still have this problem! I advise you to see a doctor.

_____

_____

5 I don't want him to go out with them. I prefer him to come with me!

_____

6 Do you want me to call your parents, Tomás?

_____

_____

7 I hope she doesn't come – I can't talk to her without her getting furious (*ponerse furioso*).

_____

_____

Reminder

◆ To form the imperfect subjunctive, take the 'they' form of the preterite. Remove the -*ron* ending and add the endings shown (the same for all verbs). Remember that verbs which have a spelling change or irregular form in the preterite third person plural will have similar changes in the imperfect subjunctive, as shown in the example of *decir*, below.

hablar	**decir**
habla**ra**	dije**ra**
habla**ras**	dije**ras**
habla**ra**	dije**ra**
hablá**ramos**	dijé**ramos**
habla**rais**	dije**rais**
habla**ran**	dije**ran**

There is another set of endings for the imperfect subjunctive, which is less common. The alternative set of endings is as follows:

hablar	**decir**
habla**se**	dije**se**
habla**ses**	dije**ses**
habla**se**	dije**se**
hablá**semos**	dijé**semos**
habla**seis**	dije**seis**
habla**sen**	dije**sen**

E Complete the following sentences with the -*ra* ending imperfect subjunctive form of a suitable verb chosen from the box below. Then translate the sentences into English on a separate sheet.

1 Esperaba que [*tú*] _____ de eso con ella antes de irte.

2 Querían que [*nosotros*] _____ con ellos, pero teníamos que salir.

3 Le pedí que me _____ con ese trabajo, pero no quiso hacerlo.

4 El médico le aconsejó que _____ de fumar, pero no le hizo caso.

5 Buscaba a alguien que _____ jugar al tenis conmigo.

6 Pidió que le [*nosotros*] _____ su número de teléfono.

7 ¡Sólo queríamos que [*tú*] _____ contenta!

8 ¡Ojalá _____ buen tiempo!

estar	comer	poder	dar	hablar
dejar	hacer	ayudar		

Reminder

◆ To form the perfect subjunctive, use the present subjunctive of *haber* with the past participle. Remember to watch out for verbs that have an irregular past participle.

F Fill the gaps using the perfect subjunctive of the verbs given.

1 Nos sorprende que todavía no [ellos] _____ . (*llegar*)

2 Siento que [él] _____ estos problemas. (*encontrar*)

3 Espero que [vosotros] _____ mi mensaje. (*recibir*)

4 ¡No creo que [tú] _____ eso! (*decir*)

5 Dudo que [ella] lo _____ . (*hacer*)

Reminder

◆ To form the pluperfect subjunctive, use the imperfect subjunctive of *haber* with the past participle.

	hablar	**poner**
hubiera		
hubieras		
hubiera	hablado	puesto
hubiéramos		
hubierais		
hubieran		

G Translate the following sentences into English.

1 No admitió que hubiera visto a Esmeralda.

2 Pilar no podía creer que Enrique se hubiera ido.

3 Esperábamos que hubieran comprendido.

4 No era verdad que te hubiéramos olvidado.

5 Si no me hubieran dado ese dinero, tendría problemas bastante graves.

Using the subjunctive
Reminder

◆ As seen in the sentences in exercises A–G above, there are many situations where the subjunctive is needed. The most common of these are practised in the following exercises. Note that you also need subjunctive forms for the imperative in Spanish (see page 60 for guidance and practice).

A Can you identify the reason why the subjunctive is used in each of the following sentences? Choose from one of the following groups of reasons.

a wish/hope	b request/advice/instruction
c doubt/improbability	d sorrow/surprise/joy/fear

1 Espero que no pierdas tu empleo. ☐
2 Dudo que encuentres un empleo. ☐
3 ¡Te aconsejo que busques un empleo! ☐
4 No es probable que encuentren un empleo. ☐
5 Estoy muy contento de que hayas encontrado un empleo, pero es una lástima que la oficina esté tan lejos. ☐ ☐

6 ¡Dígale que busque un empleo! ☐
7 Me sorprende que no haya encontrado un empleo. ☐
8 Me pidió que le ayudara a buscar un empleo. ☐
9 Querían que su hijo tuviera un empleo. ☐
10 No es verdad que hayan dicho eso. ☐

Reminder

◆ In constructions expressing a wish or hope you do not always have to use the subjunctive. If the subject of both clauses is the same (the person's wish refers to him/herself), you can use the infinitive for the second verb.
Contrast the following pairs of sentences.
Quiero que abras mis e-mails. Subjects are *yo, tú*
Quiero abrir mis e-mails. Subjects are *yo, yo*
¿Quiere que viajemos en tren? Subjects are *Vd., nosotros*
Queremos viajar en tren. Subjects are *nosotros, nosotros*

◆ Remember that you need to insert *que* before the subjunctive, but that you do not need *que* or anything else between the verbs if you are using the infinitive.

◆ After certain verbs (notice that several of them are related to permission or prohibition) you can use the infinitive even when the subject is not the same: *permitir, dejar, prohibir, consentir, aconsejar, mandar, ordenar, rogar.*
Me ***permitió entrar*** pero me ***prohibió fumar***.
Me ***mandaron esperar*** y me ***aconsejaron leer*** este folleto.

B Decide whether or not you would need the subjunctive to translate each of the following sentences into Spanish. Note 'yes' or 'no' in each case.

1 Do you hope to go to Spain next year? _____
2 They recommend that you buy these biscuits. _____
3 I'd like you to try this washing powder. _____
4 I hope we shall go to Madrid. _____
5 They'd like to visit Barcelona. _____
6 They want us to open an account. _____
7 They let me try it free for a month. _____
8 I want you to do me a favour. _____
9 They want to help you. _____
10 It's a pity you've lost your dog. _____
11 I agreed to go with them. _____
12 Did you say you wanted to go into town? _____

More verb forms

C To make sure you recognize your subjunctive tense forms, and to revise the sequence of tenses, identify the tenses of all the verbs in the following sentences. (A few of them are in the infinitive.)

1 Dudo que hayas comprendido. ——————
2 Nos pidió que le ayudáramos. ——————
3 ¿Te han permitido salir? ——————
4 Queríamos que se hiciera abogado. ——————
5 Le sorprendió que la hubiera visto. ——————
6 Me permitieron llamarte. ——————
7 Quiero que vengáis a verme. ——————
8 Tenían miedo que hubiera muerto. ——————

D For each of the following sentences, decide which combination of tenses you will need, from the choices a) and b) given below each one. Then translate the sentences into Spanish on a separate sheet.

1 I want you [*vosotros*] to do something for me.
   a) present, infinitive
   b) present, present subjunctive
2 He hopes that they haven't heard him.
   a) present, perfect subjunctive
   b) perfect, present subjunctive

3 They asked me to bring my photos.
   a) perfect, imperfect subjunctive
   b) preterite, imperfect subjunctive
4 He forbade me to speak.
   a) preterite, present subjunctive
   b) preterite, infinitive
5 I wasn't expecting you [*tú*] to ring me.
   a) preterite, infinitive
   b) imperfect, imperfect subjunctive
6 They didn't believe that you had arrived at 10 p.m.
   a) preterite, pluperfect subjunctive
   b) imperfect, imperfect subjunctive

E Translate the following into Spanish on a separate sheet.

1 I'm surprised that you don't look for your holiday on the internet.
2 It's great that this new MP3 is so cheap.
3 It's a shame they spend all their free time surfing the internet!
4 Does it worry you that so many tracks are downloaded free?

F Use the most appropriate filler from the box to complete each sentence.

1 Dudo que pueda —————— de fumar.
2 No era verdad que Paco y yo ——————.
3 No podía creer que su marido no —————— más.
4 No es probable que Mercedes —————— de acuerdo con ver un médico.
5 No es verdad que Ana y Esteban —————— drogas.

> bebe esté deje bebiera hubiéramos fumado
> hayan tomado dejar fumamos era toméis

Reminder

◆ You will find that the subjunctive is used in constructions such as the following:

¿Conoces a alguien que hable español?

But notice that the subjunctive is not needed in the following reply:

Sí, conozco a dos personas que hablan español.

… unless it is negative …

Lo siento, aquí no hay nadie que hable español.

The logic is that the subjunctive is only used when there is no certainty that the person or item that is wanted actually exists.

G Underline the subjunctive verbs in the following dialogues (not all the sentences contain one). Then translate the sentences into English.

1 Buscamos a alguien que pueda hablar con nuestros clientes rusos y alemanes. Ya tenemos una persona que habla alemán, per no hay nadie que hable ruso.

_____

_____

2 ¿Conoces alguien que sepa hacer hojas de cálculo? Sí, ¡yo sé hacerlas!

_____

_____

3 Tengo una amiga que sabe bailar el tango. Pero ¿conoces a alguien que sepa tocar la guitarra?

_____

_____

4 Necesito un ordenador que funcione sin problemas. ¡Debes estar loco! ¡No hay ordenadores que funcionen sin problemas!

_____

_____

_____

5 ¿Hay alguien aquí que haya visto a mi perro? ¿Cómo? Busco a un perro pequeño y negro que tiene las orejas blancas.
Lo siento, no hay nadie aquí que haya visto a ningún perro.

_____

_____

_____

6 Mi amigo quiere un empleo que ofrezca más responsabilidad. Lo malo es que para eso es esencial que tenga más experiencia.

_____

_____

Reminder

◆ The subjunctive is needed after these conjunctions: *de modo que, de manera que* (so that); *con tal que, siempre que* (providing that, on condition that); *a menos que, a no ser que* (unless); *mientras (que)* (as long as). With some conjunctions the subjunctive is needed only if the subjects of the two verbs are different. Compare the following pair of sentences.

Viajé toda la noche para estar contigo.

Te digo eso para que sepas cuánto te quiero.

Conjunctions that work like this are:

para que, a fin de que (in order that, so that); *sin que* (without); *a condición de que* (on condition that); *antes de que* (before).

H Match the sentence halves.

1 Te llamo para ☐
2 No voy a seguir trabajando para ellos ☐
3 Te di este dinero ☐
4 Me han explicado cómo funciona el horno ☐
5 No quería salir ☐
6 Seguiré trabajando para ellos mientras ☐

a para que pudieras pagar tu alquiler.
b sin decirles adiós.
c contarte mis noticias.
d de manera que pueda cocinar para ellos.
e a menos que me den un aumento.
f me paguen bastante.

Reminder

◆ The subjunctive is required in clauses starting with *cuando* that refer to the future.

Cuando la veas, ¡dale saludos de nuestra parte!

I Use the verbs given in the correct form to fill the gaps in these sentences.

1 Cuando _____ a Barcelona, podremos jugar unos partidos de pelota. (*tú, venir*)
2 Cuando _____ de vacaciones, voy a montar a caballo todos los días. (*ir*)
3 Cuando _____ suficientemente bien, podrán hacerse socios del primer equipo. (*jugar*)
4 Cuando _____ volverás a jugar. (*recuperarse*)
5 Cuando _____ 40 años me mantendré en forma corriendo. (*cumplir*)

Constructions with *si*

Reminder

◆ Many, but not all, *si* sentences, require the use of the conditional and the subjunctive.
You do **not** need the subjunctive in the following constructions, where the implication is that the event has already happened or is very likely to happen.

Si + present + imperative (see pages 60–61 on imperative forms)

Si te gusta, ¡cómpralo!

If you like it, buy it!

Si + present + future or present

Si le gusta, lo comprará.

If he likes it, he'll buy it.

Si is also used to mean 'if' in the sense of 'when'.

Si estaba de mal humor, gritaba a todo el mundo.

If/when she was in a bad mood she shouted at everyone.

Reminder

◆ *Si* is also used in reporting a question, i.e. to mean 'if' in the sense of 'whether'.

Dime si vas a volver.

Tell me if you're going to come back.

Le preguntó si estaría en casa.

I asked him if he would be at home.

A Translate the following sentences into English on a separate sheet.
1 Si no quieres venir, no tienes que venir.
2 Si Bernardo tiene miedo de ir en avión, no puede venir a Chile.
3 Si no te gustan las empanadas, no las comas.
4 Si quieres verme, ¡ven a Madrid!
5 Si hacía sol, pasábamos el fin de semana en la playa.
6 Si esperas ir de vacaciones, tienes que ahorrar dinero.
7 Si el tren llegaba a tiempo, me quedaban diez minutos para tomar un café antes de ir a la oficina.
8 Si estamos listos, ¡vamos!

B Match the sentence halves.
1 Si hacemos menos ruido, ☐
2 Si no te gusta la cerveza, ☐
3 Si llovía, ☐
4 Si tu madre te prohibe fumar, ☐
5 Si no quieres comer eso, ☐

a ¡escúchala!
b ¡no la bebas!
c déjalo.
d oiremos a los pájaros.
e me quedaba en casa y veía la televisión.

C Identify the tense used before and after *si* in each of the following sentences. Then translate them into English.
1 Me preguntaron si me gustaba la ciudad.
_____
2 Voy a preguntarles si estarán de vacaciones en agosto.
_____
3 Cuando llames a María, averigua si va a venir el domingo.
_____
4 ¿Preguntasteis al recepcionista si podríais entrar?
_____
5 No me ha dicho si va a trabajar aquí.
_____

D Translate the following sentences into Spanish. (For 7–10 you may want to revise imperative forms, explained and practised on pages 60–61.)
1 He asked me if I had tried the *fabada*.
_____
2 Martina is going to ask Javier if he wants to go on holiday with her.
_____
3 I wrote to ask her if I would see her at the party.
_____
4 I want to check whether they have arrived.
_____
5 They asked me if I'd like to eat with them.
_____
6 We asked her if she had enjoyed the film.
_____
7 Ask her if she has seen my suitcase.
_____
8 Tell me if you want to see us at the weekend.
_____
9 Ask them if they want something to drink.
_____
10 Check whether he has booked his hotel.
_____

Reminder

◆ Although you can use indicative tenses to translate 'if x happens, y will happen', you need the subjunctive and the conditional to translate 'if x happened, y would happen'.
Contrast the following pairs of sentences.
Si le toca la lotería, se comprará un Ferrari.
If he **wins** the lottery he **will buy** a Ferrari.
Si le tocara la lotería, compraría seis Ferraris.
If he **won** the lottery he **would buy** six Ferraris.

E Match the sentence halves. Then identify whether the verbs used in the complete sentences are present tense followed by future (PF), or imperfect subjunctive followed by conditional (ISC).

1 Si perdiera mi empleo,
2 Si pierdes tu crema solar,
3 Si me llamas mañana,
4 Si supiéramos la verdad sobre eso,
5 Si tuviéramos más dinero,
6 Si mi mujer no fuera alérgica,
7 Si te levantas a las nueve,
8 Si fueran ricos,

a tendré más tiempo para explicarte la reserva.
b comprarían una caravana.
c iríamos a las islas Maldivas.
d te prestaré la mía.
e te la diríamos.
f tendríamos tres perros.
g no podría ir de vacaciones.
h llegarás tarde.

F Choose and underline the correct alternative each time to complete the sentences.

1 Si la ves, salúdale/le saludaras de mi parte.
2 Si me marchara, ¿me olvidarías/olvidarás?
3 Si salgo/saliera mañana, ¿me acompañas?
4 Si fuéramos ricos, ¿qué harías/hagas?
5 Si fuéramos ricos, ¿qué casa compramos/compraríamos?
6 Si gana/ganara mucho dinero, haría un viaje por el mundo.
7 Si recibe/recibiera un aumento, va a cambiar de coche.
8 Si me quisieras de verdad, ¡no pasarías/pasa horas hablando con ella!
9 Si me quieres/quisieras de verdad, ¡no me dejes!
10 Si fueran más jóvenes, se irán/irían a vivir al norte.

G Complete the following sentences with the correct form of an appropriate verb chosen from the box.

1 Si estuviera de vacaciones en el campo …
Me _____ alojarme en una villa con piscina.
_____ un paseo cada mañana.
_____ a los pájaros, ¡y los tractores!
_____ un coche para hacer las compras.

2 Si estuviéramos de vacaciones en la ciudad …
_____ los museos y las galerías.
_____ al cine cada semana.
_____ con nuestros amigos en un bar todas las tardes.
_____ mucho para aparcar el coche.
No _____ ni de aire puro ni de un medio ambiente tranquilo.

3 Si estuvieras de vacaciones cerca del mar …
_____ a muchos turistas.
_____ oír las olas sobre la playa.
¿_____ a pescar?
¿_____ todos los días?
Tus padres _____ a pasar una semana contigo.

> aprender bañarse cultivar dar necesitar
> disfrutar quedar entender oír
> ir pagar poder gustar venir ver visitar

H Translate the following sentence starters into Spanish and complete each one with an idea of your own.
The minister of/for … = *El ministro/La ministra de*

1 If I won the lottery, I would buy …
2 If my friend won the lottery, he/she would …
3 If I were the minister of education, students would …
4 If I were the minister of the environment, the UK would have …
5 If I were the minister for transport, drivers would have to …
6 If I were the minister of defence, I would …
7 If I were the minister for foreign affairs, I would …
8 If I were the prime minister, I would …

More verb forms

The imperative

Reminder

◆ The imperative is used to give orders or instructions. It has several forms according to the person being instructed. Remember also that instructions can be positive or negative – this also affects their form.
Positive forms are as follows (negative forms are explained on page 61):
The *tú* form is the same as the third person singular of the present tense.   ¡*Escucha*!
For the *vosotros* form take the infinitive, and replace the final -*r* with a -*d*.   ¡*Escuchad*!
The *nosotros*, *Vd*. and *Vds*. forms are the same as the present subjunctive.
¡*Escuchemos*! ¡*Escuche*! ¡*Escuchen*!
Note that for a few common verbs, the normal *nosotros* present tense form is used instead:
¡*Vamos*! Let's go!

A Translate these phrases into English and say whether the person being instructed is *tú*, *Vd.*, *nosotros*, *vosotros* or *Vds*.
1   ¡Entra! _____
2   Repetid lo que oís. _____
3   Abra el archivo. _____
4   Guardad vuestro trabajo. _____
5   ¡Visitemos Argentina! _____
6   Recuerda estos números. _____
7   Digamos que no – porque no queremos.
_____
8   Escucha esta música. _____
9   Tomen la primera calle a la derecha.
_____
10   Visita este sitio: es muy interesante.
_____

Reminder

◆ Some verbs have irregular imperative forms (*decir, hacer, ir, poner, salir, venir*). See the tables on pages 86–93.

B Translate the following into Spanish.
1   Tell your sister the film is starting.
_____
2   Make your comments on our site <u>here</u>.
_____
3   [*Tú*] Come at eight o'clock and we'll have a drink.
_____

4   Put your opinion in the box.
_____
5   If you go to Madrid, go to the Plaza Mayor first.
_____

Reminder

◆ Object pronouns and reflexive pronouns are added to the end of imperatives. Remember that if there is a direct object pronoun and an indirect one, the indirect one comes first.
Dámelo.   Give me it.
Note that the *vosotros* form drops its final *d* when the reflexive pronoun *os* is added.

C Translate sentences 1–5 into English.
1   ¡Dadme esos libros! _____
2   ¡Sentaos! _____
3   ¡Callaos! _____
4   ¿Entendisteis la pregunta? Bueno, ¡contestadla!
_____
5   Escuchad la grabación. _____

Now use the *tú* imperative form to translate sentences 6–10 into Spanish.
6   Give me the name of that site. _____
7   Stand up! _____
8   Behave yourself! _____
9   Have you understood the problem? Well, tell me the solution! _____
10   Look at the screen. _____

Use the *nosotros* imperative form of each verb to complete sentences 11–15.
11   _____ los libros. (*esconder*)
12   _____ los bolis a la basura. (*tirar*)
13   _____ en el suelo. (*sentarse*)
14   _____ una respuesta ridícula. (*dar*)
15   _____ otra canción. (*poner*)

D Use the *Vds.* imperative form of each verb to complete the sentences.
1   Por favor, señores, _____ un libro cada uno. (*tomar*)
2   Bueno, _____ aquí. (*sentarse*)
3   _____ esta grabación. (*escuchar*)
4   _____ a la oficina y arreglaremos todo. (*venir*)
5   _____ el vino, creo que les gustará. (*probar*)

E Complete the table of positive imperatives.

	hablar	levantarse	comer	repetir
tú		levántate		
Vd.	hable			
nosotros	hablemos			
vosotros			repetid	
Vds.		coman		

Reminder

◆ For negative imperatives, the present subjunctive forms are used throughout.
Object pronouns and reflexive pronouns come before the verb rather than being attached to the end of it:
¡No me dejes!

F Complete the table of negative imperatives.

	hablar	levantarse	comer	repetir
tú		no te levantes		
Vd.	no hable			
nosotros	no hablemos			
vosotros			no repitáis	
Vds.		no coman		

G Identify whether the following instructions are for *tú*, *Vd.*, *nosotros*, *vosotros*, or *Vds*. Then make the negative commands positive.

1 ¡No me olvides!_____
2 No vengas antes de las ocho.
_____
3 ¡No se sienten allí, señoras!
_____
4 No os levantéis, por favor. _____
5 No vayamos a la playa. _____
6 No me escribas. _____
7 No comáis esos bocadillos.
_____
8 No aparquen aquí. _____
9 No salgamos hoy. _____
10 No juguéis en el parque. _____

H Translate the following negative commands into Spanish.
1 Don't forget to bring your music with you! (*tú*)
_____
2 Don't sit on that chair – it's broken. (*Vd.*)
_____

3 Don't worry, ladies! (*Vds.*)
_____
4 Don't eat those prawns, children! (*vosotros*)
_____
5 Let's not go to school tomorrow. (*nosotros*)
_____
6 Don't let your dog come into my garden, please! (*vosotros*)
_____
7 Don't put the TV on before you finish your homework. (*tú*)
_____
8 Don't use offensive language in blogs.
_____
9 When you contribute to a blog, don't put links to junk sites.
_____
10 Don't write your blog in SMS style.
_____

Reminder

◆ Remember that in Spanish the infinitive, not the imperative, is used for public instructions such as road signs, in recipes, and in instructions for constructing things.

I What is the likely wording in English for the following instructions?
1 No asomarse por la ventana.
_____
2 Añadir el azúcar y la harina.
_____
3 No aparcar aquí, por favor.
_____
4 Mantenerse a su derecha.
_____
5 Pelar las manzanas y cortarlas.
_____
6 Sujetar la parte A a la parte B con clavos C.
_____
7 No hacer ruido después de las once.
_____
8 Seguir las flechas azules.
_____
9 Poner en agua hirviendo durante cinco minutos.
_____
10 Conservar en un lugar fresco y seco.
_____

The passive and how to avoid it

Reminder

- In an active sentence, the subject 'does' the action of the verb.
  Nos ofrecen nuevos productos.
- In a passive sentence, the subject has something done to it.
  Nuevos productos son ofrecidos.
- The passive can be used when the subject of the verb is unknown. It can also be used for impact, as above, where *nuevos productos* is more prominent when it is the subject of the sentence. However, the passive is not used in Spanish as often as in English and this section includes advice and practice on common alternatives to it.

A Tick the six sentences where the passive is used. Notice that in one of them there is a passive form using *verse*.

1 Nuestra vida se ve cada vez más afectada por el cambio climático. ☐
2 Casi todo el mundo cree que es un problema grave. ☐
3 Existe una minoria que no está convencida. ☐
4 A mi modo ver, los signos a favor no han sido demostrados lo suficiente como para convencer a todos. ☐
5 Todos los países se verán afectados. ☐
6 Es esencial cambiar nuestrso modo de vida. ☐
7 Los políticos se han visto obligados a hacer suyo este problema. ☐
8 Continuamente nos vemos bombardeados con consejos y directrices en esta materia. ☐

Reminder

- The passive in Spanish is formed by using part of the verb *ser* and a past participle. The past participle must agree – masculine/feminine, singular/plural – with the subject.

  Present passive:
  *Los adultos también **son influidos** por la televisión.*
  Adults **are influenced** by television too.
  Preterite passive:
  *Los ordenadores **fueron actualizados** durante el fin de semana.*
  The computers **were upgraded** over the weekend.

B Draw up a table using the headings below. Copy out the passive phrases from exercise A into the table below and then indicate which tense each is in, and the gender (M/F) and number (sing./plur.) of the subject.

Phrase	Tense	Gender and number

C Now, on a separate sheet, translate into English the sentences you ticked in exercise A, underlining the passive construction in English, i.e. a form of the verb 'to be' and a past participle.

Reminder

- 'By' is usually translated by *por*, but after a few verbs you should use *de*, as you will see in the following exercise.

D Match up the sentence halves. Then identify three verbs that are followed by *de* in the passive.

1 Nuestra vida es cada vez más ☐
2 Personalmente, yo sé que demasiado de mi tiempo ☐
3 Cada enlace es ☐
4 Un problema es que todos somos ☐
5 Otro problema, aun más grave, es la vigilancia, que es ☐
6 Pero el problema más grave de Internet es que los niños pueden ser ☐
7 Me veo obligada a decir que el Internet nunca será ☐

a muy temido de los defensores de derechos civiles.
b amado por todos.
c seguido por muchos otros.
d puestos en peligro por los sitios y los contactos malos.
e es malgastado navegando en Internet.
f influida por el Internet.
g tentados a pasar demasiado tiempo y gastar demasiado dinero.

E Now translate the complete sentences into English on a separate sheet, underlining the passive construction each time.

F Rewrite the following active sentences in the passive, using the same verbs and tenses.

1 Marco Martínez escribió un artículo polémico.

2 Su colega Guillermo González hizo las fotos.

3 En el artículo critica a una política muy importante.

4 Acusa a esta señora de aceptar sobornos de una gran compañía de gasolina.

5 Continuamente la ven en restaurantes muy exclusivos acompañada de un directivo de esta compañía.

6 Según Martínez, la compañía ha convencido a la política para que ponga en duda el cambio climático.

7 Martínez y otros reporteros hicieron preguntas a la señora y al directivo.

8 Los dos ignoraron todas las preguntas.

Reminder

◆ In Spanish the passive tends to be used in formal contexts such as newspaper reports. Elsewhere it is common to avoid it by using other constructions.

G Find and underline the construction in each sentence that is being used to avoid the passive. Then translate the sentences into English using a passive form.

1 Aquí se habla inglés.

2 El documento secreto lo encontró un peatón en la calle.

3 Fabrican estos zapatos en México.

4 Alguien me dijo que habías llegado.

5 El café se conserva en el frigorífico.

Reminder

◆ If you use a reflexive to replace the passive, you need the *se* form in the singular or the plural according to the subject. However, be careful when using reflexive forms in this sense when referring to people. For example, *se atacó* could mean 'he attacked himself' or 'he was attacked'.
You can use *se* with people but only in the following way, using an additional object pronoun or the personal *a*:
***Se lo** atacó en su propia casa.*
***Se atacó a él** en su propia casa.*
Think of *se* as meaning 'someone' in order to get the rest of the construction right.
Note the following useful reflexive expressions: *se cree que, se dice que, se sabe que, se teme (de) que*.

H One word is missing in each of the following sentences. All the missing words are given in the box below. Identify the word and its correct position.

1 Para hacer la escalada, se un casco de seguridad.
2 Lo bueno del piragüismo es que practica todo el año.
3 El esgrima se con una espada larga y fina.
4 Si quieres hacer parapente, se mucho coraje.
5 El buceo no practica barato, el traje y el alquiler cuestan mucho.
6 Hay muchos deportes que se en el agua.
7 Las carreras sobre patines hacen sobre una pista de hielo.
8 La persona que llega primero a la meta.

necesita se practica gana lleva se
practican se

Reminder

◆ The other most common way to avoid the passive is to use the third person plural form of the verb; the subject is taken to be an impersonal 'they'.

I On a separate sheet, translate sentences 1–4 into English using passive forms. Then translate sentences 5–8 into Spanish using third person plural forms.

1 Fabrican estos juguetes en China.
2 Mandan todos los documentos por mensajero.
3 Guardan toda la comida en el frigorífico.
4 A Maribel le preguntaron si tenía alguna cosa afilada en su maleta.

5 We have been told that she is coming tomorrow.

6 They were accused of stealing the boss's computer.

7 His book was published last week.

8 Every year all our cherries are eaten by the birds!

Infinitive constructions

Reminder

◆ In a two-verb construction the first, 'dependent' verb depends on who is doing the action and the second verb is in the infinitive.
A considerable number of Spanish verbs can be used with a second verb in the infinitive. For example:
*¿Me **permite fumar**?*
*¿Quieres salir esta tarde? Sí, gracias, **me gustaría mucho tomar** una copa contigo.*
***Intentábamos abrir** la puerta.*
Verbs that operate in this way are listed below. Remember, however, that if the subject of the two verbs is not the same, you may need the subjunctive (see page 55), e.g. *Espero **verla*** but *Espero **que me veas**.*
Verbs expressing desire, hope, preference, willingness, pleasure: *desear, esperar, gustar (a), preferir, ofrecer, querer*
Verbs expressing decision, effort, intention, permission: *decidir, dejar, intentar, pensar, permitir*
Verbs expressing ability to do something: *saber, poder, lograr*
Verbs expressing necessity or obligation: *necesitar, deber*

A Give the English meaning of the verbs listed in the Reminder box.

B Underline the dependent verbs and circle the infinitives.
1 David y Margarita han decidido pasar una semana cerca del mar.
2 Les gusta relajarse en un lugar tranquilo.
3 Prefieren encontrar una pequeña playa sin demasiada gente.
4 Piensan ir a Asturias.
5 Han ofrecido llevar a Rosa con ellos.
6 Rosa quiere irse con ellos pero sus padres no le permiten viajar.
7 Tiene exámenes este año y, si quiere aprobar, debe estudiar.
8 Después de sus exámenes podrá descansar un poco.

C Construct the second sentence in each case, based on the prompts.
Example: *Julio decidió buscar trabajo en Bilbao.*
Alejandro y Manuel/Sevilla.
Alejandro y Manuel decidieron buscar trabajo en Sevilla.

1 Necesito poner un anuncio para vender mi coche. Tú / vender tu casa.

2 ¿Me permite poner la radio? ¿A él / poner la tele?

3 Con esta nueva publicidad esperan vender más coches. Nosotros / ordenadores.

4 No se puede poner publicidad de tabaco en la tele. Bebidas alcohólicas /radio

5 ¿Quieres ver este artículo? ¿Vd. / foto?

6 A mi madre le gusta ver las películas de Almodóvar. A mi padre/las películas americanas.

7 ¿Prefieres comer en casa? ¡Nosotros/en un restaurante!

8 Los estudiantes deberían escuchar al profesor. Pero ¡el profesor/los estudiantes también!

9 ¿Intentasteis contactar con la policía? Nosotros/con un médico.

10 Tu hermana piensa hacerse programadora. ¿Por qué tú no/traductor?

Reminder

◆ *Hacer* with an infinitive has the meaning of making someone do something, or getting something done. For example:
Me hizo explicarle todo. He made me explain everything to him.

D Translate the following into English.
1 Hay que hacer venir a un médico.

2 Deberías hacer arreglar tu coche.

3 ¿Es posible hacer callar a esos niños?

4 Vamos a hacer instalar una nueva cocina.

5 Hacemos pintar la casa cada tres años.
_____

Reminder

◆ The following two constructions expressing necessity or having to do something need the relative pronoun *que: tener que, hay/había que.*

E Match the sentence halves.
1 Los niños juegan en el parque ☐
2 Hoy descanso ☐
3 Tiene que irse a Madrid ☐
4 Si quieres aprobar tu examen de música ☐
5 Si ahorra el dinero ☐
6 Tuvo que salir temprano ☐
7 Cuando mi madre era joven ☐
8 Belén, ya son las ocho, ☐

a porque su avión salía a las siete.
b ¡tenemos que darnos prisa!
c pero tienen que volver a casa antes de las once.
d no tendrá que pedir prestado al banco.
e tienes que practicar todos los días.
f pero mañana tengo que trabajar.
g tenía que ir al colegio a pie.
h porque no ha logrado encontrar trabajo en su pueblo.

F Translate the following into Spanish.
1 We've got to phone her before nine o'clock. (*tener que*)
_____

2 When she arrived at the hotel she had to complete a form. (*tener que*)
_____

3 Usually you also have to show the receptionist your passport. (*hay que*)
_____

4 Will you [vosotros] have to take a taxi at the airport? (*tener que*)
_____

5 If we want to arrive in Seville before six o'clock, we have to leave right now! (*tener que*)
_____

6 We had to cancel the meeting because the boss had not arrived. (*tener que*)
_____

7 He's diabetic so he has to inject himself every day. (*tener que*)
_____

8 To get to the cinema, you have to take the bus. (*hay que*)
_____

Reminder

◆ There are more verbs that can be followed by an infinitive but these need a preposition (*a, de* or *en*). The following list shows which verbs require which preposition.
  a: *aprender a, ayudar a, comenzar/empezar a, enseñar a, invitar a, persuadir a, ponerse a, prepararse a, volver a*
  de: *cansarse de, cesar de, dejar de, olvidarse de, tener ganas de, tener miedo de, tratar de*
  en: *consentir en, convenir en, consistir en*

G From the verbs listed above, choose a suitable one and use it in an appropriate form to complete each sentence. Think carefully about which tense or form is most appropriate.
1 ¿No van a _____ hacer ese ruido?
2 En general me gusta conducir pero ¡_____ hacerlo en Madrid!
3 _____ decírtelo – ¡no quiero salir contigo!
4 Finalmente, ayer su madre _____ Jorge de arreglar su bici.
5 Emilio ya sabe tocar el piano, pero ahora _____ tocar el clarinete.
6 Señores, por favor, tienen que hacer sus maletas y _____ salir.
7 Ya hemos _____ a construir nuestra propia casa.
8 No sabía que Conchita iba a llegar ayer por la tarde, porque _____ decírmelo.
9 _____ instalar mi piscina; espero terminarla antes del verano.
10 Voy a _____ estos estudiantes a cantar.

H Translate the following into Spanish on a separate sheet.
1 I don't want to go to that restaurant because I'm afraid of seeing him there.
2 We tried to get in but the door was locked.
3 They have invited us to visit them in their new house.
4 Blanca wants to talk with you (*tú*).
5 I helped him to finish his homework.
6 The work is easy – it consists of answering the phone and welcoming the customers.
7 He stopped smoking two years ago. The sad thing is, he started smoking again two weeks ago!
8 He wanted to phone his parents because he had forgotten to give them the number of his mobile.

Verbs that require different constructions in Spanish

Reminder

◆ Several common verb constructions require careful translation because they are formed on a different pattern in Spanish. For example, Spanish uses the infinitive and the perfect infinitive (*haber* + past participle) where English uses the gerund '-ing' form, in phrases such as 'on hearing the news' and 'after having heard the news'.

The perfect infinitive is also needed to translate expressions such as 'they must have', 'they should have', 'I may have' and 'you could have'.

Reminder

◆ There are three Spanish verbs meaning 'to ask':
  – *preguntar* means to ask a question, or to ask for/after someone;
  – *pedir* means to ask for something, or (used with *que* and the subjunctive) to ask someone to do something;
  – *rogar* works like *pedir* but is more formal, and is often best translated as 'request'. It is used in the impersonal reflexive form *se ruega* on public notices.

A Translate the following sentences into English on a separate sheet.

1 Después de haber perdido el partido, los jugadores se sentían muy deprimidos.
2 ¿No recuerdas haberlo visto?
3 El entrenador debe haberse ido sin decirles nada.
4 Al llegar al club, descubrieron que había salido.
5 Después de ducharse, fueron al bar.
6 Después de hacer un análisis serio del problema, decidieron cambiar de entrenador.
7 Son las dos, todos deberían haberse ido a casa ya.

B Choose the most appropriate verb from the box, and use it in the infinitive or perfect infinitive in Spanish, to complete each sentence.

1 Después de _____ el problema durante muchos años, finalmente decidió buscar ayuda.
2 Al _____ a casa, habló francamente con su marido.
3 Le dijo que después de _____ finalmente que tenía un problema verdadero, había decidido cambiar de actitud.
4 Al _____ estas noticias, su marido se puso muy contento.
5 Después de _____ toda la noche, se acostaron a las seis de la mañana.

understand	talk	ignore	hear	arrive

C Match the sentence halves, then choose the most appropriate verb from the three given above to complete each sentence, using the verb in the correct form.

1 Siempre _____ a nuestros clientes ☐
2 Me _____ que le prestara ☐
3 Tengo un nuevo novio. Cuando vengas, te _____ ☐
4 El jefe me _____ por qué ☐
5 Se _____ a los señores pasajeros que ☐
6 Le _____ que ☐

a había llegado tarde.
b 20 euros.
c no usen su teléfono móvil en este vagón.
d que firmen el libro de visitas.
e les ayudara, pero no podía.
f tu opinión sobre él.

Reminder

◆ Because the verb 'to take' has so many meanings in English, you have to be careful in choosing which Spanish verb to use when translating it.

D Choose the most appropriate verb from the box and use it in a suitable form to fill the gaps in these sentences.

1 La señora Elena _____ su ropa de la maleta.
2 ¿Quieres que te _____ al aeropuerto?
3 A veces le dolía la cabeza pero casi nunca _____ pastillas.
4 Me gusta mucho aquella iglesia – _____ unas fotos.
5 Tiene miedo de volar así que _____ el tren.

tomar	sacar	llevar	coger

Reminder

◆ Because the verb 'to become' (or 'to get' in the sense of to become) has no direct translation in Spanish, you have to choose between a number of Spanish constructions according to the meaning and context.

– to become (as a matter of choice or effort) = *hacerse*
Se ha hecho abogado. He has become a lawyer.

– to become or to 'get' (as a matter of course) = *llegar a ser*
Mi abuela llegó a ser muy difícil cuando estaba enferma. My grandmother became very difficult when she was ill.

But note: *Se está haciendo tarde.* – It's getting late.

– to become (in a change of identity) = *convertirse en, transformarse en*
Este lugar se ha convertido en un desierto. This place has become a desert.

E How would you translate the underlined phrases into Spanish?

1 She went to university and afterwards <u>she became a nurse</u>.

2 That little company <u>has become the biggest in our town</u>.

3 <u>He became a director</u> after working here for 15 years.

4 <u>It was getting late</u> when they left.

5 I've decided <u>I'm going to be a teacher</u>.

Reminder

◆ Because the verb 'to think' can mean to believe, to have an opinion on something or to consider, you need to choose between *creer*, *opinar* and *pensar* when translating it into Spanish. Note that if you are saying you don't think (believe) something, the following verb has to be in the subjunctive.

F Translate the underlined phrases into Spanish.

1 <u>We're thinking of going</u> to Málaga.

2 She always chooses fish – <u>I don't think she eats meat</u>.

3 On holiday <u>I like to sit on the beach and think</u>.

4 Marco <u>thinks</u> this is the best bar in Seville. I'm not sure, <u>I'll have to think about it</u>.

5 <u>He's thinking of becoming a dentist</u>, but <u>I don't really believe he can do it</u>.

Time constructions

Reminder

◆ Translating 'for' or 'since' takes some care, both in choosing the right phrase and, with *desde que*, choosing the right tense for the following verb.

A In each of the following passages, underline the phrases that translate 'for' or 'since', and note the tense of each verb that is shown in bold type.

1 El e-mail de Clementina

Acabo de conocer a un chico muy amable. Voy a hablarte de él. **Vive** aquí desde hace tres meses, y **está trabajando** en nuestra oficina desde hace seis semanas. Es francés, pero **vive** en España desde hace diez ãnos y habla perfectamente español. Lo **conozco** desde solamente una semana y ¡creo que me estoy enamorando de él! Desde que **trabaja** con nosotros, hemos salido algunas veces.

2 Los recuerdos de Miguel

Cuando conocí a Ana en 2002, ella **trabajaba** en Madrid desde hacía dos años. Desde que **estaba** en Madrid, le resultaba difícil hacer amigos, porque era muy tímida. Yo **vivía** allí desde hacía muchos años y tenía algunos amigos. Se la presenté a ellos. **Estaba saliendo** con Ana desde hacía seis meses cuando decidí que quería casarme con ella. Lo triste fue que descubrí que ella **salía** con uno de estos famosos amigos desde hacía algunas semanas.

Reminder

◆ To translate 'for' in time expressions, you need *durante*, or *en*, though you only use *en* in negative sentences such as *No la había visto en muchos meses*. You should use *para* if you are referring to a specified period of time in the future, e.g. *Necesito el coche para tres días*.

B Translate the following paragraph into English on a separate sheet.

No he visitado Londres en algunas semanas. Trabajé en la capital durante tres años, y no me gustaba. Viví en un piso pequeñísimo durante dos años, y después viví en la casa de una amiga. Ella me permitió alquilar un cuarto durante un año, pero todo costaba muy caro. Finalmente me fui de la ciudad el diciembre pasado, y no pienso volver en muchos años.

Revision: more verb forms

A Complete the sentences using the conditional to explain what people would do if they won the lottery.

1 Ignacio (*comprar un Ferrari*)

_____

2 Mónica y Felicia (*viajar por el mundo*)

_____

3 Nosotros (*visitar Nueva York*)

_____

4 Tú (*buscar un nuevo piso*)

_____

5 Ella (*elegir mucha ropa nueva*)

_____

6 Vosotros (*hacer instalar una nueva cocina*)

_____

7 Vds. (*tener una casa en la ciudad y otra en el campo*)

_____

8 Yo (*no cambiar nada*)

_____

B Match the sentence halves.

1 Si no quieres verduras, ☐
2 Si llega temprano, ☐
3 Si fuera rica, ☐
4 Si fueran más simpáticos, ☐
5 Si tuviéramos más tiempo, ☐
6 Si estuvieras aquí, ☐
7 Si quiere ver al señor Roberto, ☐
8 Nos preguntaron ☐

a dígamelo y yo le llamo.
b puede tomar un café mientras me espera.
c les invitaríamos a cenar.
d iríamos más frecuentemente al cine.
e si te habíamos visto cuando estuvimos en Pamplona.
f ¡sírvete ensalada!
g te compraría una casa cerca del mar.
h podría explicarte todo.

C Choose appropriate verbs from the box, and use them in the correct form to complete the sentences.

1 Te aconsejo que _____ de verla.
2 Me han pedido que les _____ dos veces por semana.
3 Esperábamos que Ricardo nos _____ .
4 Estoy muy contento de que (*tú*) _____ a vivir a Madrid.

5 ¡Qué lástima que tu perro _____!
6 No quiero que (*vosotros*) _____ sin mí.
7 No es probable que me _____ un regalo.
8 Me sorprende que (*tú*) no le _____ , porque vive aquí desde hace dos años.

> ayudar conocer dejar venir salir dar
> llamar morirse

D Translate the following into Spanish.

1 I hope you find a new job.

_____

2 I'm surprised that you (*tú*) haven't left him!

_____

3 Ladies, we are glad that you (*Vds.*) have decided to visit our city.

_____

4 It's not likely that the train will arrive before ten o'clock.

_____

5 I don't believe that he is going to finish the work before July.

_____

6 It wasn't true that I had told them about your (*vosotros*) problems.

_____

7 I never was sure that she really loved me.

_____

8 I'm afraid that he may have had an accident.

_____

E Complete the sentences, choosing the correct imperative form according to the person or people being addressed.

1 ¿Quieres un bocadillo? ¡(*Tomar*) _____ este!
2 Cuando vengas a Londres, no (*olvidarse*) _____ de llamarme.
3 ¿Para llegar al banco? Es fácil, señores, (*doblar*) _____ a la izquierda, y lo verán enfrente del cine.
4 Niños, ¡(*callarse*) _____! Trato de leer.
5 No se permite fumar en el tren, señor – por favor, (*apagar*) _____ su cigarrillo.
6 [Vosotros] No (*comer*) _____ estas frutas – no las he lavado.
7 [Tú] (*Escucharme*) _____ – voy a decirte algo muy interesante.
8 [Vd.] (*Decirle*) _____ que venga el viernes.

F Translate the following sentences into English, using the passive.

1 En esa pastelería se venden los pasteles más ricos.

_____

2 Aquí se habla inglés.

_____

3 Programas como este no deberían ser transmitidos antes de las nueve.

_____

4 En Italia fabrican los zapatos más elegantes.

_____

5 Encontraron a la víctima en el río.

_____

6 Se entrevistaron a los candidatos el jueves.

_____

7 Se la vio en el supermercado.

_____

G Complete the translations of the following sentences, using the prompts to help you avoid using the passive.

1 Meat, cheese, clothes and fruit are sold in the market.
Se venden _____

2 The boys were seen in that bar.
Se vieron _____

3 Spanish is spoken in many parts of the world.
Se _____

4 The money was found by a child.
El dinero _____

5 It's feared that he has disappeared.
Se teme que _____

6 It's believed that the minister should resign.
Se _____

H Give the Spanish equivalent of each verb, noting what preposition, if any, is required if a second verb in the infinitive follows.

1	to learn	
2	to wait for	
3	to prefer	
4	to prepare for/to	
5	to offer	
6	to consent, agree to	
7	to stop (doing something)	
8	to go back to (doing something)	
9	to be able to	
10	to think of	
11	to start	
12	to have to	
13	to be afraid to	
14	to know how to	

I Translate the following into English.

1 Después de haber trabajado con ella, estaba seguro que no me fallaría.

_____

2 Al llegar al restaurante, buscamos a nuestros amigos.

_____

3 Después de haberla entrevistado, le pidió empezar a trabajar en mayo.

_____

4 Al llegar al hotel, nos rogaron rellenar un formulario.

_____

5 Tomemos una copa, y después cojamos el bus para ir al centro; podemos llevar al perro.

_____

6 Va a hacerse ingeniero, pero su madre quiere que se haga médico como su padre.

_____

J Choose the right word from the box to fill each gap in the following paragraph.

¡Estudio (**1**) _____ hace tantos años! Me gustaría (**2**) _____ en España y espero trabajar allí durante un año (**3**) _____ de ir a la universidad. Mi (**4**) _____ mayor (**5**) _____ en la universidad de Pamplona desde hace (**6**) _____ años, y (**7**) _____ allí desde hace tres años; (**8**) _____ en un restaurante (**9**) _____ el primer año. Desde que (**10**) _____ en Pamplona, ha (**11**) _____ muchos nuevos amigos, y no ha venido a vernos (**12**) _____ algunos meses.

hermano dos desde hecho trabajó estudia en
vivir durante vive está antes

Additional grammar for A2

The future perfect

Reminder

- The future perfect is used to say what will have happened in the future. It is made up of the future tense of *haber* and a past participle.

A Choose a suitable verb in the future perfect from the box to complete the description of what will have happened by the end of the year.
Antes del fin de año ...

1 Tú ——————————— de empleo.
2 Manuela y Felipe ———————————.
3 Pedro ——————————— su libro.
4 Vosotros ——————————— un hijo.
5 Vds. ——————————— su coche.
6 Nosotros ——————————— la casa.
7 Yo ——————————— mis examenes.
8 ¡Todo ———————————!

> habréis tenido   se habrán casado   habré aprobado
> habrá cambiado   habrá terminado
> habrás cambiado   habremos hecho pintar
> habrán vendido

Reminder

- Remember that in constructions beginning with a time preposition such as *cuando, para cuando, tan pronto como, hasta que* you must use the subjunctive when they refer to the future.

B Choose between the alternatives to complete each sentence. Underline the correct one.

1 Cuando habrás terminado/termines tu trabajo, ven a verme.
2 Tan pronto como habré perdido/pierda seis kilos, saldremos para comer una cena magnífica.
3 Para cuando habrán llegado/lleguen, sin duda ya coman/habrán comido.
4 Antes del fin de semana, habrá comprado/compre esa bici.
5 Hasta que habrán ahorrado/ahorren dinero, no podrán comprar un nuevo coche.

Reminder

- The future perfect is also used to imply the assumption, for example, that 'he must have'. It indicates speculation about something that is likely to have happened.
Habrá llegado a Madrid. He must have arrived in Madrid (by now).

C Translate the following into Spanish.

1 She must have misunderstood.
   _____

2 They must have learned a lot from that experience.
   _____

3 You will have finished that job by tomorrow, won't you?
   _____

4 He must have been surprised.
   _____

5 What are you saying? You must have had too much to drink!
   _____

The conditional perfect

Reminder

- The conditional perfect is used to say what would have happened. It is made up of the conditional of *haber* and a past participle. It is used after phrases such as 'I'd have thought that' and 'They expected that'. Remember, however, that if the expectation is negative, you need the subjunctive.

A Underline the conditional perfects and circle or highlight the subjunctives in the following sentences.

1 Creía que habría salido.
2 No fue probable que hubiera salido.
3 Estaba seguro que la habrías visto.
4 No podía creer que la hubieras visto.
5 Creíamos que me habrían llamado.
6 No me sorprendió que no me hubieran llamado.

Reminder

♦ In situations where the event could have happened but evidently has not, here is the construction using *si*:
*Si le **hubiera tocado** la lotería, **habría comprado** un Ferrari.*
If he **had won** the lottery, he **would have bought** a Ferrari.
The pluperfect subjunctive is followed by the conditional perfect.

B Complete the report on Guillermo, who has been convicted of his first crime, by writing a suitable ending for each sentence. The phrases you need are given in the box below. Then translate the sentences into English.

1 Si los padres de Guillermo se hubieran interesado más por su hijo, —————————

—————————

2 Si Guillermo hubiera estudiado más en el colegio,

—————————

3 Si no hubiera visto tantas películas violentas,

—————————

4 Si hubiera logrado encontrar trabajo,

—————————

abría sido más motivado estado
no habría tenido tantas ideas románticas sobre la violencia estado
se habrían dado cuenta que tenía amigos violentos estado
habría ido a la universidad estado

The passive – more forms

Reminder

♦ You have already worked on ways of avoiding the passive and use of the passive in the present and preterite tenses. The passive can also be encountered in other tenses, but it is always formed from the appropriate part of *ser* with the past participle, as shown here for *ver*.

present	soy, eres etc. visto/a(s)
preterite	fui, fuiste etc. visto/a(s)
imperfect	era, eras etc. visto/a(s)
perfect	he sido, has sido etc. visto/a(s)
pluperfect	había sido, habías sido etc. visto/a(s)
future with *ir*	voy, vas etc. a ser visto/a(s)
simple future	seré, serás etc. visto/a(s)

C Form the conditional perfect of these verbs.

1	hablar	[ella]
2	poner	[yo]
3	abrir	[Vds.]
4	decir	[tú]
5	saber	[nosotros]
6	hacer	[ellos]
7	ver	[Vd.]
8	descubrir	[vosotros]

	hablar	levantarse	comer	repetir
tú		levántate		
Vd.	hable			
nosotros	hablemos			
vosotros			repetid	
Vds.		coman		
	hablar	levantarse	comer	repetir
tú		no te levantes		
Vd.	no hable			
nosotros	no hablemos			
vosotros				no repitáis
Vds.			no coman	

A Identify the tense of the passive verb in each of the following sentences. Then translate them into English.

1 Hemos sido vistos en este pueblo de vez en cuando. —————————

—————————

2 Josefina es vista en el mercado cada semana.

—————————

—————————

3 Antes eran vistos en el casino todos los días.

—————————

—————————

4 Javier fue visto en la playa cuando debía estar en el colegio. —————————

—————————

5   A mi ver, su obra no será comprendida antes de su muerte. _____

6   Las chicas habían sido vistas en el bar el mes anterior. _____

7   La actriz va a ser criticada por los periódicos. _____

The subjunctive – more uses

Reminder

◆ You need to use the subjunctive in clauses starting with the following expressions, but only when the reference is to an event that has not happened yet or may not happen.

cuando, después de que, tan pronto como, desde que, cada vez que, hasta que, siempre que (whenever), *a pesar de que* (despite), *aunque* (although)

When the reference is to an event that has already happened, you can use the indicative. Compare:

Voy a esperar hasta que llegue with *Esperó hasta que llegó.*

The subjunctive is always needed after certain conjunctions:

de modo que, de manera que (so that)

con tal que, siempre que (providing that, on condition that)

a menos que, a no ser que (unless)

mientras (que) (as long as)

With some conjunctions the subjunctive is needed only if the subjects of the two verbs are different. Compare the following pair of sentences:

Viajé toda la noche para estar contigo.

Te digo eso para que sepas cuánto te quiero.

Conjunctions that work like this are:

para que, a fin de que (in order that, so that)

sin que (without)

a condición de que (on condition that)

antes de que (before)

A   Translate the following sentences into Spanish.
1   I'm not going to go out unless I finish my work!

_____

2   He didn't want to do it without speaking to you.

_____

3   I'll buy that house on condition that they mend the roof.

_____

4   I'm ringing to ask you how your mother is.

_____

5   Could you (*Vd.*) ring the bell before you come in?

_____

6   She left before I arrived.

_____

7   He has saved lots of money so that they can go on holiday.

_____

8   He's gone to Madrid to look for a job.

_____

B   Translate the following into Spanish.
1   He will keep on asking you (*Vds.*) to help until you agree!

_____

2   Although I explained it to her, she didn't understand.
3   As soon as you (*tú*) finish your work, we can have dinner.

_____

4   Since she started her new job, I haven't seen her!

_____

5   When you (*vosotros*) see him, he will no doubt ask you how I am.

_____

Reminder

◆ Remember that you need to use the subjunctive in relative clauses like the one in the question below:

*¿Conoces a **alguien que hable** portugués?*

where there is an element of doubt because the person referrred to has not yet been identified and is not certain to exist.

C   Translate the following into Spanish.
1   Do you know anyone who speaks Russian?

_____

2 I'm looking for a mobile phone that my grandparents can use without problems.

_____

_____

3 Is there someone here who can tell me where calle Mercurio is?

_____

_____

4 I'm sorry, there's no-one here who knows where that street is.

_____

5 There's never anyone in that shop who can help me.

_____

Revision: additional grammar for A2

A For each sentence, write a corresponding sentence in the future perfect to describe what will have happened by the end of the week, as in the example.
Antes del fin del domingo ...

Example:
El lunes, Verónica va a escribir una carta a sus padres.
Verónica habrá escrito una carta a sus padres.

1 El martes por la mañana, Ignacio va a ver a sus amigos en Madrid.

_____

2 El miércoles por la tarde, vamos a dar un paseo en bici.

_____

3 El jueves por la mañana, Elena y Luisa van a visitar a los abuelos de Luisa.

_____

4 El jueves por la tarde, vas a ver la nueva película de Almodóvar.

_____

5 El viernes, voy a terminar mis tareas domésticas.

_____

6 El sábado, vais a hacer las compras.

_____

7 El sábado por la tarde, vamos a cenar en un restaurante.

_____

8 El domingo por la mañana, Enrique y Pablo van a volver de Pamplona.

_____

B Use the verbs given in the subjunctive or the future perfect as required to complete these sentences correctly.

1 Cuando [*tú, ir*] _____ al supermercado, ¿podrías comprarme dos litros de agua mineral?

2 Tan pronto como [*terminar*] _____ su trabajo, Jorge va a salir con sus amigos.

3 Antes de mayo, [*nosotros, comprar*] _____ un nuevo ordenador.

4 Para cuando [vosotros, llegar] _____ al banco, va a estar cerrado.

5 Antes del fin de agosto, [*ellos, firmar*] _____ ese contrato.

6 Hasta que [ella, decirme] _____ su número de teléfono, no puedo llamarle.

C Choose the most suitable ending for each sentence and complete the sentences with the prompted verb in the correct form.

1 Si hubiera escuchado la pregunta ☐

2 Estoy seguro que si hubieras pedido dinero a tu hermano ☐

3 Si hubiéramos recibido su carta ☐

4 Si la hubieran visto ☐

5 Si hubiera querido estar con nosotros ☐

a te lo [*dar*] _____.

b me lo [*decir*] _____.

c ¡[*poder*] _____ contestarla!

d nos [*acompañar*] _____.

e no [*preocuparse*] _____.

D On a separate sheet, re-write this passage by putting the sentences in the correct order. (The first sentence is in the right place.) Then translate the passage into English.

Tan pronto como el viejo señor Ruíz hubo llegado a su pueblo natal, descubrió que todo era diferente ...
En cuanto hubo pagado, se marchó.
El señor Ruíz se sentó y pidió una sopa.
Cuando hubo terminado de mirar los nuevos edificios, decidió comer algo.
Pidió la cuenta apenas hubo comido.
Por suerte quedaba el viejo bar – después de que se hubo muerto el viejo Manolito, su hijo Manuel continuó con la tradición familiar.

E Express the following passive sentences in another way, as in the example.

Example: *Un ministro ha sido criticado por los periódicos porque tiene una amante. Los periódicos han criticado a un ministro porque tiene una amante.*

1 Los políticos siempre han sido criticados por los periódicos.

_____

2 Es bueno que los periódicos no sean impedidos de criticar los errores de nuestros líderes.

_____

3 Pero ¿no te parece que los periódicos mismos deben ser más controlados?

_____

4 A mi ver, los individuos tienen el derecho de que su privacided sea respetada.

_____

5 Por ejemplo, si es decubierto que un ministro casado tiene una amante, ¿es necesario que todo el mundo sea informado de los detalles?

_____

6 Yo creo que es más importante que el país tenga un gobierno estable y competente – ¡los periódicos deberían ser regulados más estrictamente!

_____

7 Lo siento, pero no estoy de acuerdo. Lo más importante es que la libertad de prensa sea mantenida. Si no son permitidos revelar lo que descubren, los derechos civiles se verían limitados – es comprendido por todos que estos derechos son más importantes que la privacidad de los políticos.

_____
_____
_____
_____

F Decide whether the subjunctive is required in each of the following sentences and choose the correct form of the most appropriate verb from the table below.

1 ¡Te lo digo para que _____ lo que dicen de ti!
2 No podemos salir sin que él _____ sus deberes.
3 ¿Cuánto tiempo vas a esperar? Hasta que

_____.

4 Ahorramos dinero para _____ a nuestro hijo un ordenador para su cumpleaños.
5 No podremos irnos de vacaciones a menos que me _____ un aumento.
6 A pesar de que _____ un poco locos, me gustan estos chicos.
7 Te diré la verdad a condición de que _____ no enfadarte.
8 Cuando nos _____, vamos a pasarlo bomba.
9 Una vez que _____ aquí me siento más relajada.
10 Siempre que me _____, hablamos durante una hora o más.

llegamos	llegaramos	lleguen
estés	estoy	soy
den	damos	dan
termines	termine	terminado
visiteis	visitaremos	visitan
sabes	sabe	sepas
regalamos	regalar	regaléis
llames	llamo	llamaré
fueron	sean	están
prometimos	prometes	prometas

Revision of the whole book

A Choose nouns from the box to complete the following passage. You will need to decide each time whether to use a singular or plural form and a definite or indefinite article. Remember also that accents may be affected by your choice of singular or plural forms.

Según (**1**) _____ reciente, (**2**) _____ no comen más como antes. (**3**) _____ ha tenido (**4**) _____ fenomenal, sobre todo entre (**5**) _____, a quienes les gusta comer de prisa. No les interesan más (**6**) _____ tradicionales, y no quieren comer a (**7**) _____ con (**8**) _____. Prefieren comer (**9**) _____ de (**10**) _____ a (**11**) _____ y prefieren (**12**) _____ a (**13**) _____ tinto.

> joven español éxito familia comida rápida
> comida sondeo fabada vino patata frita
> coca-cola porción mesa

B Translate the following sentences into Spanish.
1 This new law is important for Spain's rural economy.

_____

2 Many old Spanish cars are a major source of pollution.

_____

3 Shopping on the internet is quick and easy, and it can be cheap, but it's difficult to know whether the items are of good quality.

_____

_____

4 Evidently the former prime minister wanted to help the poorest families.

_____

_____

5 Many English students want to become wealthy IT specialists.

_____

6 My grandparents love their quiet farm, and the traffic in the large town is too loud for them.

_____

_____

C Choose the appropriate possessive pronoun for each gap to complete the following sentences.

(**1**) _____ padres son mucho más estrictos que los [*tú*] (**2**) _____; me parece que es porque soy chica. Por ejemplo, le permiten a

(**3**) _____ hermano salir con
(**4**) _____ novia sin pedirle que vuelva a casa antes de la medianoche, pero cuando yo salgo con el novio (**5**) _____ y pido a (**6**) _____ padre (**7**) _____ permiso para no volver hasta tarde, siempre me dice que no. Los padres de (**8**) _____ novio no lo entienden – les parece que (**9**) _____ padres no tienen confianza en (**10**) _____ hijos. Pero en (**11**) _____ familia hay tres chicos – en la (**12**) _____ somos dos chicas y todo es diferente para nosotras.

D Translate the following sentences into Spanish.
1 Which part of Spain do you [*tú*] prefer? This region or the north?

_____

2 The villages in this region are much poorer than the towns in that one.

_____

_____

3 What is the main reason for the poverty in this region?

4 This soil is very poor, and do you see that river? It's not usually like that; it's dry from May to October so all these farms suffer from a shortage of water.

_____

_____

5 What crops do the farmers grow?

6 Well, on this large farm we grow oranges and avocados; on that little farm you see on the hill, they just grow what they need for themselves and for their animals.

_____

_____

_____

E Give the Spanish for the following phrases.
1 much more important _____
2 completely different _____
3 not very fast _____
4 quite interesting _____
5 too expensive _____
6 many times _____
7 especially difficult _____
8 really unbelievable _____
9 very carefully _____
10 totally impossible _____

75

Revision of the whole book

A Choose the appropriate preposition from the box to complete each sentence. You may not need all of the prepositions, but you will need to use some of them more than once.

1 Llegaron _____ las nueve _____ la mañana.

2 Tomamos una siesta _____ las dos _____ las cuatro.

3 Te esperaré en el café _____ la iglesia.

4 Yo vivo _____ Pamplona pero mi novio vive _____ 50 kilómetros _____ la ciudad; cada semana viene a verme en autobús.

5 Entrevistaron _____ Felipe el jueves; _____ día siguiente le llamaron _____ ofrecerle el puesto.

6 _____ lo que dicen, el gobierno ha decidido nombrar un nuevo ministro _____ salud.

7 _____ empezar, dobla _____ la derecha; después, sigue _____ la calle Fuentes y verás el cine _____ banco.

8 Los ciclistas pasarán _____ aquí _____ llegar _____ Sevilla.

9 _____ vez _____ cuando vamos _____ Madrid _____ tren _____ ir _____ compras.

10 _____ los cuarenta años todavía jugaba _____ tenis dos veces _____ la semana.

> enfrente de   según   a   al lado del   para
> hasta   en   al   por   de   hasta

B Write out the following sentences replacing the nouns in bold with pronouns. Remember that the pronoun is unlikely to appear in the same position as the noun.

1 Me gusta la televisión; veo **la televisión** cada tarde.

_____

2 Pusieron el partido en la televisión ayer por la tarde. ¿Viste **el partido**? No, no me interesan los programas de deporte – nunca veo **los programas de deporte**.

_____
_____
_____

3 Y ¿las noticias? Sí, encuentro **las noticias** más interesantes.

_____

4 ¿Has enviado esa carta a tu abuela? Sí, he enviado **la carta a mi abuela** ayer.

_____

5 ¿Tienes tus llaves? No, he perdido **mis llaves**, estoy buscando **mis llaves**. ¿Has visto **mis llaves**?

_____

6 Si no te gusta la carne, deja **la carne**.

_____

7 Lorenzo, ¿has terminado tus deberes? Hay que terminar **tus deberes** antes de ver la televisión.

_____

8 Este libro es para Maribel. Si encuentras **a Maribel**, ¿podrías dar **el libro a Maribel**?

_____
_____

C Translate the following sentences into Spanish.

1 I saw him on Sunday and I'm going to see him again tonight.

2 Look at these flowers! My parents sent me them.

_____

3 Esteban, you haven't eaten your salad. Eat it, please.

_____

4 I've seen a great computer game and I know my brother would like it. I'm going to buy him it and that way I'll be able to borrow it as well.

_____
_____
_____

5 Have you seen Antonio Banderas's new film? You must see it – we loved it.

_____
_____

6 That's my sandwich! Give me it, please!

_____

7 They saw her yesterday and told her that he had gone.

_____

8 If you (Vd.) see Manuela and Gerardo, tell them to ring me.

_____

D Choose the appropriate relative pronoun or expression from the options given in each sentence and underline it.

1 La ciudad española que/quien prefiero es Salamanca.
2 Mis padres acaban de vender la casa en el cual/en la que viven desde hace veinte años.
3 Ese es el hombre con quien/cuya foto vimos en el periódico ayer.
4 No comprendí el mensaje el cual/que dejaste.
5 El coche de mi profesora, que/el cual es rojo, es muy viejo.
6 La ruta por quien / donde habéis venido es la más larga.
7 No puedo ir más al restaurante donde/en los cuales la conocí a ella.
8 La contaminación es un problema para quien/el cual tenemos que encontrar una solución.
9 La amiga con quien/con el cual pasé mis vacaciones estudia matemáticas.
10 El amigo que/de quien me prestaba el ordenador de vez en cuando ha decidido venderlo.

E Translate the following questions and answers into Spanish.

1 There are two red rucksacks – which is yours (*tú*)? That one, the larger one.

_____

_____

2 Which photos do you want to keep? This one and this one – I don't like those.

_____

_____

3 Whose house do you prefer – theirs or ours? Yours, of course.

_____

4 Which car is yours (*Vd.*)? That one.

_____

5 I've just finished my chores – I'm not going to do yours as well!

_____

6 Which jeans are you going to buy? Those – they're like yours!

_____

7 My dog is much more affectionate than his – even he prefers mine!

_____

8 Which glasses are yours? Those.

_____

Pages 32–37

A For each sentence, choose a suitable verb from the box and use it in the correct form of the present tense, to fill the gap. In some cases you should use the present continuous. You may use some of the verbs more than once.

1 Los señores Gómez _____ en una casa moderna.
2 Yolanda siempre _____ los sábados por la tarde, y nunca _____ temprano el domingo por la mañana.
3 Felicia y yo nos _____ muy bien – _____ en la misma calle desde hace muchos años. Me _____ mucho Felicia; es muy simpática.
4 No molestes a tu padre – está muy cansado y _____ .
5 Todos los meses Mercedes y su marido _____ a los abuelos de Mercedes. _____ un buen almuerzo con ellos, _____ una siesta después, y por la tarde _____ y _____ música.
6 (Yo) _____ de recibir un mensaje y ahora _____ otra llamada telefónica.

7 ¿(Vosotros) _____ antes de la medianoche generalmente? Sí, _____ la televisión hasta las once y después _____ .
8 Nunca _____ con Enrique cuando _____ , porque siempre _____ furioso si le _____ .

> vivir esperar ver acostarse gustar tomar
> dormir salir molestar hablar comer
> visitar escuchar levantarse charlar ponerse
> conocer hablar acabar poner

B For each sentence, use the prompted verb in the correct form of the present tense, to fill the gap.

1 Normalmente Antonio [jugar] _____ al fútbol cada domingo, pero hoy no [poder] _____ jugar porque no [sentarse] _____ bien; [tener] _____ dolor de cabeza y le [doler] _____ los ojos.
2 ¿Mi rutina diaria? Bueno, [despertarse] _____ a las siete, [levantarse] _____ a las siete y cuarto y [salir] _____ a las ocho. [Tener] _____ que tomar el autobús para ir al centro. A veces, antes de ir a la oficina,

[quedar] _____ con mi amiga en el café para desayunar. A la una, [ir] _____ al bar enfrente de la oficina – unos amigos [venir] _____ conmigo de vez en cuando. La oficina [cerrar] _____ a las seis y media, y [volver] _____ a casa a las siete. [Cenar] _____ a las nueve; después [ver] _____ la televisión o [tocar] _____ la guitarra.

3 ¿Adónde [*tu/ir*] _____?
[*Ir*] _____ al centro – [*hacer*] _____ las compras, ¡como de costumbre! ¿Y vosotros, adónde [*ir*] _____?
[*Ir*] _____ a la playa, y Carmen [*venir*] _____ con nosotros.
¿De verdad? [*Yo/pensar*] _____ que eso es una gran idea.

C Decide which of *ser* or *estar* would be the appropriate choice to translate the verb 'to be' in the following sentences, and explain why in each case.

1 I'**m** here – in the kitchen!
_____

2 His mother [a] **is** a really difficult person but today at least she [b] **is** in a good mood.
_____

3 That boy who [a] **is** on the stage just now [b] **is** very tall, isn't he? Yes, he [c] **is** taller than my brother – you know, the one who [d] **is** in Madrid.
_____

4 We [a] **are** younger than them but they [b] **are** fitter than us, because I [c] **am** ill and Helen [d] **is** depressed. They [e] **are** good friends of ours and [f] **are** always nearby if we need help.
_____

5 Her new boyfriend [a] **is** from Brazil; he [b] **is** an engineer and [c] **is** studying for some more qualifications. However, they [d] **are** on holiday at the moment.
_____

D Translate the following sentences into Spanish.

1 He always arrives on time, doesn't he?
_____

2 I never eat hamburgers but I have to admit that I like chips.
_____

3 I'm ringing them again this morning but no-one ever answers the phone in that house.
_____

4 When they go shopping, he buys lots of things and she buys nothing! She doesn't even go into the shops – she doesn't like any of them.
_____
_____
_____

5 I've got no beers left, no wine and no coffee. Nothing to offer my visitors! The good thing is, I never have any visitors. I have no-one to talk to – peaceful, isn't it!
_____
_____
_____

6 Neither Carlos nor José speaks English, and I don't speak Spanish, so we never have anything to say to each other!
_____
_____

Pages 38–51

A Complete the sentences with the perfect tense of a suitable verb chosen from the box. Use each verb once only.

1 Juan _____ tus llaves – las _____ allí, en la mesa.
2 Luisa me _____ que vas a venir a Madrid.
3 Julio, ¿ _____ la nueva película de Antonio Banderas?

4 Hola, Diego, ¿qué _____ hoy?
_____ un muy buen día. _____ a mis amigos, _____ mis tareas, y _____ mis vacaciones.
5 Te llamo para decirte que _____ a casa.
6 El ayuntamiento _____ coches en la plaza.

> decir telefonear terminar volver prohibir
> encontrar hacer pasar reservar poner ver

B Rewrite the following sentences in the preterite tense.

1 Hago mis ejercicios.

_____

2 El ayuntamiento está construyendo un nuevo parking en el centro de la ciudad.

_____

3 No puedo contactarte el jueves.

_____

4 ¿Vais a Salamanca? Sí, vamos a la universidad para visitar a mi hermana.

_____

5 Salimos a las ocho y volvemos a las once.

_____

6 ¿Venden Vds. su casa?

_____

7 Ana y Esteban tienen un hijo.

_____

8 Cuando viene a vernos, a su horrible perro.

_____

9 El sábado comemos en un restaurante, pero el domingo mis padres vienen a comer con nosotros en casa.

_____

10 ¿Viajas a Gerona en tren? No, tomo el autobús.

_____

C Complete the following passage with the **preterite** or the **imperfect** tense of the verbs given in brackets, as appropriate.

Hace treinta años la mayoría de los españoles (**1** *fumar*) _____ y los cigarrillos no (**2** *costar*) _____ mucho. Todo el mundo (**3** *fumar*) _____ por todas partes.
Después, los científicos (**4** *descubrir*) _____ que el tabaco es una causa del cáncer, y el gobierno (**5** *tomar*) _____ medidas para reducir su consumo. Antes, la gente (**6** *tener*) _____ el derecho de fumar en los cines, en el transporte público y en los restaurantes, pero las nuevas leyes (**7** *obligar*) _____ a los empresarios a creer zonas donde está prohibido fumar. La semana pasada, nuestra reportera (**8** *hablar*) _____ con unos clientes sobre este tema. Algunos (**9** *decir*) _____ que la ley (**10** *hacer*) _____ comprender a los fumadores que lo que hacen no es muy sociable. Otros (**11** *preocuparse*) _____ porque a su ver, la ley (**12** *representar*) _____ una reducción de los derechos civiles.

D Use the preterite and imperfect continuous forms to translate the following sentences into Spanish.

1 When they came in, I was reading the paper.

_____

2 When you called, I was having a bath.

_____

3 When you arrived, we were still getting the dinner ready.

_____

4 When I saw him, he was sleeping in the garden.

_____

5 I'm sorry, you told me your name but I wasn't listening.

_____

E Complete these sentences with an appropriate verb from the box in the pluperfect tense.

1 Filomena sacó una mención especial en su examen porque _____ _____ mucho vocabulario.

2 El peatón tuvo que repetir algunas veces que no _____ _____ el accidente.

3 Hoy por la mañana, perdí el tren porque el autobús _____ _____ muy tarde.

4 Los pasajeros estaban todos muy cansados porque su vuelo _____ _____ cuatro horas.

5 Cuando la policía llegó, _____ _____ a la señora al hospital y el agresor _____ _____.

6 La víctima dijo que no _____ _____ a su agresor porque estaba demasiado oscuro.

ver (x2)   llevar   retrasarse   aprender
escaparse   llegar

F Complete these sentences in the future tense.

1 Dentro de veinte años, _____ menos contaminación. (*haber*)

2 Todo el mundo _____ al trabajo a pie. (*ir*)

3 [Nosotros] _____ solamente productos biológicos. (*comprar*)

4 [Nosotros] No _____ más basura en la calle. (*ver*)

5 Nuestros hijos _____ bañarse en los ríos y el mar sin preocuparse. (*poder*)

6 Los ingenieros _____ nuevos coches más limpios. (*inventar*)

7 Nuevas leyes _____ la selva tropical. (*proteger*)

8 Cada persona _____ todo lo posible para conservar el medio ambiente. (*hacer*)

9 [Nosotros] _____ menos energía. (*consumir*)

10 ¡Nuestro planeta _____ salvado! (*ser*)

A Translate the following sentences into Spanish using the conditional tense of the prompted verbs.

1 I would like to travel in Argentina and Peru. (*gustar*)

_____

2 He told me he would arrive at half past ten. (*llegar*)

_____

3 I wouldn't go out with Rafael – he's boring! (*salir*)

_____

4 In your place I would leave my job. (*dejar*)

_____

5 Could you explain this decision to her? (*poder*)

_____

6 A fit person would get there in three hours; I would need four hours! (*llegar, necesitar*)

_____

7 I wouldn't see that film if I were you. (*ver*)

_____

8 My mother would say you should be more careful. (*decir, deber*)

_____

_____

B Choose the most appropriate form from the options given to complete each sentence.

1 Voy a pedirle que me ayudara/ayude con estas tareas.

2 Prefieren que no lleguemos/hayan llegado demasiado tarde.

3 Me sorprende que no hayas terminado /terminaras ese trabajo.

4 Nuestro jefe no permite que hayan fumado /fumemos en el comedor.

5 Su padre no quería que saliera/salga conmigo.

6 No me gusta que mi madre te hayan hablado/hable así.

7 Espero que Manuela hubiera escuchado/haya escuchado el mensaje que dejé.

8 Fue una lástima que no pudieran/puedan venir con nosotros.

9 Nadia, necesito que me hiciera/hagas un favor.

10 Siento que tu hermano haya encontrado/encuentras tantas dificultades.

C Complete the following sentences with an appropriate form of a suitable verb chosen from the box. You may have a choice of verbs and a choice of tenses.

1 ¡No creo que un amigo mío _____ eso de mí!

2 Espero que _____ que nunca te mentiría.

3 ¿No quieres que mi marido y yo _____ contigo?

4 Cuando _____ a Perú, van a llamarnos.

5 Me sorprendió que _____ allí.

6 Necesitan que les _____ a comprar un piso.

7 Dígale que me _____ en la oficina mañana.

8 Mis padres no permiten que mi hermana y yo _____ películas violentas.

9 No me sorprende que Mario _____ con ella.

10 No pienso que _____ los señores Gómez a Gerona.

11 Sin que me _____ un aumento, no podré ir de vacaciones este año.

12 Le presté mi ordenador para que _____ buscar la información que necesitaba en Internet.

> estar   ayudar   salir   saber   venir   llamar   dar
> decir   poder   ver   ir   llegar

D Translate the following into Spanish, deciding whether or not you need the subjunctive in each case.

1 If you (*tú*) see her, tell her to get in touch with me.

_____

2 If he saw her he would not speak to her.

_____

3 If they don't arrive soon, we shall go out without them.

_____

4 If they arrived on time, I would be amazed.

_____

5 If I could, I would come with you (*Vds.*).

_____

6 If we lived in Madrid, we'd go out every night!

_____

7 If you (*tú*) had explained your problems to me, I would have tried to help you.

_____

8 If he had listened to me, he would not have had these difficulties!

_____

9 If I save up enough money, I'll move to a larger flat, but if I won a million euros, I would leave this town.

_____

10 If you (*vosotros*) had been with us on Sunday, we could all have seen that film.

_____

Pages 60–69

A Complete the following sentences with the correct imperative form as prompted.

1 Hace mucho frío – ¡ —————— los abrigos, niños! (*ponerse*; *vosotros*)

2 No —————— de enviarme un e-mail. (*olvidarse*; *tú*)

3 ¿Tienes el martillo? ——————, por favor. (*pasar*; *tú*)

4 Pablo, ¡—————— al bar y —————— una copa con nosotros! (*venir, tomar, tú*)

5 ¡No ——————, señores! (*preocuparse*; *Vds.*)

6 No —————— los artículos de vidrio y de papel – ¡—————— al centro de reciclaje! (*tirar, llevarse*; *Vds.*)

7 ¡No —————— al perro, niños! (*tocar*; *vosotros*)

8 —————— al cine mañana por la tarde. (*ir*; *nosotros*)

9 ¡No me —————— que has perdido tus llaves otra vez! (*decir*; *tú*)

10 ¡—————— y ——————, chicos! (*levantarse, ducharse*; *vosotros*)

B Translate the following sentences into Spanish, finding an alternative to avoid using the passive form.

1 He is often seen in the bar.

_____

2 They were seen in the Marina restaurant yesterday.

_____

3 Señor Martín's shop has been closed down – nowadays fruit and vegetables are sold in the supermarket.

_____

_____

4 I don't like the films that are shown on television in the mornings.

_____

5 These shoes are made in Spain, but those clothes are all made in Korea.

_____

_____

6 My computer has been upgraded and now it is much quicker.

_____

7 She was described as shy but she never stops talking!

_____

8 The building won't be finished before the end of the year.

_____

9 It's feared that many people were killed by the hurricane.

_____

10 It's said that women talk more than men, but by whom is that said?

_____

_____

C Translate the following sentences into Spanish using a verb chosen from the box plus the infinitive of the second verb.

1 Do you (*vosotros*) want to see our photos?

_____

2 I'm hoping to arrive before dinner.

_____

3 He likes playing tennis.

_____

4 They offered to help us but it wasn't necessary.

_____

5 I prefer to travel by train.

_____

6 We're thinking of visiting Barcelona.

_____

7 Do you (*tú*) know how to make gazpacho?

_____

8 He wouldn't let me pay for the meal.

_____

9 We managed to open the door.

_____

10 You've got to read that book!

_____

11 I couldn't understand anything he said.

_____

12 We're having the car mended.

_____

13 They had to sell their house.

_____

14 They made me sing in front of all those people!

_____

15 I need to ask you something.

_____

| lograr hacer ofrecer gustar saber desear |
| saber preferir necesitar permitir poder |
| esperar pensar tener que hay/había que |

Revision of the whole book

D Translate the following into English.

1 Al llegar a Madrid, descubrieron que Michaela había salido.

2 No recuerdo haberlo dicho.

3 David debería haber recibido tu mensaje.

4 Después de haber visto la película, fuimos a un restaurante mexicano.

5 Me han pedido acompañarles.

6 Se ruega no fumar.

7 No me preguntes por qué he hecho eso.

8 Después de haber sacado unas fotos, tomaron una cerveza en la plaza.

9 ¿Quieres que te lleve al aeropuerto? No es necesario, voy a tomar el autobús.

10 Quiero hacerme traductora.

11 Esta ciudad se ha transformado en un centro importante.

12 Trabajo para esta empresa desde hace diez años.

13 Julio vivía en Pamplona desde hacía tres meses cuando la conoció.

14 No la hemos visto en algunos días.

15 Desde que estoy aquí he hecho muchos nuevos amigos.

Pages 70–74

A On a separate sheet, rewrite the following paragraph in full, using the prompted verbs in the future perfect to fill the gaps.

Antes del fin de semana, Hernando (*comprar*) un nuevo teléfono móvil; vosotros (*hacer pintar*) la casa; yo (*escribir*) mi artículo; tú (*aprobar*) tu examen; nosotros (*terminar*) nuestro proyecto; Cristina (*elegir*) su nuevo coche; y Enrique e Isabel (*volver*) de sus vacaciones.

B Translate the following into English.

1 No estaba seguro de que hubiera cerrado la puerta.

2 ¿No creías que yo hubiera salido sin ti?

3 No me parecía probable que les hubieras dicho algo sobre eso a ellos.

4 Me sorprendió que hubieran olvidado su nombre.

5 Esperábamos que hubieran comprendido la situación.

6 ¿No os sorprendió que se hubieran casado?

7 Si hubieran tenido bastante dinero, se habrían comprado un coche.

8 Si mi hermana hubiera aprobado sus exámenes, se habría ido a Madrid para estudiar.

9 Si Tomás hubiera encontrado un puesto, se habría quedado en su pueblo natal.

10 Sabes que si te hubiera visto, te habría saludado.

C Use the subjunctive of the verbs given in the box to translate the following into Spanish.

1 I'm not going to talk to her unless she apologizes.

_____

2 They will want to leave as soon as he arrives.

_____

3 I will keep on trying until I succeed.

_____

4 I don't think they paid much for that computer.

_____

5 Do you know anyone who speaks German?

_____

6 I'm looking for someone who can mend my car.

_____

7 We're looking for a present for Marisol but we can't find anything she might like!

_____

_____

8 I'm telling you this so that you can prepare yourself for their questions.

_____

_____

9 I'll come to the party on condition that you invite Antonio.

_____

10 Unless we all make an effort, the problems of the environment will go from bad to worse.

_____

_____

> invitar reparar pagar hacer un esfuerzo
> tener éxito gustar disculparse prepararse
> llegar hablar

D Find another way of expressing the following passive sentences in Spanish.

1 Aquel ministro va a ser expulsado antes de fin del año.

_____

2 Los chicos habían sido advertidos que no jugaran allí.

_____

3 [Ella] ha sido vista aquí de vez en cuando.

_____

4 Le escucharé pero no seré convencido por nada que pueda decir.

_____

5 Cuando estaba enferma, era visitada por toda la familia.

_____

6 No me dijo que había sido entrevistada para ese puesto.

_____

Verb tables

85

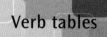

Regular verbs

infinitive present participle past participle	present indicative	imperfect indicative	simple future indicative	preterite indicative
-ar verbs hablar hablando hablado	hablo hablas habla hablamos habláis hablan	hablaba hablabas hablaba hablábamos hablabais hablaban	hablaré hablarás hablará hablaremos hablaréis hablarán	hablé hablaste habló hablamos hablasteis hablaron
-er verbs comer comiendo comido	como comes come comemos coméis comen	comía comías comía comíamos comíais comían	comeré comerás comerá comeremos comeréis comerán	comí comiste comió comimos comisteis comieron
-ir verbs vivir viviendo vivido	vivo vives vive vivimos vivís viven	vivía vivías vivía vivíamos vivíais vivían	viviré vivirás vivirá viviremos viviréis vivirán	viví viviste vivió vivimos vivisteis vivieron

conditional	present subjunctive	imperfect subjunctive	imperative
hablaría	hable	hablara	–
hablarías	hables	hablaras	habla
hablaría	hable	hablara	hable
hablaríamos	hablemos	habláramos	hablemos
hablaríais	habléis	hablarais	hablad
hablarían	hablen	hablaran	hablen
comería	coma	comiera	–
comerías	comas	comieras	come
comería	coma	comiera	coma
comeríamos	comamos	comiéramos	comamos
comeríais	comáis	comierais	comed
comeríais	coman	comieran	coman
viviría	viva	viviera	–
vivirías	vivas	vivieras	vive
viviría	viva	viviera	viva
viviríamos	vivamos	viviéramos	vivamos
viviríais	viváis	vivierais	vivid
vivirían	vivan	vivieran	vivan

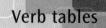

Verb tables

Irregular verbs

infinitive present participle past participle	present indicative	future indicative	preterite indicative	imperfect indicative
dar dando dado *to give*	doy das da damos dais dan	daré	di diste dio dimos disteis dieron	daba
decir diciendo dicho *to say*	digo dices dice decimos decís dicen	diré	dije dijiste dijo dijimos dijisteis dijeron	decía
estar estando estado *to be*	estoy estás está estamos estáis están	estaré	estuve estuviste estuvo estuvimos estuvisteis estuvieron	estaba
haber habiendo habido *to have* (auxiliary)	he has ha hemos habéis han	habré	hube hubiste hubo hubimos hubisteis hubieron	había
hacer haciendo hecho *to do*	hago haces hace hacemos hacéis hacen	haré	hice hiciste hizo hicimos hicisteis hicieron	hacía
ir yendo ido *to go*	voy vas va vamos vais van	iré	fui fuiste fue fuimos fuisteis fueron	iba ibas iba íbamos ibais iban

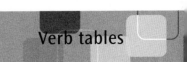

conditional	present subjunctive	imperfect subjunctive	imperative
daría	dé	diera/diese	
	des		da
	dé		
	demos		
	deis		dad
	den		
diría	diga	dijera/dijese	
	digas		di
	diga		
	digamos		
	digáis		decid
	digan		
estaría	esté	estuviera/estuviese	
	estés		está
	esté		
	estemos		
	estéis		estad
	estén		
habría	haya	hubiera/hubiese	
	hayas		he
	haya		
	hayamos		
	hayáis		habed
	hayan		
haría	haga	hiciera/hiciese	
	hagas		haz
	haga		
	hagamos		
	hagáis		haced
	hagan		
iría	vaya	fuera/fuese	
	vayas		ve
	vaya		
	vayamos		
	vayáis		id
	vayan		

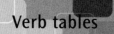

Verb tables

Irregular verbs

infinitive present participle past participle	present indicative	future indicative	preterite indicative	imperfect
oír oyendo oído *to hear*	oigo oyes oye oímos oís oyen	oiré	oí oíste oyó oímos oísteis oyeron	oía
poder pudiendo podido *to be able*	puedo puedes puede podemos podéis pueden	podré	pude pudiste pudo pudimos pudisteis pudieron	podía
poner poniendo puesto *to put*	pongo pones pone ponemos ponéis ponen	pondré	puse pusiste puso pusimos pusisteis pusieron	ponía
querer queriendo querido *to want/love*	quiero quieres quiere queremos queréis quieren	querré	quise quisiste quiso quisimos quisisteis quisieron	quería
reír riendo reído *to laugh*	río ríes ríe reímos reís ríen	reiré	reí reíste rió reímos reísteis rieron	reía
saber sabiendo sabido *to know*	sé sabes sabe sabemos sabéis saben	sabré	supe supiste supo supimos supisteis supieron	sabía

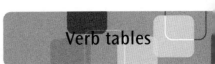

conditional	present subjunctive	imperfect subjunctive	imperative
oíria	oiga	oyera/oyese	
	oigas		oye
	oiga		
	oigamos		
	oigáis		oíd
	oigan		
podría	pueda	pudiera/pudiese	
	puedas		puede
	pueda		
	podamos		
	podáis		poded
	puedan		
pondría	ponga	pusiera/pusiese	
	pongas		pon
	ponga		
	pongamos		
	pongáis		poned
	pongan		
querría	quiera	quisiera/quisiese	
	quieras		quiere
	quiera		
	queramos		
	queráis		quered
	quieran		
reiría	ría	riera/riese	
	rías		ríe
	ría		
	riamos		
	riáis		reíd
	rían		
sabría	sepa	supiera/supiese	
	sepas		sabe
	sepa		
	sepamos		
	sepáis		sabed
	sepan		

infinitive present participle past participle	present indicative	future indicative	preterite indicative	imperfect
salir saliendo salido *to go out*	salgo sales sale salimos salís salen	saldré	salí saliste salió salimos salisteis salieron	salía
ser siendo sido *to be*	soy eres es somos sois son	seré	fui fuiste fue fuimos fuisteis fueron	era eras era éramos erais eran
tener teniendo tenido *to have*	tengo tienes tiene tenemos tenéis tienen	tendré	tuve tuviste tuvo tuvimos tuvisteis tuvieron	tenía
traer trayendo traído *to bring*	traigo traes trae traemos traéis traen	traeré	traje trajiste trajo trajimos trajisteis trajeron	traía
venir viniendo venido *to come*	vengo vienes viene venimos venís vienen	vendré	vine viniste vino vinimos vinisteis vinieron	venía
ver viendo visto *to see*	veo ves ve vemos veis ven	veré	vi viste vio vimos visteis vieron	veía

conditional	present subjunctive	imperfect subjunctive	imperative
saldría	salga	saliera/saliese	
	salgas		sal
	salga		
	salgamos		
	salgáis		salid
	salgan		
sería	sea	fuera/fuese	
	seas		sé
	sea		
	seamos		
	seáis		sed
	sean		
tendría	tenga	tuviera/tuviese	
	tengas		ten
	tenga		
	tengamos		
	tengáis		tened
	tengan		
traería	traiga	trajera/trajese	
	traigas		trae
	traiga		
	traigamos		
	traigáis		traed
	traigan		
vendría	venga	viniera/viniese	
	vengas		ven
	venga		
	vengamos		
	vengáis		venid
	vengan		
vería	vea	viera/viese	
	veas		ve
	vea		
	veamos		
	veáis		ved
	vean		

ánimo

Grammar Workbook Answers

Note: Where students are required to circle answers in their workbook, the answers appear in bold in this answer booklet.

Nouns and determiners

Gender (page 5)

A Students' choice of answers

B 1 la 2 la 3 el 4 la 5 la 6 el 7 la 8 el 9 la 10 el 11 la 12 el

C 1 maquinista 2 portuguesa 3 fundadora 4 estudiante 5 madrileña 6 profesora 7 joven 8 enfermera 9 americana 10 turista

Singular and plural nouns (page 6)

A 1 las manos 2 los anuncios 3 los cafés 4 los ingleses 5 los sofás 6 las revoluciones 7 los reyes 8 las cabezas 9 las comunidades 10 los ordenadores

B 1 las luces 2 los lunes 3 las voces 4 los autobuses 5 los andaluces

C 1 la ropa 2 la aduana 3 vacaciones 4 deberes

D 1 familias 2 compras 3 supermercados 4 cientos 5 coches 6 mercados 7 colores 8 frutas/verduras 9 verduras/frutas 10 voces 11 vendedores

Suffixes (page 6)

A 1 a hefty bloke 2 a nasty bout of the flu 3 a very small girl 4 a little dog 5 a little while 6 a little bell 7 a short little chap 8 a huge door

Definite and indefinite articles (page 7)

A 1 el 2 unos 3 unas, un, una 4 una, unos 5 un, unos, las, las 6 la, el, los, el 7 los, las 8 los, unas 9 los, las 10 la, un, el, la, un, la, un, unos, los, el, unas, la, la

B 1 Pablo es dentista. 2 Conchita espera hacerse profesora. 3 Mi hermano es ingeniero y mi hermana es estudiante. 4 Me gustaría hacerme/ser traductor(a). 5 Su sueño es hacerse jugador de tenis.

C 1 Los, Manolo Blahnik shoes are very expensive. 2 La, Life in Madrid is very interesting. 3 las, What's your opinion – is it important to support regional traditions, or not? 4 El, Spanish wine is cheaper than French wine. 5 las, la I love tapas and Spanish beer.

D 1 Venezuela es un pais hermoso. 2 Las enchiladas chilenas son deliciosas. 3 Me gustaría hacerme periodista, pero ¡es probable que me haga secretaria! 4 Los coches alemanes son populares en toda Europa, pero los coches españoles no son tan caros. 5 La mayoría de las casas tradicionales andaluzas son blancas. 6 Le gustan los deportes, sobre todo el baloncesto y la pelota. 7 Mi padre es fontanero y mi hermano es enfermero. 8 Se ha hecho daño en la cabeza y en la mano – ¡está de mal humor!
9 No me gustan mucho las ciudades modernas, pero me encantan los pueblecitos bonitos. 10 Es alérgica a los mejillones, así que no come paella.

E 1 The good thing is that in our area we have an exceptional climate. The bad thing is that in summer, there are too many people! 2 The good thing is that building provides lots of employment. The bad thing is that now we have many holiday apartments that aren't selling. 3 The good thing is that around here we have some really lovely golf courses. The bad thing is that to keep them so lovely requires huge quantities of water.

F 1 al 2 del 3 del 4 al 5 del

G 1 La directora del departamento de marketing está enferma. 2 Vio a un toro en el centro del campo. 3 Ana va a mandar un e-mail al banco. 4 Le dio una zanahoria al caballo. 5 He sacado cien euros del cajero y ahora voy al mercado.
6 Voy a llamar al hospital.

Possessive adjectives (page 8)

A 1 mis hermanos 2 nuestros abuelos 3 tus deberes 4 sus vaqueros 5 sus libros 6 su coche 7 nuestras hermanas 8 vuestra casa

B 1 sus 2 sus 3 su 4 sus 5 mis 6 su 7 su 8 su 9 sus 10 tu 11 tus 12 tus

C 1 Your boyfriend is better looking than mine. 2 These keys are ours, they're not yours. 3 The ham sandwich is yours; the cheese one is mine.

Adjectives and adverbs

Agreement of adjectives; shortened adjectives (page 9)

A 1 For me, Salamanca is a perfect university city. 2 It has a very old and attractive centre. 3 I also like the modern commercial part of the city. 4 University life is lively and interesting. 5 There are Spanish, foreign, young and mature/older students.

B 1 turística 2 histórico, bonito 3 moderno, próspero 4 preferido, gótica

C 1 conocido 2 británicos 3 lógico 4 cercano 5 turística 6 famosas 7 innumerables 8 mediterránea 9 cálida

10 preferida.

D 1 interesante **2** encantadora **3** barcelonesa **4** verde **5** holgazana **6** española

E 1 buen **2** primer **3** mal **4** ningún **5** abierto **6** segundo **7** gran **8** aburrida **9** tercer

Position of adjectives (page 10)

A 1 famosa, a famous person **2** serio, a serious actor **3** <u>interesante</u>, an interesting interview **4** <u>personales</u>, some personal questions **5** <u>difícil</u>, a difficult situation

B 1 un día agradable **2** una familia feliz **3** los estudiantes inteligentes **4** unos exámenes importantes **5** la música clásica **6** un regalo magnífico **7** una respuesta estúpida **8** los niños tímidos **9** mis amigos franceses **10** una crisis permanente

C Tomorrow poor Antonio's going to have a bad day. It's the day of the great theatre awards, and a young director is going to receive the first prize which Antonio dreams of winning.

D 1 long-time, big **2** great, poor (financially) **3** new (different), new (brand new)

E 1 Haven't you bought enough olives? **2** Yes, I've brought too many olives! **3** In my town there are lots of bars and several restaurants but we haven't got a top chef. **4** In the library I didn't see a single student, but I did see some other people – for example, some old men who were asleep.

F 1 La actriz conducía un coche pequeño y negro. **2** Llevaba un vestido blanco y fabuloso. **3** Se queda en una hermosa villa privada. **4** Había unas buenas fotos en el periódico regional.

Comparative and superlative adjectives (page 11)

A 1 menos, que **2** menos, que **3** más, que, tan, como **4** tan, como **5** más, que

B montañosa, pobre, seco, seco, largo, turístico **1** Nicaragua es menos montañosa que Guatemala. **2** Chile es menos pobre que Bolivia. **3** El clima de Argentina es más seco que el de Ecuador, pero no es tan seco como el de Uruguay. **4** Panamá no es tan largo como Perú. **5** Chile es más turístico que Colombia.

C 1 mejor **2** mejor **3** menor, mayor **4** más grandes

D 1 la más, I think Salamanca is the most beautiful city in Spain. **2** los más, In many countries Aids is one of the most serious problems for doctors. **3** el más, I can't say which country is more interesting, Mexico or Chile – both are fascinating. **4** las más, I wouldn't like to live in Bogotá, it's one of the most dangerous cities in the world. **5** las más, Mexican comedies are among the most popular films.

E 1 peligrosas **2** sucias **3** alta **4** ricas **5** climáticos, graves

F 1 animadísima **2** dificilísimo, bellísimo

More determiners: demonstrative and indefinite adjectives (page 12)

A 1 esa dieta **2** estas sustancias **3** este descubrimiento **4** esos alimentos **5** estos niños

B 1 aquel **2** esa **3** estas **4** esos **5** este

C 1 These trainers are more expensive than those. **2** What are those trees? Those are apple trees, but these are pear trees.

3 Which sandwich do you prefer? This ham one or that cheese one? **4** Which is your rucksack? This one or that one? **5** I need to buy some postcards but I don't like these. **6** Which sweater are you going to buy? That blue one or this red one? **7** I like them both, but I have to choose – I'll take this one. **8** Children, can you see those horses? There, in front of that house. **9** These jeans are too small. Can I try those? **10** Do you see that man? He's the one that gave me those flowers.

D 1 <u>toda</u> **semana**. (f sing) **2** <u>todos</u> **pasteles** (m pl) **3** <u>todas</u> **comidas** (f pl) **4** <u>todos</u> **kilos** (m pl) **5** <u>todo</u> **queso** (m sing)

E 1 toda **2** todos **3** todo **4** todas

Interrogatives and exclamations (page 13)

A dónde, Cómo, Qué, Cuántas, Cómo, Por qué, Qué, Cuánto, Cuándo, qué

B 1 ¿Cuál es la capital de Venezuela? **2** ¿Quién es el presidente de Argentina? **3** ¿Qué solución propones? **4** ¿Quiénes son esos hombres? **5** ¿Cuál es la diferencia entre el español de España y el español colombiano, por ejemplo? **6** ¿Quién ha llamado hoy? **7** ¿Con quién va a la conferencia, Señor Ramón? **8** ¿Cuáles fueron las causas de la Guerra Civil? **9** ¿Quién fue presidente de España después de la muerte de Franco? **10** ¿Cuál es tu/su opinión? ¿Quién va a ganar las elecciones?

C Listen, Mercedes, I've got some surprising news about Miguel and Ana ... What news? Are they going to get divorced? What a shame! No, but Miguel has finally left her. What? Miguel has left Ana? But what a surprise! I'd have thought Ana was going to leave Miguel. Well, what news! Yes, such a nice man, and her, well, I don't want to give you my opinion of her ... Yes, what a disgrace.

Adverbs, intensifiers and quantifiers (page 14)

A 1 frecuentemente (frequently) **2** fácilmente (easily) **3** tristemente (sadly) **4** mal (badly) **5** tranquilo/ tranquilamente (quietly) **6** bien (well)

B 1 peor **2** más claramente **3** mucho mejor **4** más frecuentemente que **5** menos fácilmente que **6** menos rápido que **7** más seriamente

C 1 <u>de una manera muy franca</u>, *My trainer spoke to me very bluntly*. **2** <u>bastante barato</u>, In this country you can ski quite cheaply. **3** <u>Por fin</u>, In the end we arrived at the stadium. **4** <u>de un modo bastante independiente</u>, Federico trains fairly independently. **5** <u>juntos muy contentos</u>, The members of the team work together very happily.

D 1 <u>felizmente</u>, very **2** <u>imposible</u>, completely **3** <u>fácil</u>, quite, fairly **4** caro, too **5** <u>importante</u>, much more **6** <u>rápido</u>, more and more **7** <u>difícil</u>, particularly **8** <u>complicado</u>, extremely **9** <u>frecuente</u>, even less **10** <u>ridículo</u>, totally **11** <u>prudente</u>, not very **12** <u>fantástico</u>, really, truly

E 1 mucho más importante / especialmente difícil / sumamente complicado / totalmente ridículo **2** completamente imposibles / sumamente complicadas / totalmente ridículas / realmente fantásticas **3** cada vez más rápido **4** completamente imposible / demasiado cara / sumamente complicada / totalmente ridícula / realmente fantástica **5** cada vez más rápido

F Students' choice of answers

G Los robos ocurren cada vez más frecuente mente. Todo el mundo está muy preocupado. La policía dice que la solución del crimen es sumamente complicada y demasiado cara, pero yo creo que esa excusa es completamente ridícula. Están completamente obsesionados con la detención de automovilistas que conducen con poco cuidado; claro, ese problema es muy importante pero en mi opinión, los robos son mucho más graves.

Revision: nouns, determiners, adjectives, adverbs (pages 16–17)

A 1 sistema 2 frase 3 avión 4 pena 5 problema

B 1 departamento 2 lenguas 3 suerte 4 ordenadores 5 programas 6 pares 7 investigaciones 8 proyectos 9 estadísticas 10 datos 11 vida 12 materiales 13 vídeos 14 libros 15 biblioteca 16 diccionarios 17 obras 18 referencia 19 mapas 20 países

C 1 el, –, la 2 un, el, un 3 unos, la, el, las, la 4 los, unos, del, la, un 5 al, el, las, los, lo, la, los, el, la, el, –

D 1 su jefe y su enorme sueldo 2 nuestra región y sus problemas de tráfico 3 mi vida y mis planes para el futuro 4 Sus amigos viven cerca de los nuestros. 5 Esa es su/tu/vuestra opinión pero no la mía. 6 He aparcado mi coche al lado del suyo.

E 1 Mis amigos portugueses quieren un piso nuevo con un balcón grande y vistas bonitas. 2 No estoy de acuerdo con todas sus ideas políticas, pero es un buen amigo y un colega simpático. 3 ¡La hermana mayor de mi amiga madrileña va a casarse con un gran torero colombiano!

F 1 Su familia es más grande que la mía, pero más unida. 2 La mayor parte de las universidades españolas son más pequeñas que las británicas. 3 El vegetarianismo no es tan popular en España como en el Reino Unido. 4 La comida biológica no es siempre más cara, pero es más común en los mercados que en los supermercados. 5 Las verduras y las frutas son más baratas que el queso y la carne, ¡y más sanas también! 6 Conduce con menos cuidado que su esposa, pero ella conduce más rápido/rápidamente. 7 Escribe mucho mejor que ella, pero mucho más lentamente.

G 1 aquellas 2 este 3 este, esas 4 ese, esta

H 1 ¡Qué desastre! ¿Cómo va a reaccionar? 2 ¿Se ha ido? ¡Qué lástima! ¿Cuándo salió? 3 ¿Cuál es la capital de Costa Rica? Y ¿quién es el líder del país? 4 ¿Por qué te levantas? ¿Qué hora es? ¡Ay no, qué lata – voy a llegar tarde al trabajo! 5 ¿Cuáles son las diferencias entre la vida en España y la vida en Chile? ¡Qué pregunta! ¿Cuánto tiempo tienes?

Prepositions, conjunctions and pronouns

Prepositions (pages 18–20)

A 1 enfrente de, entre 2 en 3 detrás de, al lado del 4 dentro de 5 delante del 6 sobre/en, en, debajo de

B 1 durante 2 antes de 3 después de 4 hacia 5 por 6 desde 7 hasta 8 a

C 1 Estuvimos bailando desde las diez hasta las dos de la mañana. 2 Llegaré hacia las ocho y te esperaré delante del cine que está enfrente de la catedral. 3 Dame ese libro: mira, está en el suelo, debajo del periódico, entre el sofá y la silla. 4 Si salimos por la tarde, después de la hora punta, llegaremos en dos horas.

D 1 on time; the next day/on the following day 2 50 km from 3 twice a week; about the weather 4 in the sun, in the shade 5 nine-year-old 6 to go shopping 7 by bike, by bus 8 on the table, onto the floor 9 at around two o'clock

E 1 Según nuestros cálculos, sobre sesenta mil, according to our calculations, around/about sixty thousand 2 ante el tribunal, a mi mode de ver, de todos, before the court, in my view, of them all 3 Por fin, bajo la lluvia, desde las once, at last, in the rain, from eleven o'clock 4 por la escalera, ante esa situación, con prisa, down the stairs, faced with that situation, in a rush

F 1 Según mi padre, delincuentes como esos deberían aparecer ante un juez. 2 Ante estos problemas, el gobierno debería tomar decisiones – ¡y de prisa! 3 De todos los bares de Madrid, este es el más grande – en mi opinión, hay sobre quinientas personas aquí.

G 1 para 2 para 3 para 4 por, para 5 por 6 para 7 para 8 por, para

H 1 El maratón pasa por el centro de la ciudad por la tarde. 2 Para empezar compró una bicicleta de ejercicio para ponerse en forma, pero ahora corre por la orilla del río cada mañana. 3 Buscamos un cajero automático: ¿hay uno por aquí? Sí, tomen la calle a la derecha y crucen el puente. Hay un cajero en la esquina. 4 Andaba por el mercado buscando un regalo para mi madre.

I 1 de seda, She was wearing a silk shirt. 2 de acuerdo, I don't agree with you. 3 de moda, Red isn't in fashion. 4 de ocho pisos, del siglo XX, That eight-storey building dates from the 20th century. 5 de Madrid, de sus negocios, The gentleman from Madrid was talking about his business. 6 De vez en cuando, de compras, From time to time I go shopping with my mother. 7 de dos años, de veras, My sister has a two-year-old son, Oh really? 8 de madera, Juan's lorry was already full of wood.

J Students' choice of answers

K 1 a finales de año 2 al día siguiente 3 a la izquierda 4 a tiempo 5 a 10 euros el kilo 6 a la sombra 7 cinco veces al mes 8 a los ochenta años 9 a 20 km de mi casa 10 a veces

L 1 A veces se pueden comprar manzanas en el mercado a dos euros el kilo. 2 Toma esa carretera a la derecha y podremos aparcar a la sombra. 3 A los sesenta años todavía nadaba tres veces a la semana. 4 Al día siguiente un accidente tuvo lugar a unos metros de la casa de mi madre. 5 A finales de año voy a tomar unas vacaciones. 6 No vas a terminar a tiempo, estoy seguro.

M 1 golpeó a 2 Odia a 3 mató a 4 Engañó a 5 Pidió al 6 Echa de menos a

Conjunctions (page 21)

A 1 d, así que, therefore 2 a, después, then 3 g porque, because 4 e, y, and 5 b cuando, when 6 h, sin, without 7 c, o, or 8 f, pero, but

B 1 para que 2 antes de 3 a menos que 4 cuando 5 después de que 6 sin que 7 mientras

C 1 Antonio no fuma porque hace mucho deporte. 2 Bebe vino de vez en cuando pero nunca ha bebido demasiado. 3 Come mucha fruta porque trata de mantenerse en forma. 4 Corre cada mañana antes de/después de tomar el desayuno. 5 Cuando hace buen tiempo, va al trabajo en bici. 6 Hace ejercicios mientras ve la televisión.

D 1 Me gustaría hacerme traductor(a) pero sé que es difícil. 2 Cuando era joven fumaba mucho más. 3 Mientras sus amigos estaban en el cine, ella estaba trabajando. 4 Mucha gente es vegetariana porque cree que las verduras son más sanas que la carne. 5 No se puede ganar mucho dinero sin trabajar duro. 6 Voy a ducharme antes de salir. 7 ¿Quieres ir a un bar después de comer, o prefieres irte a casa?

Personal and reflexive pronouns (page 22)

A 1 for emphasis/contrast 2 because the verb endings do not reveal who the subject is 3 because the verb endings do not reveal who the subject is 4 for politeness 5 because the verb endings do not make it clear who is being referred to

B 1 vosotros 2 usted. 3 tú 4 ustedes . 5 vosotros 6 tú

C 1 me 2 Nos, se, se, Me 3 se 4 me, me 5 nos, nos 6 se 7 nos 8 nos, me

D 1 Se quieren. 2 Se llaman por teléfono cada día 3 Se ven en la plaza cada tarde. 4 A menudo se dan pequeños regalos. 5 Todo el mundo se pregunta cuándo se van a casar.

Direct object pronouns (page 23)

A 1 <u>la</u>, I hate oldfashioned music, I never listen to it. 2 <u>la</u>, Still, I really like classical music, I always listen to it when I'm studying. 3 <u>los</u>, I also love jazz programmes on the radio, I listen to them to relax. 4 <u>los</u>, Have you got those CDs? No, I've lost them. 5 <u>las</u>, Did you buy those tickets for the concert? No, I didn't buy them, they were too expensive.

B 1 <u>la</u>, They're listening to it/her! 2 <u>lo</u>, I love that CD – I'm going to buy it. 3 <u>la</u>, That music's too loud. Turn it down please! 4 <u>lo</u>, His/her new CD? He/she is listening to it. 5 <u>la</u>, Everyone loves Shakira's music, but I don't, I hate it! 6 <u>las</u>, Have you got your tickets, ladies? I need to see them, please! 7 <u>lo</u>, I haven't got David Bisbal's latest CD, but I think I'm going to get it from my sister for my birthday.
8 <u>lo</u>, Where's the remote? I don't know, I'm looking for it.

C 1 No, no los tengo. 2 No, no lo espero. 3 No, no la descargo. 4 No, no lo grabamos.

D Bueno, hoy hacemos una ensalada de frutas, con naranjas, un melón, y uvas. Vamos a sazonar<u>la</u> con jengibre y menta. Bueno, aquí tengo las naranjas – <u>las</u> he pelado y <u>las</u> voy a cortar en rodajas .... y las uvas, lo mejor es pelar<u>las</u>, pero si no hay tiempo de hacer<u>lo</u>, no importa. Lo importante es cortar<u>las</u> en dos y quitar<u>les</u> las pepitas. Yo <u>las</u> he pelado, como ven ustedes ... también el melón <u>lo</u> he cortado en pedazos. Bueno, ahora tomo todas las frutas y <u>las</u> mezclo en este bol. Es buena idea rociar<u>las</u> con jugo de limón, para que no se descoloren ... Ahora, el jengibre... tenemos que pelar<u>lo</u> y cortar<u>lo</u> en pedazos muy pequeños ... voy a añadir<u>los</u> a la ensalada. Para acabar, la menta. Tengo unas doce hojas, y <u>las</u>

voy a cortar. Lo mejor es hacer<u>lo</u> en el último momento, para mantener<u>las</u> frescas.Y aquí tenemos una ensalada riquísima de frutas – ¡aún más rica si la comen con nata montada!

Well, today we're making a fruit salad, with oranges, a melon and grapes. We're going to season it with ginger and mint. Now, here I've got the oranges, I've peeled them and I'm going to slice them ... and the grapes, the best thing is to peel them, but if there isn't time to do it, it's not important. The main thing is to cut them in half and take out the pips. I've peeled them, as you can see ... also the melon, I've cut it into chunks. OK, now I take all the fruit and mix it in this bowl. It's a good idea to sprinkle it with lemon juice so it doesn't discolour. Now, the ginger – we have to peel it and cut it into tiny pieces ... I'm going to add them to the salad. Finally, the mint. I've got a dozen or so leaves, and I'm going to chop them up. The best thing is to do it at the last minute, to keep them fresh. And here we have a delicious fruit salad – even more delicious if you eat it with whipped cream!

E 1 No me gusta mucho la música clásica, así que no la escucha. 2 ¿Puedes explicar estas instrucciones? No las comprendo. 3 Daniel ha perdido su MP3 otra vez, lo has visto? 4 Busco a Felicia y Xavier. ¿Les has visto? 5 ¿Dónde está ese florero? ¿Lo ha roto? 6 Compré unos pasteles – ¿Vamos a comerlos? 7 Me encanta la música y voy a estudiarla en la universidad. 8 No pude resistir esas botas – ¡tuve que comprarlas!

Indirect object pronouns (page 24)

A me, les, le, nos, me, me, le
my parents gave me tickets, I gave them some DVDs, my parents gave him a new guitar, my grandmother sent us money, I'm going to buy myself a new MP3, the kinds of music I need, I'll give her the old one. She was forever asking me to lend her my player but I always said no (to her).

B 1 regalar 2 dar 3 enviar 4 comprarse 5 faltar 6 pedir 7 prestar 8 contestar

C 1 Les llamé ayer. 2 Le preguntamos por qué se había ido. 3 Mi amigo me prestó dinero. 4 Nos llamaron la semana pasada. 5 Le has dado un regalo. 6 Te he dicho la verdad. 7 Va a escribirles el lunes. 8 Voy a darle el cheque mañana.

D 1 My ears hurt. 2 She/he has broken her/his leg. 3 His/her eyes hurt. 4 Come here, Manuelito, I'm going to wash your hands. 5 Why are you taking that aspirin? Have you got a headache?

E 1 Alberto le pidió que le prestara su nuevo CD. 2 El médico le aconsejó que jugara menos frecuentemente. 3 Siempre les estoy pidiendo que bajen la televisión. 4 Mi padre les ha prohibido que vayan a bailar a este club. 5 Su amigo le dijo que escuchase ese CD de salsa, pero no le gustó nada. 6 Mis padres no le permiten que aprenda a tocar la batería.

F 1 Le pedí a Enrique que me enseñara a tocar la guitarra, pero me dijo que no era posible. 2 Invitó a mi amigo a ir a un concierto, pero a ella le dijo que le dejara en paz. 3 No permite a su perro entrar en la habitación cuando está tocando el piano.

Order of pronouns (page 25)

A 1 <u>Me</u>, Those CDs? He/she gave <u>me them</u> yesterday. 2 <u>Te</u>,

Those tracks? We've already sent you them. **3 te**, **me**, They told you but they haven't told me. **4 Me (x2)**,You've told me a thousand times – don't tell me again! **5 me**, Conchita, what are you doing with my headphones? Give them to me please! **6 Me**, Those tickets need to reach me tomorrow. Send **me them** this evening please.

B 1 I always give them to her. **2** He gives it to them. **3** I've told him/her. **4** Maria gave **him it**. **5** I'm going to give **her them**. **6** I'm going to tell **him them**.

Pronouns after prepositions (page 26)

A 1 a ella, a él **2** a usted, a ellas

B 1 Pablo, ¿quieres venir de vacaciones con nosotros? **2** Esta carta es para usted, señora. **3** Mandó el mensaje con ella. **4** No puedo ir sin ti. ¡Ven conmigo! **5** No veo porque hay alguien está delante de mí.

Relative pronouns (pages 26–27)

A 1 la revista que prefiero, the magazine (that) I prefer **2** el grupo que ha ganado, the group that won **3** los detalles que buscabas, the details (that) you were looking for **4** el autógrafo que me dio, the autograph (that) he/she gave me **5** los cantantes que escriben, singers who write

B 1 El hombre que acaba de llegar es el padre del actor/ de la actriz. **2** La gente que la critica no comprende la situación. **3** La persona que me encantaría conocer es Christina Aguilera. **4** El grupo que me más gusta es El sueño de Morfeo. **5** La revista que compré ayer tiene unas fotos fantásticas de la familia real.

C 1 con quienes **2** de quien **3** con quien **4** a que **5** de quien **6** a quien

D 1 It's a prize for which the competitors have to perform in front of an audience, who chose three finalists. **2** That competitor you voted for didn't win. **3** The shelf I put my books on has fallen down! **4** By the door there's a flower pot, in which you will find the keys. **5** The route you came along is very pretty.

E 1 the house **2** the cat **3** the friends

F 1 Este es el lugar donde tenemos que doblar a la izquierda. **2** Estoy visitando a amigos en la ciudad de nací. **3** Esta es la plaza donde solíamos tomar una cerveza.

G 1 cuyo **2** cuyos **3** cuyas

Possessive and demonstrative pronouns (page 28)

A 1 los tuyos **2** la vuestra **3** la suya **4** la nuestra **5** los tuyos, los míos **6** el nuestro **7** el suyo

B 1 el suyo **2** los suyos **3** la nuestra, la suya **4** el mío **5** los míos

C 1 que ese **2** comer estos **3** son aquellas **4** y aquel **5** esto **6** Esa es

Indefinite pronouns and adjectives (page 29)

A 1 algo **2** Alguien **3** Algo, alguien **4** algo **5** algo **6** Alguien **7** algo

B 1 Algunas **2** alguna **3** algún **4** algunas **5** algunos

C Do you want something to eat? Well, I don't know … I'm not very hungry … shall we have something light? Yes, I'm sure there's something tasty in the fridge. Do you prefer something sweet? No, thanks, I'd prefer something savoury – have we got any spaghetti, for example? Spaghetti? But you said you wanted something light!

D 1 muchas **2** muchos **3** todo **4** poco **5** mucho **6** tantos

E 1 We have to find another solution. **2** I've got to choose – this shirt or the other one? **3** You can take any of the books. **4** He gave them each a present. **5** Each student has various books to read.

F 1 Cuáles **2** Qué **3** Cuál **4** Cuáles **5** Qué

Revision: prepositions, conjunctions and pronouns (pages 30–31)

A (1) **Para** encontrar la casa, siga estas instrucciones. Estamos (2) **cerca de** Santa Felicia, (3) **a 20 km de** San Miguel. Primero, vaya (4) **hasta** el centro de San Miguel y siga el camino que le lleva (5) **hacia** Santa Felicia. Cuando salga de Santa Felicia, (6) **antes de** cruzar el puente, doble (7) **a la** izquierda, (8) **enfrente del** colegio. Hay una carnicería (9) **en** la esquina. Continúe (10) **hasta** un lago que verá (11) **a la** derecha. (12) **Después del** lago, busque un pequeño camino (13) **al lado de** una cruz. Tómelo, y continúe (14) **por** este camino. (15) **Después de** unos dos kilómetros, verá nuestra casa (16) **delante de** usted. Si sale a las diez, debería llegar (17) **hacia** las diez y media.

B 1 de, a **2** de, a **3** A, a **4** a, al **5** de **6** en, de

C 1 cuando, pero, cuando, She always chats for an hour when I ring her, but when she rings me we only talk for five minutes! **2** porque, y, It's difficult to understand him because he talks very fast and he's lost his teeth.
3 sin/antes de, I can't decide without/before talking to you. **4** y, así que, después de, The journey is very long and it's very hot so I'll need to shower after I arrive. **5** Cuando, pero, When you are studying in Madrid you'll make new friends, but don't forget us!

D 1 Se **lo me**, I've explained it to them twice but they don't listen (to me). **2** lo **se la**, Slice the lemon and add it to the sangría. The sangría is now ready for your guests – serve it to them straight away. **3** se las **le se** lo **me** lo **Me**, Darling, have you got the car keys? Give them to my mother, please, because I've promised to lend her it for the weekend. What are you saying (to me)? I need it to go to the airport! You'll drive me crazy!

E 1 ¿Dónde están mis gafas de sol? Nadia, ¿las has cogido prestadas otra vez? ¡Dámelas, por favor! **2** Ana quiere hablar contigo. Está pidiendo ese mapa. ¿Qué? ¿Ya lo ha perdido? ¡Pero si se lo di ayer! **3** El profesor de historia siempre está haciéndome preguntas difíciles. No las comprendo y él no me gusta. **4** ¿Te acuerdas de ese CD que mencionó José? Bueno, lo ha comprado finalmente y está eschuchándolo ahora. ¿Te gustaría oírlo? **5** Me gustaría mucho salir contigo, pero a mi novio (eso) no le gustaría. Es muy posesivo conmigo. ¡Lo siento!

F 1 quien, donde **2** que, quien **3** donde/en que, que **4** la que, donde, quien

G 1 That glass is mine, isn't it? Yes, it's yours, and this one is mine. **2** Her/his mother is a programmer and his/her brother is an engineer. And his/her cousin works for my father! **3** A friend of mine wants to go out with that man over there. That one, the chubby guy in black? No, no, that one, the tall one in jeans. Oh, that one. **4** Where's the book I was reading? It's (over) there, under(neath) mine. But that book's not very good – you should read this other one, it's much better. **5** Does your father still live in that same house? No, that house was too big for him and now he lives in town, very near one of my sisters. He was hoping to live with her in her flat, but her husband said no because his own mother already lives there! **6** We're inviting all our friends to a party. Do you want to come with your boyfriend? My boyfriend's left me for one of my friends. But I could ask a friend to come with me …

H **1** algunos **2** poco, algo **3** algunos, todos, algo **4** Algún, alguien **5** alguien, algún, todos **6** cualquiera, todos

The main tenses of verbs

The present tense: regular verbs; the present continuous, the present participle

Regular verbs (page 32)

A **1** a Vas **2** b voy **3** a Vas **4** b juega **5** b es **6** a Vas **7** b das

B **1** d **2** b **3** a **4** e **5** f **6** c

C **1** charlo, I chat **2** cantas, you sing **3** baila, Pablo dances **4** visita, you visit **5** tomamos, we take/have **6** viajamos, Marisol and I travel **7** gastáis, you spend **8** pasan, they pass/spend

D **1** comemos, We always eat in a restaurant on Fridays. **2** debes, You shouldn't smoke so much. **3** venden, In our market they sell delicious fruit. **4** saben, Do you know when the train from Madrid arrives?

E **1** Las tiendas abren a las tres. **2** Mi novio me escribe poesía. **3** Mi padre vive a **10** km de nuestra casa. **4** En su artículo describe el paisaje de Navarra.

The present continuous, the present participle (page 33)

A **1** **Están** preparando, they're making **2** **Estamos** viendo, we're watching **3** **está** trabajando, she's working **4** **Estás** durmiendo, are you sleeping/asleep? **5** **estoy** cortándolas, I'm chopping them **6** **nos estamos** bañando, se **está** sacudiendo, **estás** salpicando, we're bathing, he's shaking himself, you're splashing

B **1** Por favor, hablad más bajo, niños, ¡estoy escuchando la música! **2** Miguel está en el baño desde las ocho. Siempre dice que está leyendo *El País*, pero yo creo que está durmiendo. **3** ¿Dónde están los chicos? Están viendo el partido del Barça con los vecinos. **4** ¿Puedes volver a llamar dentro de media hora? Estamos levantándonos.

C **1** sigue leyendo **2** Llevan dos años estudiando **3** siguen jugando **4** Va subiendo **5** seguiré trabajando **6** sigues enviándome

D **1** the following day **2** running water **3** the coming week **4** living plants **5** a surprising idea

The present tense: reflexive verbs; spelling change verbs, common irregular verbs

Reflexive verbs (page 34)

A **1** Nico, are you getting up? It's eleven o'clock! **2** My brother has been building himself a house for a year. **3** He's called Xavier, like his father and his grandfather, but his sons are called Antonio and Ramón. **4** Come on children, we must hurry to get there on time. **5** Are you having a good time in Madrid? Yes, very. We're treating ourselves and we're staying in a nice hotel. We're going out every night. We're getting to bed at two in the morning!

B nos levantamos, me baño, se ducha, nos vestimos, nos divertimos, nos vamos, se llena, no nos llevamos nunca, nos damos el gusto, nos acostamos, no nos damos prisa, nos sentimos

Spelling change verbs and common irregular verbs (page 34)

A **1** Mi equipo juega muy mal. Jugamos todos muy mal, ¿no queremos ganar? Menos Diego, naturalmente. ¡Oye, Diego, juegas muy bien!

2 What a day! I go shopping at quarter to twelve and I don't find anyone there; the shop closes at 11.30 today because the shopkeeper is playing in a football team. I come home, but I can't get in because my keys are in the kitchen. It's raining hard and I think I'm going to end up soaked. Finally I ask the neighbour to let me get in via his balcony. I'm feeling very tired.

B **1** salgo, hago, veo **2** doy, sé **3** conozco, pongo **4** Estoy, tengo

C No hago nunca mis deberes, porque salgo cada noche. Ya lo sé, ¡te conozco bastante bien! Bueno, te doy mis apuntes – ¡pero esta es la última vez!

D **1** dicen **2** van **3** Oigo **4** tengo **5** tienen **6** venimos **7** digo **8** tenemos

Ser and estar (page 35)

A es, es, son, está, está, está, está, es
su casa es grande – *ser* because it's describing a long-term characteristic
su mujer es modelo – *ser* when giving someone's job
sus dos hijos son inteligentes – *ser* for a long-term characteristic
su mujer está en Brasil – *estar* because it's describing location
su madre está enferma – *estar* because it's describing a temporary condition
su padre está un poco deprimido – *estar* because it's describing a temporary condition
su hermano está en la cárcel – *estar* because it's describing location
su hija es heroinómana – *ser* because it's describing a long-term characteristic

B **1** están **2** estoy, es **3** son **4** es, somos **5** está, está **6** son, están **7** está, es, es

Modes of address; gustar (page 36)

A **1** tú **2** usted **3** vosotras **4** ustedes **5** vosotros **6** tú **7** tú **8** usted **9** vosotros **10** usted

B **1** gusta, gustan, I like the idea of the programme, but I don't like the presenters. **2** gustan, gustan, Do you like reality shows?, Yes, I like some, but I prefer the ones on the home, interiors, I don't like *Supervivientes*. **3** gustan, gusta, I like the ads, but apart from that I don't like TV very much. **4** gusta, gustan, They like to watch films and the news, but they don't like series or reality shows.

Negatives (page 36)

A **1** Según este artículo, no es demasiado tarde para salvar el medio ambiente. **2** No debemos vivir sin preocuparnos del futuro. **3** Mi coche, por ejemplo, no consume mucha gasolina. **4** En mi familia no nos gusta comprar productos con mucho envoltorio de plástico. **5** A los niños no les interesa este problema. **6** No tiran basura por la calle y no olvidan la importancia del reciclaje.

B **1** You've seen this interview, haven't you? I don't think so. I haven't seen the paper. **2** Don't you like reading the papers? Of course I do, but I don't have time for it! **3** But you watch the TV, don't you? Of course not, I have too much work. **4** But aren't you interested in the news, what's going on in the world? I suppose so, but my friends keep me up to date.

C **1** nadie **2** ni, ni **3** ninguno **4** nada **5** ningún **6** no ... más **7** tampoco **8** jamás/nunca **9** siquiera **10** nadie

D **1** nada que **2** nada que, ningún ... que, ningunos ... que

E **1** They didn't even say hello to us. **2** No-one has left me a message? No-one. **3** They will never find the solution to this problem. **4** Neither my father not my mother is happy. Neither am I. **5** Nada ha cambiado. **6** Ni siquiera abrió su correo electrónico. **7** Sé que me olvidarás. No, nunca. **8** Ni el profesor ni tus amigos te comprenden. Yo tampoco.

F **1** My grandad still doesn't like the internet, he prefers to read his paper. **2** Have you bought my paper? No, not yet. **3** He left without her and without saying goodbye. **4** We'll get there by eleven with no problem.

The perfect tense (page 38)

A **1** <u>han llegado</u>, <u>ha llamado</u>, Rosa and Jaime have arrived, but Carlos has called to say he has a problem with his car – he'll be here at ten. **2** <u>¿Han visto?</u>, Have you seen this article on tourism in Chile? **3** <u>hemos visitado</u>, <u>hemos estado</u>, We haven't visited the Old Cathedral, but we've been to almost all the other main sights and now we're going to have a cold drink. **4** <u>has visto</u>, <u>he comprado</u>, Have you seen this guidebook? Yes, but I'm not going to buy it because I've already bought another one, with a map.

B **1** han **2** han **3** has **4** habéis **5** hemos

C **1** invitado **2** comprado **3** comido **4** hablado

D **1** ¿Le has dicho a Manuel el resultado del partido? **2** He perdido mi bolso. ¿Lo has visto? **3** No sé lo que he hecho, pero se hiegan a llamarme. **4** Hemos puesto el equipaje en el coche, y ahora esperamos a nuestro amigo.

E **1** no he entendido, I've never understood physics. **2** ha dicho, He has never told anyone, but he's not working. **3** han mandado, Haven't they sent you that money yet? **4** hemos recibido, We haven't received any information about them.

F **1** acaban de salir, (my friends) have just gone out **2** acaba de telefonearme, (my mother) has just phoned me **3** acabáis de cenar, you have just had dinner **4** acabamos de decidir, (we) have just decided

The preterite tense (page 39)

A **1** wrote **2** started **3** refused **4** watched, explained **5** received, got very excited **6** bumped into **7** rang up, talked **8** saw, decided, lost

B Roberto: **1** Habló con Isabel por teléfono. **2** La invitó a ir con él a la playa. **3** Descubrió que a Isabel no le gusta el mar. **4** Llamó a Susana. **5** Le dejó un mensaje al padre de Susana. **6** No recibió ninguna respuesta de Susana. **7** Salió solo y comió muchas patatas fritas.
Vosotros: **1** cenasteis con la familia **2** leísteis los periódicos **3** comprasteis algunas cosas para la casa **4** lavasteis el coche **5** escribisteis algunos correos electrónicos
Yo ... / pero ellos: **1** Yo perdí mi empleo, pero ellos ganaron diez mil euros. **2** Yo tomé una cerveza, pero ellos bebieron tres botellas de Rioja. **3** Yo vendí mi bici, pero ellos compraron un coche. **4** Yo comí en casa, pero ellos salieron con sus amigos a un restaurante. **5** Yo decidí no ir de vacaciones, pero ellos reservaron un hotel.

C Ayer el señor Martín llegó a la empresa a las ocho. Entró en su oficina, se quitó su chaqueta y se sentó. Tomó un café y sacó sus papeles. Trabajó (durante) dos horas, preparándose para una reunión importante. A las diez, sus invitados llegaron. Les ofreció café y todo el mundo se congregó en la sala de reuniones. Pasaron tres horas hablando de derechos y de honorarios. Finalmente todos firmaron un contrato. Después, salieron y tomaron un buen almuerzo. El señor Martín no volvió a la olicina por la tarde.

D **1** hicieron, fuimos **2** dio, pusieron **3** supe, dije **4** vinieron, trajeron

E **1** Busqué la Guía TV pero no la encontré. **2** Preferían la pantalla más cara pero eligieron la más barata. **3** Ayer Margarita se divirtió, condujo a la playa y leyó toda una novela. **4** Yo pagué nuestra cena porque la tarjeta de crédito de Esteban no funcionó; se sintió muy incómodo, porque el camarero se rió.

F **1** fui **2** me alojé **3** estuvieron **4** tuve **5** se rieron **6** corrigieron **7** visitamos **8** entendí **9** ripetió **10** gustaron **11** hicimos **12** fuimos **13** condujo **14** dio **15** busqué **16** encontré **17** puse **18** regalé **19** dijo

The imperfect tense (page 41)

A **1** vivíais, Where did you live? **2** teníais, How many children did you have? **3** Trabajabais, Did you both work? **4** ganaba, How much did a typical worker earn in those days? **5** ibais, Where did you go on holiday? **6** hacíais, What did you do to relax? **7** comíais, Did you eat the same food as nowadays? **8** Erais, Were you happy?

B

C **1** d **2** j **3** g **4** c **5** a **6** h **7** f **8** e **9** i **10** b

D **1** escribía **2** estudiabas **3** prometían **4** trabajaban **5** veían

E **1** íbamos **2** era **3** iba **4** era **5** era **6** erais, ibais

F **1** estudiaba **2** era **3** iba **4** pasaba **5** organizaba **6** escribía **7** soñaba

G **1** La abuela habla: estaba, iba, tenía, trabajaban, lavaban, limpiaban, cocinaban

2 Los padres hablan: éramos, jugábamos, dábamos, teníamos, hacíamos, tomábamos, salíamos, vivíamos, comíamos

3 El joven habla: comía, interesaba, pasaba, acostaba, iba, bebía, fumaba, estaba, me sentía

The imperfect continuous (page 43)

A **1** estaba comiendo **2** estaba escuchando **3** estaba haciendo **4** estaban criticando **5** estaba describiendo **6** estaba sacando **7** estaba bebiendo **8** estaban telefoneando

B **1** estaba trabajando **2** estaba pasando **3** estaba durmiendo **4** estaba diciendo, estaba perjudicando **5** me estaba poniendo, estaba tomando **6** estaba bebiendo **7** estaba ignorando

C **1** He was waking up when the rain started. **2** He was having a bath when the storm started. **3** He was shaving when the lightning started. **4** An hour later, the wind was dying down as he left the house. **5** Estaba levantándome cuando el teléfono sonó. **6** Estaba duchándome cuando llegaste. **7** Estaba vistiéndome cuando el teléfono sonó otra vez. **8** Me estaba poniendo furioso pero tú contestaste.

D **1** Cuando alguien rompió la ventana, Raimundo estaba jugando al voleibol. **2** Cuando alguien se llevó mi bici, Raimundo estaba paseando al perro en el parque. **3** Cuando el matón atracó a la señora, Raimundo estaba viendo la televisión con su novia. **4** Cuando el ladrón entró en la tienda de ordenadores, Raimundo estaba bebiendo una cerveza en el bar. **5** Cuando alguien se llevó la radio de mi coche, Raimundo estaba haciendo las compras en el supermercado.

Using contrasting past tenses (page 44)

A **1** I **2** P **3** I **4** I **5** P **6** I **7** P

B **1** Nació **2** murió **3** vivía **4** empezó **5** gustaba **6** cambió, encontró **7** eran **8** estaba, terminó, tenía **9** Dejó, fue

1	comprábamos	compraba	I bought (was buying, used to buy)
2	jugábamos	jugaba	I played (was playing, used to play)
3	lavábamos	lavaba	I washed (was washing, used to wash)
4	bebíamos	bebía	I drank (was drinking, used to drink)
5	veíamos	veía	I saw (was seeing, used to see)
6	traíamos	traía	I brought (was bringing, used to bring)
7	conducíamos	conducía	I drove (was driving, used to drive)
8	escribíamos	escribía	I wrote (was writing, used to write)
9	salíamos	salía	I left (was leaving, used to leave)

10 Empezó **11** trabajó **12** estaba viviendo, conoció **13** era, trabajaba **14** era, gustó **15** salían **16** Iban, daban, bailaban, iban **17** se casaron **18** vivieron **19** decidieron, estaba **20** tuvieron, estaban

C **1** ¿Has visto mi libro sobre Joaquín Rodrigo? Lo estaba leyendo cuando entraste. **2** Rodrigo ya estaba estudiando piano y violín cuando decidió irse a París. **3** Carmen lha llamado otra vez. ¿Le has enviado esos billetes? No, lo siento, no los he enviado. Estaba preparándolos cuando un invitado llegó, y después me olvidé de ellos. **4** El cantante estaba cantando con los ojos cerrados cuando se cayó del escenario. Se cayó sobre un espectador que estaba bailando en la primera fila. El cantante está bien pero el espectador está en tratamiento por el shock y se ha roto la muñeca. **5** Cuando estaba conduciendo de Casares a Estepona, mi coche se estropeó. Llamé al taller pero estaba cerrado. Hacía mucho calor, así que me dormí. Cuando me desperté, eran las tres. Llamé otra vez al taller, y un camión llegó después de media hora. El conductor me dio algo de beber porque tenía mucha sed y no tenía agua.

The pluperfect tense (page 45)

A **1** g **2** d **3** e **4** b **5** a **6** c **7** f

B **1** Luisa didn't pass her exam because she <u>had not revised</u>. **2** She wrote a good essay because she <u>had learned</u> lots of vocabulary. **3** She was very cold because she <u>hadn't put on</u> her coat. **4** She arrived late because she <u>had missed</u> the bus. **5** She didn't take part in the PE class because she <u>had forgotten</u> her trainers.
6 Señora Ramona told her off because she <u>had not finished</u> her homework. **7** She argued with Carla because Carla <u>had not phoned</u> her as she promised.

C Antes de salir … Michaela había llevado al perro a la casa de su madre; Julia había dado a los vecinos nuestro número de teléfono móvil; Selina y Michaela habían hecho las maletas; yo había visto al médico porque necesitaba pastillas; y Marco había comprado unos bocadillos para el viaje.

D **1** El jefe le gritó a Francisca porque esta mañana había perdido unos documentos importantes. **2** El lunes, los ordenadores estaban estropeados porque los ingenieros no habían hecho su trabajo durante el fin de semana. **3** Durante toda la semana los clientes no pudieron contactar con el jefe de marketing, porque se le había olvidado su teléfono móvil en el tren. **4** El señor Ramírez no participó en la reunión porque se había dormido en su oficina. **5** No podían oír lo que decía el jefe porque el micrófono se había estropeado.

E **1** Antes del triunfo del Concierto de Aranjuez en el año **1939**, Rodrigo había encontrado muchas dificultades en la vida. **2** De niño había contraído difteria. **3** Como consecuencia de esta enfermedad se había quedado ciego. **4** Había aprendido braille para poder estudiar piano y violin. **5** Se había ido a París para trabajar con otros compositores. **6** Había vivido en la pobreza.

Direct and indirect speech (page 46)

A **1** 'La policía ha llegado.' **2** 'Entran en la casa.' **3** 'Ahora salen con un hombre.' **4** 'Hay también una mujer.' **5** 'La mujer parece muy nerviosa.' **6** 'El hombre parece totalmente loco, – grita y gesticula.' **7** 'La policía se ha llevado al hombre y a la mujer y todo el mundo vuelve a su casa.'

B **1** Dice que ha hecho sus maletas y que se va a ir. **2** Dice que tiene dos maletas enormes. **3** Dice que va a llamar un taxi para ir a la estación. **4** Dice que piensa comprarse un bocadillo en el tren. **5** Dice que no es necesario darle nada de comer. **6** Dice que espera llegar a las dos. **7** Dice que tiene su móvil consigo, va a darme el número.

C **1** Me pregunta dónde está nuestra casa. **2** Me pregunta si estamos lejos de la estación. **3** Pregunta si puedo ir a buscarle en la estación. **4** Me pregunta qué tipo de coche tengo. **5**

Pregunta si puedo llamarle si hay algún problema.

D 1 'No quiero verla más.' 2 'Nunca voy a volver.' 3 'Mi vida comienza de nuevo.' 4 '¿Esta noticia te interesa?' 5 'Salgo con tu amigo Federico desde el año pasado, así que no me importa mucho.'

E Alicia: 1 Dice que decidió dejar su trabajo. 2 Dice que quería pasar más tiempo con su hijo. 3 Dice que también prefería tener un horario menos rígido. 4 Dice que Alejandro y ella estaban preocupados porque el niño no estaba muy robusto. 5 Dice que está muy contenta con su decisión.
Bárbara: 6 'Tuve que volver al trabajo por razones económicas.' 7 'Encontré a una muy buena niñera.' 8 'Volví al trabajo seis meses después del nacimiento de mi hijo.' 9 'No quería quedarme en casa.' 10 'No me arrepiento de haber mantenido mi independencia.'

F Dijeron que ......
habían llegado a Gerona el lunes y habían hecho algunas visitas. El jefe de la empresa les había invitado a hacer una visita a la fábrica, lo cual habían hecho el jueves. Habían hablado con algunos empleados. También habían participado en algunas reuniones y habían firmado un contrato. Por la tarde habían salido con el jefe y su mujer, habían ido al teatro y después habían comido en un restaurante.

G 1 Le había gustado la visita. 2 Nunca había ido a Barcelona. 3 Siempre había querido ver la ciudad. 4 La gente había sido muy simpática. 5 Había visitado la Sagrada Familia dos veces. 6 Siempre había admirado la obra de Gaudí.

The immediate future (page 48)

A 1 Voy a hacerme socio de un centro deportivo. 2 Guillermo va a jugar al fútbol con sus hijos. 3 Lorenzo va a comprar una bici de ejercicio. 4 Luisa va a hacer una hora de natación cada mañana. 5 Vamos a dar paseos en bici. ¿Os apuntais? 6 Consuelo y Mercedes van a renunciar al queso y al chocolate. 7 ¿(Tú) vas a hacer algo, Paco?

B 1 Tomás dice que va a ir al gimnasio con su hermano. 2 Eso no va a durar, a mi modo de ver. 3 No sé, dice que va a hacerse socio. 4 ¡Una pérdida de dinero! Nunca va a ser una persona deportista – no le gusta el deporte. 5 Quizás, pero dice que va a ir una vez por seman y que va a perder 10 kilos. 6 Si quiere perder 10 kilos, ¡ tendrá que ir una vez al día, no una vez por semana!

The future tense (page 48)

A 1 Compraré 2 ganará 3 estudiará, trabajará 4 Vivirás, encontraré 5 se casarán 6 Volveréis, os quedaréis

B 1 Harán un nuevo contrato al entrenador. 2 Se retirará después de otros dos años. 3 Así que seguro que podremos ganar la copa el próximo año. 4 ¿Vendréis a ver el final con nosotros como de costumbre? 5 Después, ¡saldremos a cenar e iremos de fiesta! 6 El único problema es que Manolo no querrá celebrar, porque no es de nuestro equipo. 7 Es sencillo: ¡tendrá que cambiar de equipo!

C Acuario: recibirá, encontrará, dará; Piscis: tendrá, cogerá, podrá, necesitará; Aries: traerá, ofrecerá, tendrá; Tauro: será, verá, conocerá, gastará; Géminis: deberá, se sentirá, faltará, verá, dirá; Cáncer: dejará, se sentirá, intentará, contestará;

Leo: preocupará, hará, sabrá, pensará, tomará; Virgo: será, mostrará, comenzará, hará; Libra: estará, comprenderá, ayudará, descubrirá; Escorpio: preocuparán, ganará, gastará, terminará, deberá

Revision: the main tenses of verbs (page 49)

A 1 juegan 2 duermes 3 pienso 4 pedimos 5 quieren 6 corregís 7 juego 8 pueden 9 vuelve 10 entiende 11 encuentras 12 llueve 13 sienten 14 prefiero 15 muestra

B 1 sé 2 dices 3 salgo 4 vamos 5 estoy 6 oye 7 pongo 8 tienen 9 viene 10 dice 11 vas 12 tengo 13 son 14 hago 15 es

C 1 son 2 está 3 Son, es 4 están 5 Es, ser 6 estaba 7 estaba 8 estaba, fue 9 estaba, era 10 han sido

D 1 Nunca he visitado Londres/No he visitado nunca Londres. 2 Nadie te ha dejado un/ningún mensaje. 3 No vi a nadie en el bar. 4 No les gusta ninguna de esas personas. 5 No llama jamás/nunca a su madre – no la llamó ni siquiera en su cumpleaños. 6 No tengo nada que decirles.

E 1 ha visto, Enrique hasn't seen her today. 2 habéis levantado, Girls, haven't you got up yet? 3 han dicho, he dicho, They've told me the news but I haven't told her. 4 he hecho, ha puesto, I've packed the cases and Pablo has put them in the car. 5 has venido, me he duchado, me he vestido, Why have you come so early? I've had my shower but I haven't got dressed.

F 1 ¿Qué te dieron? 2 No pude abrir la puerta, así que llamé al timbre. 3 Leyó el periódico y le dijo las noticias. 4 Perdí mis gafas ayer. Las busqué por todas partes y finalmente las encontré sobre la televisión. 5 Fuimos a los Picos de Europa en mayo. Condujimos desde San Sebastián. 6 Isabel vino a vernos la semana pasada. ¡Trajo cuatro maletas!

G 1 Estaba leyendo 2 Leía, estaba 3 trabajaba, iba 4 Estaba conduciendo, estaba durmiendo 5 gustaba, visitábamos, estaban escuchando

H 1 La semana pasada se fue de vacaciones; había hecho sus maletas el fin de semana. 2 Dijo que me había dicho las fechas de sus vacaciones. 3 En realidad, ¡había decidido irse sin decírmelo! 4 Cuando llegó a la casa, no pudo entrar, se había dejado las llaves en el restaurante. 5 Descubrió que también se había olvidado la tarjeta de crédito. 6 Llamó al restaurante, por suerte, habían encontrado sus cosas y se las habían guardado.

More verb forms

The conditional (page 52)

A 1 Deberían, They should give up smoking. 2 gustaría, We'd like to do a tennis course. 3 vería, You said you'd meet me at the pool at ten o'clock. 4 compraría, If I were you, I'd buy a new exercise bike. 5 Podrías, Could you bring a litre of milk? I haven't got time to go out. 6 viviría, Raquel told me she would never live in the city. 7 hablaría, If I were you I'd talk to her to explain everything. 8 podríais, Could you please tell us where the sports centre is?

B 1 comerías 2 iría 3 elegirían 4 beberíais 5 vendería 6 sabría 7 saldría 8 vendríais 9 deberíamos 10 harían 11 podría 12 pondrían 13 verían 14 podríamos preguntar/invitar a Pilar 15 debería contestar

C 1 se entrenaría 2 comería 3 trabajaría 4 estudiaría

5 bebería **6** cuidaría **7** haría **8** tendría **9** participaría **10** se acostaría

D En un medio ambiente más limpio ... estaríamos todos más sanos. Los problemas de tráfico desaparecerían, menos niños sufrirían de asma y las calles estarían menos sucias. También podríamos salvar las especies en peligro.

The forms and uses of the subjunctive (present, imperfect, perfect, pluperfect) (page 53)

A **1** vengas **2** ayuden **3** esperara **4** conduzcas **5** haya muerto **6** tomara **7** llamaras **8** hayan recibido **9** diéramos **10** haya hecho

1 e 2 i 3 h 4 b 5 d 6 g 7 a 8 f 9 j 10 c

B **1** Pr.S. **2** Pr. S. **3** Imp.S. **4** Pr.S. **5** Perf.S. **6** Imp.S. **7** Imp.S. **8** Perf.S. **9** Imp.S. **10** Perf.S.

C **1** Pilar, I need you to do me a favour. I want you to go to the supermarket and do the shopping. **2** You must put your cigarette out – the boss doesn't let us smoke in the office. **3** I prefer you to come on Friday because on Thursday I have to work. **4** Do you want me to help you, sir? **5** The doctor has advised my sister not to work. **6** Tell him/her to send me an e-mail. **7** I'm going to ask them to make less noise. **8** It's a pity you can't come. **9** I'm surprised that you don't like Monica. **10** I doubt if he's enjoying himself in Madrid – he hates cities. **11** I need someone who knows how to drive. **12** We'll go to Barcelona so that you can see the Sagrada Familia. **13** Unless it's too cold, we'll go for a walk on the beach. **14** I want you to do your homework before we go out. **15** Unless you tell me, I can't know what the problem is.

D **1** Me sorprende que vaya a su casa. **2** Necesito que me dejes tu portátil porque mi módem se ha estropeado. **3** No creo que quiera invitarla, no creo que la vea hoy en día. **4** ¡Quiero que sepas que no estoy contento de que tengas todavía este problema! Te aconsejo que veas a un médico. **5** No quiero que salga con ellos. ¡Prefiero que venga conmigo! **6** ¿Quieres que llame a tus padres, Tomás? **7** Espero que no venga. No puedo

verb	tense	translation into English
comenzaba	imperfect	was beginning
extender	infinitive	to extend
llegamos	preterite	arrived
es	present	is
se ven elevarse	present	can be seen rising
rodean	present	surround
parecen	present	appear, seem
han abatido	perfect	have descended (from)
apagar	infinitive	quench, slake
conduce	present	leads
remontando	present participle	working its way upstream
siguiendo	present participle	following
se encuentra	present	you come to, you come
son	present	are
se apoya	present	is supported
conduce	present	leads
ha cubierto	perfect	has covered
ha roto y carcomido	perfect	has broken and eaten away/crumbled
crecen	present	grow
suben enredándose	present	twine their way up
sirve	present	serves, acts
había adelantado	pluperfect	had gone ahead of
deteniendo	present participle	stopping
contemplaba	imperfect	contemplated (for a while)
se agolpó	preterite	crowded into
unían	imperfect	brought together

hablar con ella sin que se ponga furiosa.

E **1** hablaras **2** comiéramos **3** ayudara **4** dejara **5** pudiera **6** diéramos **7** estuvieras **8** hiciera **1** I hoped you would talk to her before you left. **2** They wanted us to eat with them but we had to leave. **3** I asked him to help me with that work but he didn't want to (do it). **4** The doctor advised him/her to give up smoking but he/she didn't pay any attention. **5** I was looking for someone who could play tennis with me. **6** He/she asked us to give him her phone number. **7** We just wanted you to be happy! **8** If only the weather was good!

F **1** hayan llegado **2** haya encontrado **3** hayáis recibido **4** hayas dicho **5** haya hecho

G **1** He didn't admit that he had seen Esmeralda. **2** Pilar could not believe that Enrique had left. **3** We hoped they had understood. **4** It wasn't true that we had forgotten you. **5** If they hadn't given me that money, I'd have serious problems.

Using the subjunctive (pages 55–57)

A 1 a 2 c 3 b 4 c 5 d (x2) 6 b 7 d 8 b 9 a 10 c

B 1 no 2 yes 3 yes 4 yes 5 no 6 yes 7 yes 8 yes 9 no 10 yes 11 no 12 no

C 1 present, perfect subjunctive 2 preterite, imperfect subjunctive 3 perfect, infinitive 4 imperfect, imperfect subjunctive 5 preterite, pluperfect subjunctive 6 preterite, infinitive 7 present, present subjunctive 8 imperfect, pluperfect subjunctive

D 1 b) Quiero que hagáis algo por mí. 2 a) Espero que no le hayan oído. 3 b) Me pidieron que trajera mis fotografías. 4 b) Me prohibió hablar. 5 b) No esperaba que me llamaras. 6 a) No creyeron que hubieras llegado a las diez de la noche.

E 1 Me sorprende que no busques tus vacaciones por Internet. 2 Es fantástico que este nuevo MP3 sea tan barato. 3 Es una lástima que pasen todo su tiempo libre navegando por Internet. 4 ¿Te preocupa que tantas canciones se puedan descargar gratis?

1 deje 2 hubiéramos fumado 3 bebiera 4 sea 5 hayan tomado

G 1 pueda, hable 2 sepa 3 sepa 4 funcione, funcionen 5 haya visto, haya visto 6 ofrezca, tenga

1 We're looking for someone who can talk to our Russian and German clients. We already have a person who speaks German, but there's no one who speaks Russian. 2 Do you know anyone who knows how to do spreadsheets? Yes, I can do them 3 I have a friend who can dance the tango. But do you know anyone who can play the guitar? 4 I need a computer that works without any problems. Are you crazy? There's no such thing as a computer that works without any problems. / There are no computers that work without any problems. 5 Is there anyone here who's seen my dog? Sorry? I'm looking for a little black dog with white ears. Sorry, no-one here has seen any dog. 6 My friend wants a job with more responsibility. The problem is that for that he has to have more experience.

H 1 c 2 e 3 a 4 d 5 b 6 f

I 1 vengas 2 vaya 3 juegan 4 te recuperes 5 tenga

Constructions with *si* (page 58)

A 1 If you don't want to come, you don't have to come. 2 If Bernard is frightened of taking the plane, he can't come to Chile. 3 If you don't like the pasties, don't eat them. 4 If you want to see me, come to Madrid! 5 When it was sunny, we spent the weekend on the beach. 6 If you hope to go on holiday, you need to save some money. 7 If the train arrived on time, I used to have ten minutes to have a coffee before going to the office. 8 If we're ready, let's go!

B 1 d 2 b 3 e 4 a 5 c

C 1 preterite, imperfect; They asked me if I liked the city. 2 immediate future, future; I'm going to ask them whether they'll be on holiday in August. 3 present, (imperative), immediate future; When you ring Maria, find out if she's going to come on Sunday. 4 preterite, conditional; Did you ask the receptionist if you could go in? 5 perfect, immediate future; He didn't tell me whether he's going to work here.

D 1 Me preguntó si había probado la fabada. 2 Martina le va a preguntar a Javier si quiere acompañarla de vacaciones/ir de vacaciones con ella. 3 Le escribí para preguntarle si la veía en la fiesta. 4 Quiero averiguar si han llegado. 5 Me preguntaron si me gustaría comer con ellos. 6 Le preguntamos si le había gustado la película. 7 Pregúntale si ha visto mi maleta. 8 Dime si quieres vernos el fin de semana. 9 Pregúntales si quieren beber algo. 10 Averigua si se ha reservado su hotel.

E 1 g I S C 2 d P F
3 a P F 4 e I S C
5 c I S C 6 f I S C 7 h P F 8 b I S C

F 1 salúdale 2 olvidarías 3 salgo 4 harías 5 compraríamos 6 ganara 7 recibe 8 pasarías 9 quieres 10 irían

G 1 Si estuviera de vacaciones en el campo … me gustaría alojarme en un villa con piscina daría un paseo cada mañana. Oiría a los pájaros – ¡y los tractores! Necesitaría un coche para hacer las compras. 2 Si estuviera de vacaciones en la ciudad … visitaríamos los museos y las galerías. Iríamos al cine cada semana. Quedaréamos con nuestros amigos en un bar todas las tardes. Pagaríamos mucho para aparcar el coche. Disfrutaríamos ni de aire puro ni de un medio ambiente tranquilo.
3 Si estuvieras de vacaciones cerca del mar … verías a muchos turistas. podrías escuchar las olas sobre la playa. ¿Aprenderías a pescar? ¿Te bañarías todos los días? Tus padres vendrían a pasar una semana contigo.

H Completion of sentences depends on students' personal choices. 1 Si me tocara la lotería, compraría … 2 Si a mi amigo/a le tocara la lotería, … 3 Si fuera ministro/a de educación, los estudiantes… 4 Si fuera ministro/a del medio ambiente, el Reino Unido tendría… 5 Si fuera ministro/a de transportes, los conductores tendrían que… 6 Si fuera ministro/a de defensa, … 7 Si fuera ministro/a de asuntos exteriores, … 8 Si fuera primer ministro/primera ministra, …

The imperative (page 60)

A 1 Come in. (tú) 2 Repeat what you hear. (vosotros) 3 Open the file. (usted) 4 Save your work. (vosotros) 5 Let's visit Argentina! (nosotros) 6 Remember these numbers. (tú) 7 Let's say no – because we don't want to. (nosotros) 8 Listen to this music. (tú) 9 Take the first street on the right. (ustedes) 10 Visit this site – it's very interesting. (tú)

B 1 Dile a tu hermana que empieza la película. 2 Haz tus comentarios sobre nuestra página <u>aquí</u>. 3 Ven a las ocho y tomaremos una copa. 4 Pon tu opinión en la casilla. 5 Si vas a Madrid, ve primero a la Plaza Mayor.

C 1 Give me those books! 2 Sit down! 3 Be quiet! 4 Did you understand the question? Well, answer it! 5 Listen to the recording. 6 Dime el nombre de aquel sitio. 7 ¡Levántate! 8 ¡Pórtate bien! 9 ¿Has comprendido el problema? Bueno, ¡dime la solución! 10 Mira la pantalla. 11 Escondamos 12 Tiremos 13 Sentémonos 14 Demos 15 Pongamos

D 1 tomen 2 siéntense 3 escuchen 4 Vengan 5 prueben

E

F

G 1 tú, Olvídame. 2 tú, Ven antes de las ocho. 3 Vds., Siéntense allí, señoras. 4 vosotros, Levantaos, por favor. 5 nosotros, Vamos a la playa. 6 tú, Escríbeme. 7 vosotros,

Comed esos bocadillos. **8** Vds., Aparquen aquí. **9** nosotros, Salgamos hoy. **10** vosotros, Jugad en el parque.

H 1 No te olvides de traer tu música. **2** No se siente en esa silla, está rota. **3** ¡No se preocupen, señoras! **4** ¡No comáis esas gambas, niños! **5** No vayamos al colegio mañana.
6 ¡No permitáis a vuestro perro entrar en mi jardín, por favor! **7** No pongas la televisión antes de terminar los deberes. **8** No utilices lenguaje ofensivo en los blogs. **9** Cuando contribuyas a un blog, no pongas enlaces a sitios 'basura'. **10** No escribas en los blogs en estilo SMS.

I 1 Don't lean out of the window. **2** Add the sugar and the flour. **3** No parking here, please. **4** Keep to the right. **5** Peel the apples and chop them. **6** Attach part A to part B with nails C. **7** Don't make a noise after 11 p.m. **8** Follow the blue arrows. **9** Place in boiling water for five minutes.
10 Keep in a cool dry place.

The passive and how to avoid it (pages 62–63)

A 1 3 4 5 7 8

B

C 1 Our lives <u>are</u> increasingly <u>influenced</u> by climate change. **3** There is a minority who <u>are not convinced</u>. **4** In my view, <u>we have not been shown</u> enough evidence to convince everyone. **5** Every country <u>will be affected</u>. **7** Politicians <u>have been forced</u> to take up this issue. **8** We're constantly bombarded with advice and guidelines on this subject.

D 1 f **2** e **3** c **4** g **5** a **6** d **7** b
seguir, temer, tentar

E 1 Our life <u>is</u> increasingly <u>influenced</u> by the Internet. **2** Personally, I know that too much of my time <u>is wasted</u> surfing the Internet. **3** Each link <u>is followed</u> by many others. **4** One problem is that we <u>are</u> all tempted to spend too much time and money. **5** Another more serious problem is surveillance, which <u>is</u> greatly <u>feared</u> by defenders of civil rights. **6** But the most serious problem of the Internet is that children can <u>be endangered</u> by the wrong sites and contacts. **7** I'm forced to say that the Internet <u>will</u> never be <u>loved</u> by everyone.

F 1 Un artículo polémico fue escrito por Marco Martínez. **2** Las fotos fueron hechas por su colega Guillermo González. **3** En el artículo una política muy importante es criticada. **4** Esta señora es acusada de aceptar sobornos de una gran compañía de gasolina. **5** Continuamente es vista en restaurantes muy exclusivos, acompañada por un directivo de esta compañía. **6** Según Martínez, la política ha sido convencida por la compañía para que ponga en duda el cambio climático. **7** La señora y el directivo fueron preguntados por Martínez y otros reporteros. **8** Todas las preguntas fueron ignoradas por los dos.

G 1 se habla inglés **2** lo encontró **3** Fabrican **4** Alguien me dijo **5** se conserva
1 English is spoken here. **2** The secret document was found in the street by a pedestrian. **3** These shoes are made in Mexico. **4** I was told that you had arrived. **5** The coffee is kept in the fridge.

H 1 Para hacer la escalada, se **lleva** un casco de seguridad. **2** Lo bueno del piragüismo es que **se** puede practicar todo el año. **3** La esgrima se **practica** con una espada larga y fina. **4** Si quieres hacer parapente, se **necesita** mucho coraje. **5** El buceo no **se** practica barato, el traje y el alquiler cuestan mucho. **6** Hay muchos deportes que se **practican** en el agua. **7** Las carreras en patines **se** hacen sobre una pista de hielo. **8 Gana** la persona que llega primero a la meta.

I 1 These toys are made in China. **2** All documents are sent by courier. **3** All the food is kept in the fridge. **4** Maribel was asked if she had any sharp objects in her case. **5** Nos han dicho que viene mañana. **6** Les han acusado de robar el ordenador del jefe. **7** Publicaron su libro la semana pasada. **8** ¡Cada año los pájaros comen todas nuestras cerezas!

Infinitive constructions (pages 64–65)

A 1 desear – to wish, want **2** esperar – to hope **3** gustar (a) – to like, enjoy **4** preferir – to prefer **5** ofrecer – to offer
6 querer – to want **7** decidir – to decide **8** dejar – to allow, let **9** intentar – to try, intend **10** pensar – to think about, consider **11** permitir – to allow, permit **12** saber – to know how to **13** poder – to be able to **14** lograr – to succeed in, manage to **15** necesitar – to need to **16** deber – to have to

B 1 <u>han decidido</u> **pasar 2** <u>gusta</u> **relajarse 3** <u>Prefieren</u> **encontrar 4** <u>Piensan</u> **ir 5** <u>Han ofrecido</u> **llevar 6** <u>quiere</u> **irse**, <u>permiten</u> **viajar 7** <u>quiere</u> **aprobar**, <u>debe</u> **estudiar 8** <u>podrá</u> **descansar**

C 1 Necesitas poner un anuncio para vender tu casa. **2** ¿Le

phrase	tense	gender and number
es influida	present	F. sing.
está convencida	present	F. sing.
ha sido demostrada	perfect	F. sing.
serán afectados	future	M. pl.
han sido obligados	perfect	M. pl.

permite poner la radio? **3** Con esta nueva publicidad esperamos vender más ordenadores. **4** No se puede poner publicidad de bebidas alcohólicas en la radio. **5** ¿Quiere usted ver esta foto? **6** A mi padre le gusta ver las películas americanas. **7** ¡Nosotros preferimos comer en un restaurante! **8** El profesor también debería escuchar a los estudiantes. **9** Nosotros intentamos contactar con un médico. **10** ¿Por qué tú no piensas hacerte traductor?

D **1** We have to get a doctor to come. **2** You should have your car repaired. **3** Is it possible to make those children shut up? **4** We're going to have a new kitchen put in. **5** We have the house painted every three years.

E **1** c **2** f **3** h **4** e **5** d **6** a **7** g **8** b

F **1** Tenemos que telefonearle antes de las nueve. **2** Cuando llegó al hotel, tuvo que rellenar un formulario. **3** Generalmente también hay que mostrar el pasaporte a la recepcionista. **4** ¿Tendréis que tomar un taxi en el aeropuerto? **5** Si queremos llegar a Sevilla antes de las seis, ¡tenemos que salir ahora mismo! **6** Tuvimos que cancelar la reunión porque el jefe no había llegado. **7** Es diabético, así que tiene que inyectarse cada día. **8** Para llegar al cine, hay que coger el bus.

G **1** dejar de **2** tengo miedo de **3** me canso de **4** ha persuadido/ persuadió a **5** aprende a **6** prepararse a **7** empezado / comenzado / tratado **8** se había olvidado de **9** he empezado a /comenzado a **10** enseñar a

H **1** No quiero ir a ese restaurante porque tengo miedo de encontrarlo allí. **2** Tratamos de entrar, pero la puerta estaba cerrrada con llave. **3** Nos han invitado a visitarles en su nueva casa. **4** Blanca quiere hablar contigo. **5** Le ayudé a terminar sus deberes. **6** El trabajo es fácil, consiste en contestar el teléfono y darles la bienvenida a los clientes. **7** Dejó de fumar hace dos años. ¡Lo triste es que empezó a fumar otra vez hace dos semanas! **8** Quería llamar a sus padres porque se había olvidado de darles su número de móvil.

Verbs that require different constructions in Spanish

(pages 66–67)

A **1** Having lost the match, the players felt very depressed. **2** Don't you remember seeing it? **3** The trainer must have left without saying anything to them. **4** On arriving at the club, they found that he had left. **5** After having a shower, they went to the bar. **6** Having analysed the problem seriously, they decided to change their trainer. **7** It's two o'clock – they must have all gone home by now.

B **1** haber ignorado **2** llegar **3** haber reconocido **4** oír **5** haber hablado

C **1** d, rogamos **2** b, pidió **3** f, pediré **4** a, preguntó **5** c ruega **6** e, habían pedido

D **1** sacó **2** lleve **3** tomaba **4** voy a sacar **5** va a coger

E **1** se hizó enfermera **2** se ha convertido en la más grande de nuestra ciudad **3** llegó a ser director **4** se estaba haciendo tarde **5** Voy a hacerme profesor(a)

F **1** pensamos ir **2** No creo que coma carne **3** me gusta sentarme en la playa y pensar **4** Marco cree que, tendré que pensarlo **5** Piensa hacerse dentista, no creo en realidad que pueda hacerlo

Time constructions (page 67)

A **1** El e-mail de Clementina
He conocido a un chico muy amable. Voy a hablarte de él. **Vive** (pres.) aquí <u>desde hace</u> tres meses, y **está trabajando** (pres. cont.) en nuestra oficina <u>desde hace</u> seis semanas. Es francés, pero **vive** (pres.) en España <u>desde hace</u> diez años y habla perfectamente español. Lo **conozco** (pres.) <u>desde</u> hace solamente una semana y ¡creo que me estoy enamorando de él! <u>Desde que</u> **trabaja** (pres.) con nosotros, hemos salido algunas veces.
2 Los recuerdos de Miguel Cuando conocí a Ana en 2002, ella **trabajaba** (imperf.) en Madrid <u>desde hacía</u> dos años. <u>Desde que</u> **estaba** (imperf.) en Madrid, le resultaba difícil hacer amigos, porque era muy tímida. Yo **vivía** (imperf.) allí <u>desde hacía</u> muchos años y tenía algunos amigos. Se los presenté. **Estaba saliendo** (imperf. cont.) con Ana <u>desde hacía</u> seis meses cuando decidí que quería casarme con ella. Lo triste fue que descubrí que ella **salía** (imperf.) con uno de estos famosos amigos <u>desde hacía</u> algunas semanas.

B I haven't visited London for some weeks. I worked in the capital for three years and I didn't like it. I was living in a tiny flat for two years, and then I lived in a friend's house. She let me rent a room for a year but everything was very expensive. Finally I left the city last December and I don't intend going back for many years.

Revision: more verb forms (pages 68–69)

A **1** Ignacio compraría un Ferrari. **2** Mónica y Felicia viajarían por el mundo. **3** Nosotros visitaríamos Nueva York. **4** Tú buscarías un nuevo piso. **5** Ella elegiría mucha ropa nueva. **6** Vosotros haríais instalar una nueva cocina. **7** Vds. tendrían una casa en la ciudad y otra en el campo. **8** Yo no cambiaría nada.

B **1** f **2** b **3** g **4** c **5** d **6** h **7** a **8** e

C **1** dejes **2** llame **3** ayudara **4** vengas **5** se haya muerto **6** salgáis **7** den **8** conozcas

D **1** Espero que encuentres un nuevo empleo. **2** Me sorprende que no le hayas dejado. **3** Señoras, estamos contentos de que hayan decidido visitar nuestra ciudad. **4** No es probable que el tren llegue antes de las diez. **5** No creo que vaya a terminar el trabajo antes de julio. **6** No era verdad que les hubiera hablado de vuestros problemas. **7** Nunca estuve seguro de de que me quisiera de verdad. **8** Tengo miedo de que haya tenido un accidente.

E **1** toma **2** te olvides **3** doblen **4** callaos **5** apague **6** no comáis **7** escúchame **8** dígale

F **1** The most delicious cakes are sold in that cake shop. **2** English is spoken here. **3** Programmes like this should not be shown before nine o'clock. **4** The most elegant shoes are made in Italy. **5** The victim was found in the river. **6** The candidates were interviewed on Thursday. **7** She was seen in the supermarket.

G **1** Se venden carne, queso, ropa y fruta en el mercado. **2** Se vieron con los chicos en ese bar. **3** Se habla español en muchas partes del mundo. **4** El dinero lo encontró un niño. **5** Se teme que haya desaparecido. **6** Se cree que el ministro debe dimitir.

H **1** aprender a **2** esperar – **3** preferir – **4** prepararse a

5 ofrecer – 6 consentir en 7 dejar de 8 volver a 9 poder –
10 pensar – 11 comenzar/empezar a 12 deber – 13 tener
miedo de 14 saber –

I 1 Having worked with her, I was sure she would not let me
down. 2 When we arrived at the restaurant we looked for our
friends. 3 After interviewing her, he asked her to start work in
May. 4 When we arrived at the hotel, they requested us to fill
in a form. 5 Let's have a drink and then get the bus to go into
the centre; we can take the dog with us. 6 He's going to
become an engineer, but his mother wants him to become a
doctor like his father.

J 1 desde 2 vivir 3 antes 4 hermano 5 estudia 6 dos 7 vive
8 trabajó 9 durante 10 está 11 hecho 12 en

Additional grammar for A2

The future perfect (page 70)

A Antes del fin de año … 1 habrás cambiado 2 se habrán casado
3 habrá terminado 4 habréis tenido 5 habrán vendido 6
habremos hecho pintar 7 habré aprobado
8 habrá cambiado

B 1 termines 2 pierda 3 lleguen, habrán comido 4 habrá
comprado 5 ahorren

C 1 Habrá comprendido mal. 2 Habrán aprendido mucho de esa
experiencia. 3 Habrás terminado esa tarea para mañana, ¿no?
4 Habrá estado sorprendido. 5 ¿Qué dices? Habrás bebido
demasiado.

Conditional perfect (page 70)

A 1 habría salido 2 hubiera salido 3 habrías visto 4 hubieras
visto 5 habrían llamado 6 hubieran llamado

B 1 Si los padres de Guillermo se hubieran interesado más por
su hijo, se habrían dado cuenta que tenía amigos violentos. 2
Si Guillermo hubiera estudiado más en el colegio, habría ido a
la universidad. 3 Si no hubiera visto tantas películas violentas,
no habría tenido tantas ideas románticas sobre la violencia. 4
Si hubiera logrado encontrar trabajo, habría estado más
motivado.

C 1 habría hablado 2 habría puesto 3 habrían abierto
4 habrías dicho 5 habríamos sabido 6 habrían hecho
7 habría visto 8 habríais descubierto

The past anterior (page 71)

A 1 hubo oído, **vino**, As soon as he had heard the news, he came
to see me. 2 hubieron terminado, **se marcharon**, When they
had finished their work, they left the house.
3 hubieron desaparecido, **olvidaron**, After they had
disappeared, everyone forgot them. 4 se hubieron acostado,
oyeron, They had scarcely gone to bed when they heard once
more the gentle laugh of a child. 5 hubo dejado, **se escapó**, As
soon as the thief had left his usual emblem – a broken mirror
– he escaped.

The passive – more forms (page 72)

A 1 perfect; We have been seen in this village from time to time.
2 present; Josefina is seen in the market every week.
3 imperfect; At one time they were seen in the casino every
day. 4 preterite; Javier was seen on the beach when he should
have been in school. 5 future; In my opinion, his work will not

be understood before his death. 6 pluperfect; The girls had
been seen in the bar the month before. 7 immediate future;
The actress is going to be criticized by the papers.

The subjunctive – more uses (page 72)

A 1 No voy a irme sin terminar mi trabajo. 2 No quería hacerlo
sin decírtelo. 3 Compraré esa casa a condición de que/con tal
de que/siempre que reparen el tejado. 4 Te llamo para
preguntarte cómo está tu madre. 5 ¿Podría tocar el timbre
antes de entrar? 6 Salió antes de que yo llegara. 7 Ha
ahorrado mucho dinero de manera que/de modo que/a fin de
que/para que puedan ir de vacaciones. 8 Ha ido a Madrid
para buscar un empleo.

B 1 ¡Va a seguir pidiéndoles que le ayuden hasta que consientan!
2 Aunque se lo expliqué, no lo comprendió.
3 Tan pronto como termines tu trabajo, podemos cenar.
4 Desde que empezó su nuevo trabajo, ¡no la he visto! 5
Cuando le veáis, sin duda va a preguntaros cómo estoy.

C 1 ¿Conoces a alguien que hable ruso? 2 Busco un teléfono
móvil que mis abuelos puedan usar sin problemas. 3 ¿Hay
alguien aquí que pueda decirme dónde está la calle Mercurio?
4 Lo siento, aquí no hay nadie que sepa dónde está esa calle. 5
Nunca hay nadie en esa tienda que pueda ayudarme.

Revision – Additional grammar for A2 (pages 73–74)

A 1 Ignacio habrá visto a sus amigos en Madrid. 2 Habremos
dado un paseo en bici. 3 Elena y Luisa habrán visitado a los
abuelos de Luisa. 4 Habrás visto la nueva película de
Almodóvar. 5 Habré terminado mis tareas domésticas.
6 Habréis hecho las compras. 7 Habremos cenado en un
restaurante. 8 Enrique y Pablo habrán vuelto de Pamplona.

B 1 vayas 2 termine 3 habremos comprado 4 lleguéis
5 habrán firmado 6 me diga

C 1 Si hubiera escuchado la pregunta, ¡habría podido
contestarla! 2 Estoy seguro de que si le hubieras pedido
dinero a tu hermano, te lo habría dado. 3 Si hubiéramos
recibido su carta, no nos habríamos preocupado. 4 Si la
hubieran visto, me lo habrían dicho. 5 Si hubiera querido
estar con nosotros, nos habría acompañado.

D Tan pronto como el viejo señor Ruíz hubo llegado a su pueblo
natal, descubrió que todo era diferente. Cuando hubo
terminado de ver los nuevos edificios, decidió comer algo. Por
suerte quedaba el viejo bar – después de que se hubo muerto
el viejo Manolito, su hijo Manuel continuó con la tradición
familiar. El señor Ruíz se sentó y pidió una sopa. Pidió la
cuenta apenas hubo comido. En cuanto hubo pagado, se
marchó. As soon as old Sr Ruíz had arrived in his home town,
he discovered that everything was different. When he had
finished looking at the new buildings, he decided to eat
something. Luckily the old bar was still there – after old
Manolito had died, his son Manuel continued the family
tradition. Sr Ruíz sat down and ordered some soup. He asked
for the bill when he had scarcely finished eating. As soon as
he had paid,
he left.

E Answers depend on students' own choice of forms

F 1 sepas 2 termine 3 lleguen 4 regalar 5 den 6 sean
7 prometas 8 visitéis 9 estoy 10 llama

Revision of the whole book

Pages 5–17 (page 75)

A 1 un sondeo 2 los españoles 3 la comida rápida 4 un éxito 5 los jóvenes 6 las comidas 7 la mesa 8 la familia 9 una porción 10 patatas fritas 11 una fabada 12 la coca-cola 13 al vino

B 1 Esta nueva ley es importante para la economía rural de España. 2 Muchos coches viejos españoles son una fuente importante de contaminación. 3 Hacer las compras en Internet es rápido y fácil, y puede ser barato, pero es difícil saber si los artículos son de buena calidad. 4 Aparentemente el antiguo primer ministro quiso ayudar a las familias más pobres. 5 Muchos estudiantes ingleses quieren hacerse informáticos ricos. 6 A mis abuelos les gusta su granja tranquila, y la tráfico en el gran ciudad es demasiado ruidoso para ellos.

C 1 Mis 2 tuyos 3 mi 4 su 5 mío 6 mi 7 su 8 mi 9 mis 10 sus 11 su 12 nuestra

D 1 ¿Qué parte de España prefieres? ¿Esta región o el norte? 2 Los pueblos de esta región son mucho más pobres que las ciudades de aquella. 3 ¿Cuál es la razón principal de la pobreza en esta región?

4 Esta tierra es muy pobre, y ¿ves ese río? Generalmente no es así; está seco de mayo a octubre así que todas estas granjas sufren de falta de agua. 5 ¿Qué productos cultivan los agricultores? 6 Bueno, en esta hacienda cultivamos naranjas y aguacates; en esa granja que ves en aquella colina, sólo cultivan lo que necesitan para ellos y para sus animales.

E 1 mucho más importante 2 completamente diferente 3 no muy rápido 4 bastante interesante 5 demasiado caro 6 muchas veces 7 especialmente difícil 8 realmente increíble 9 con mucho cuidado 10 totalmente imposible

Pages 18–31 (page 76)

A 1 a, de 2 desde, hasta 3 enfrente de 4 en, a, de, en 5 a, al, para 6 según, de 7 para, a, hasta, al lado del, 8 por, para, a 9 de, en, a, en, para, de 10 a, al, a

B 1 Me gusta la televisión; la veo cada tarde. 2 Pusieron el partido en la televisión ayer por la tarde. ¿Lo viste? No, no me interesan los programas de deporte, nunca los veo. 3 Y ¿las noticias? Sí, las encuentro más interesantes. 4 ¿Has enviado esa carta a tu abuela? Sí, **se la** envié ayer. 5 ¿Tienes tus llaves? No, **las** he perdido, estoy buscándo**las**. ¿**Las** has visto? 6 Si no te gusta la carne, déjala. 7 Lorenzo, ¿has terminado tus deberes? Hay que terminar**los** antes de ver la televisión. 8 Este libro es para Maribel. Si la encuentras, ¿podrías dár**selo**?

C 1 Le vi el domingo y voy a verle otra vez esta noche. 2 ¡Mira estas flores! Mis padres me las enviaron. 3 Esteban, no has comido tu ensalada. ¡Cómetela, por favor! 4 He visto un juego de ordenador fantástico y sé que le gustaría a mi hermano. Voy a comprárselo y así yo podré cogerlo prestado también. 5 ¿Has visto la nueva película de Antonio Banderas? Tienes que verla, nos gustó mucho. 6 ¡Ese es mi bocadillo! ¡Dámelo, por favor! 7 La vieron ayer y le dijeron que había salido. 8 Si ve a Manuela y Gerardo, dígales que me llamen.

D 1 que 2 en la que 3 cuya 4 que 5 el cual 6 por la cual 7 donde 8 el cual 9 con quien 10 que

E 1 Hay dos mochilas rojas – ¿cuál es la tuya? Esa, la más grande. 2 ¿Qué fotos quieres guardar? Esta y esta, no me gustan esas. 3 ¿Qué casa prefieres, la suya o la nuestra? La vuestra, por supuesto. 4 ¿Qué coche es el suyo? Aquel. 5 Acabo de terminar mis tareas domésticas, ¡no voy a hacer las tuyas también! 6 ¿Qué vaqueros vas a comprar? Aquellos, ¡son como los tuyos! 7 Mi perro es mucho más cariñoso que el suyo, ¡hasta él prefiere el mío! 8 ¿Qué gafas son las tuyas? Esas.

Pages 32–37 (page 77)

A 1 viven 2 sale, se levanta 3 conocemos, vivimos, gusta 4 está durmiendo 5 visitan, Comen, toman, charlan, escuchan 6 Acabo, estoy esperando 7 Os acostais, vemos, nos acostamos 8 hablo, está trabajando, se pone, molesto

B 1 juega, puede, se siente, tiene, duelen 2 me despierto, me levanto, salgo, tengo, encuentro, voy, vienen, cierra, vuelvo, ceno, veo, toco 3 vas, voy, hago, vais, vamos, viene, pienso

C 1 *estar* because it describes location. 2 [a] *ser* because it describes an aspect of her personality; [b] *estar* because it describes a temporary state. 3 [a] *estar* because it describes location; [b] *ser* because it describes a physical characteristic; [c] as [b]; [d] *estar* because it describes location. 4 [a] *ser* because it describes a physical characteristic; [b] *estar* because it describes a temporary state; [c] and [d] as [b]; [e] *ser* because it describes a long-term characteristic; [f] *estar* because it describes location. 5 [a] *ser* because it describes a long-term characteristic; [b] as [a]; [c] *estar* because it describes a current activity and forms part of a verb in the present continuous; [d] *estar* because it describes location and/or a temporary situation.

D 1 Siempre llega a tiempo, ¿no? 2 Nunca como hamburguesas pero tengo que admitir que me gustan las patatas fritas. 3 Les he llamado otra vez hoy por la mañana, pero nadie contesta nunca el teléfono en esa casa. 4 Cuando van de compras, él compra muchas cosas, ¡y ella no compra nada! No entra siquiera en las tiendas, no le gusta ninguna de ellas. 5 No me quedan cervezas, ni vino ni café. ¡Nada para ofrecer a los invitados! Lo bueno es que nunca tengo invitados. No tengo a nadie con quien hablar, tranquilo, ¿no? 6 Ni Carlos ni José hablan inglés, y yo no hablo español, así que ¡nunca tenemos nada que decirnos!

Pages 38–51 (page 78)

A 1 ha encontrado, ha puesto 2 ha dicho 3 has visto 4 has hecho, he pasado, he telefoneado, he terminado, he reservado 5 hemos vuelto 6 ha prohibido

B 1 Hice mis ejercicios. 2 El ayuntamiento construyó un nuevo parking en el centro de la ciudad. 3 No pude contactarte el jueves. 4 ¿Fuisteis a Salamanca? Sí, fuimos a la universidad a visitar a mi hermana. 5 Salimos a las ocho y volvimos a las once. 6 ¿Vendieron ustedes su casa? 7 Ana y Esteban tuvieron un hijo. 8 Cuando vino a vernos, trajo a su horrible perro. 9 El sábado comimos en un restaurante, pero el domingo mis padres vinieron a comer con nosotros en casa. 10 ¿Viajaste a Gerona en tren? No, cogí el autobús.

C 1 fumaba 2 costaban 3 fumaba 4 descubrieron 5 tomó

6 tenía **7** obligaron **8** habló **9** dijeron **10** hizo **11** se preocupaban **12** representaba

D **1** Cuando entraron, estaba leyendo el periódico. **2** Cuando me llamaste, estaba bañándome. **3** Cuando llegasteis, todavía estábamos preparando la cena. **4** Cuando le vi, estaba durmiendo en el jardín. **5** Lo siento, me dijo su nombre pero no estaba escuchando.

E **1** había aprendido **2** había visto **3** había llegado **4** se había retrasado **5** habían llevado, se había escapado **6** había visto

F **1** habrá **2** irá **3** compraremos **4** veremos **5** podrán **6** inventarán **7** protegerán **8** hará **9** consumiremos **10** será

Pages 52–59 (page 80)

A **1** Me gustaría viajar en Argentina y Perú. **2** Me dijo que llegaría a las diez y media. **3** No saldría con Rafael, ¡es aburrido! **4** Yo que tú/en tu lugar, dejaría el puesto. **5** ¿Podrías explicarle esta decisión? **6** Una persona en forma llegaría en de tres horas; ¡yo necesitaría cuatro horas! **7** Yo que tú/en tu lugar no vería esa película.
8 Mi madre diría que deberías ser más prudente.

B **1** ayude **2** lleguemos **3** hayas terminado **4** fumemos **5** saliera **6** hable **7** haya escuchado **8** pudieran **9** hagas **10** haya encontrado

C (suggested answers) **1** dijera/haya dicho **2** sepas **3** vengamos/estemos/salgamos **4** lleguen **5** estuvieran **6** ayude **7** llame **8** veamos **9** salga/haya salido/esté **10** vayan/hayan ido **11** den **12** pudiera

D **1** Si la ves, dile que se ponga en contacto conmigo. **2** Si la viera, no le hablaría. **3** Si no llegan pronto, saldremos sin ellos. **4** Si llegaran a tiempo, me sorprendería mucho. **5** Si pudiera, vendría con ustedes **6** Si viviéramos en Madrid, ¡saldríamos cada noche! **7** Si me hubieras explicado tus problemas, habría tratado de ayudarte. **8** Si me hubiera escuchado, no habría encontrado estas dificultades.
9 Si ahorro bastante dinero, me cambiaré a un piso más grande, pero si ganara un millón de euros, dejaría esta ciudad. **10** Si hubierais estado con nosotros el domingo, todos habríamos podido ver esa película.

Pages 60–69 (page 81)

A **1** poneos **2** te olvides **3** pásamelo **4** ven, toma **5** se preocupen **6** tiren, llévenselos **7** tocad **8** vamos **9** digas **10** levantaos, duchaos

B **1** Siempre se le ve en el bar. **2** Los vieron en el restaurante Marina ayer. **3** La tienda del señor Martín se ha cerrado/Han cerrado la tienda del señor Martín – las frutas y las verduras se venden hoy en día en el supermercado. **4** No me gustan las películas que ponen en la televisión por la mañana. **5** Fabrican estos zapatos en España, pero fabrican toda esa ropa en Korea. **6** Han actualizado mi ordenador y ahora es mucho más rápido.
7 La describieron como tímida, pero ¡nunca deja de hablar! **8** No van a terminar el edificio antes del fin de año.
9 Se teme que mucha gente haya muerto en el huracán. **10** Se dice que las mujeres hablan más que los hombres, pero ¿quién ha dicho eso?

C **1** ¿Queréis ver nuestras fotos? **2** Espero llegar antes de la cena. **3** Le gusta jugar al tenis. **4** Ofrecieron ayudarnos pero no era necesario. **5** Prefiero viajar en tren. **6** Pensamos visitar Barcelona. **7** ¿Sabes hacer gazpacho? **8** No me dejó pagar la comida. **9** Logramos abrir la puerta. **10** ¡Tienes que leer ese libro! **11** No pude comprender nada de lo que dijo. **12** Nos están reparando el coche. **13** Tuvieron que vender su casa. **14** ¡Me hicieron cantar delante de toda esa gente! **15** Necesito preguntarle algo.

D **1** On arriving in Madrid they found that Michaela had left. **2** I don't remember having said that. **3** David should have received your message. **4** After seeing the film, we went to a Mexican restaurant. **5** They have asked me to go with them. **6** No smoking. **7** Don't ask me why I did that. **8** After taking some photos, they had a beer in the square. **9** Do you want me to take you to the airport? It's not necessary, I'm going to take the bus. **10** I want to become a translator. **11** This town has become an important centre. **12** I've worked for this company for ten years. **13** Julio had been living in Pamplona for three months when he met her. **14** We haven't seen her for a few days. **15** Since I've been here I've made lots of new friends.

Pages 70–74 (page 82)

A Antes del fin de semana, Hernando habrá comprado un nuevo teléfono móvil; vosotros habréis pintado la casa; yo habré escrito mi artículo; tú habrás aprobado tu examen; nosotros habremos terminado nuestro proyecto; Cristina habrá elegido su nuevo coche; y Enrique e Isabel habrán vuelto de sus vacaciones.

B **1** He was not sure that he had shut the door. **2** Didn't you believe I had gone without you? **3** It seemed unlikely to me that you would have said anything about that to them. **4** I was surprised that they'd forgotten your name. **5** We were expecting/hoping that they would have understood the situation. **6** Didn't it surprise you that they had got married? **7** If they'd had enough money they would have bought a car. **8** If my sister had passed her exams she would have gone to study in Madrid. **9** If Tomás had found a job, he would have stayed in his home town. **10** You know that if I had seen you I would have said hello.

C **1** No voy a hablarle si no se disculpe. **2** Querrán salir tan pronto como llegue. **3** Seguiré intentando hasta que tenga éxito. **4** No creo que pagaran mucho por ese ordenador. **5** ¿Conoces a alguien que hable alemán? **6** Busco alguien que pueda reparar mi coche. **7** ¡Buscamos un regalo para Marisol, pero no encontramos nada que le guste!
8 Te digo esto para que puedas prepararte para sus preguntas. **9** Vendré a la fiesta con tal que/siempre que invites a Antonio. **10** A menos que todos hagamos un esfuerzo, los problemas del medio ambiente irán de mal en peor.

D **1** Van a expulsar a aquel ministro antes de fin de año.
2 A los niños les habían advertido que no jugaran allí.
3 Se la ha visto aquí de vez en cuando. **4** Le escucharé pero no me convencerá nada de lo que pueda decir. **5** Cuando estaba enferma, toda la familia la visitó. **6** No me dijo que la habían entrevistado para ese puesto.

MEL BAY'S
Mandolin Chords

This book was created in response to many requests
for a catalog of mandolin chords arranged in a photo-diagram form
for maximum ease in understanding and playing.

Mel Bay

Online Video

To Access the Online Video Go To:
dv.melbay.com/93257 - download
or
www.melbay.com/93257V - YouTube

INDEX OF CHORDS

THE CORRECT WAY TO HOLD THE
MANDOLIN

THIS IS THE PICK

Hold it in

this manner ⟶

firmly between the

thumb and first finger.

Use a medium

soft pick.

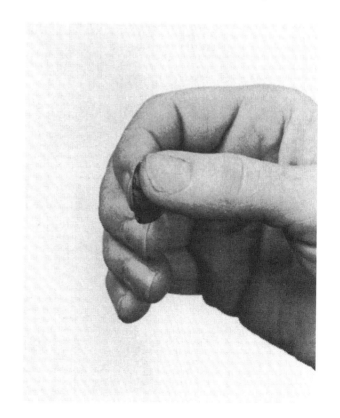

4

THE LEFT HAND

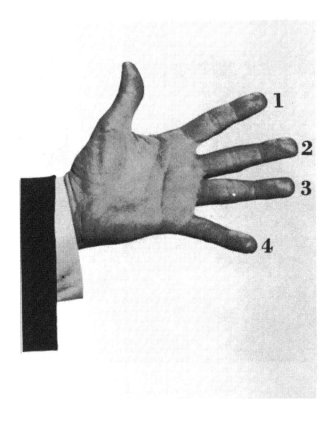

Practice
holding the
Mandolin
in this
manner.

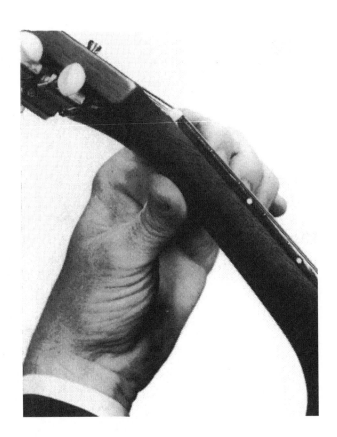

Keep the palm
of the hand
away from the
neck of the
instrument.

THE FINGERBOARD

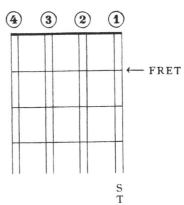

← FRET

S T R I N G

The vertical lines
are the strings.

The horizontal lines
are the frets.

The encircled numbers
are the number of the strings.

Striking the Strings

⊓ = Down stroke
of the pick.

TUNING THE MANDOLIN

First String . . . . E ①
Second String . . . . A ②
Third String . . . . D ③
Fourth String . . . . G ④

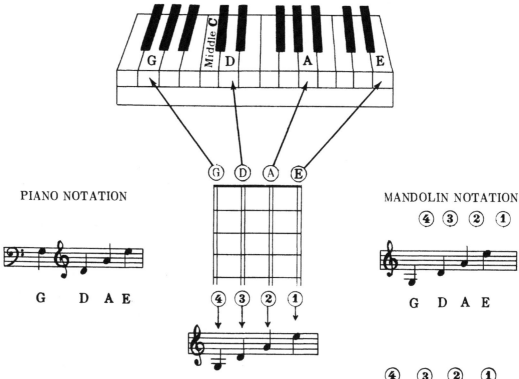

PIANO NOTATION

G   D A E

MANDOLIN NOTATION

④ ③ ② ①

G D A E

ANOTHER METHOD OF TUNING

PLACE THE FINGER BEHIND THE SEVENTH FRET OF THE FOURTH
STRING TO OBTAIN THE PITCH OF THE THIRD STRING (D).

PLACE THE FINGER BEHIND THE SEVENTH FRET OF THE THIRD
STRING TO OBTAIN THE PITCH OF THE SECOND STRING (A).

PLACE THE FINGER BEHIND THE SEVENTH FRET OF THE SECOND
STRING TO OBTAIN THE PITCH OF THE FIRST STRING (E).

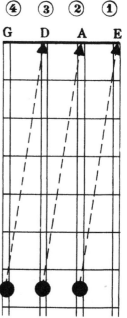

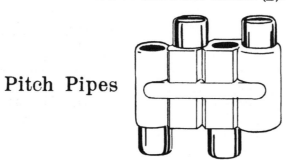

Pitch Pipes

PITCH PIPES FOR THE MANDOLIN (VIOLIN) MAY BE PURCHASED
AT ANY MUSIC STORE. EACH PIPE WILL HAVE THE CORRECT PITCH
OF EACH MANDOLIN STRING. THESE ARE AN EXCELLENT INVESTMENT.

THE MAJOR CHORDS

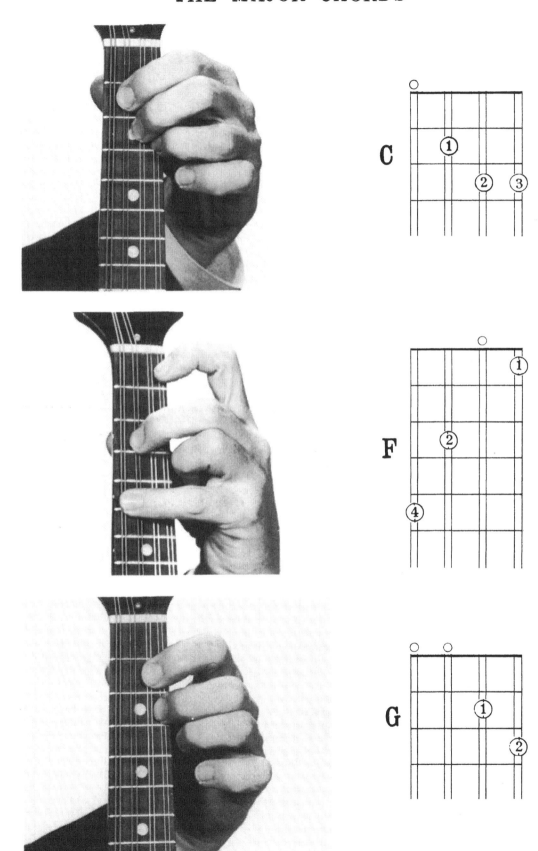

SEE THE MEL BAY "FUN WITH THE MANDOLIN"

THE MAJOR CHORDS

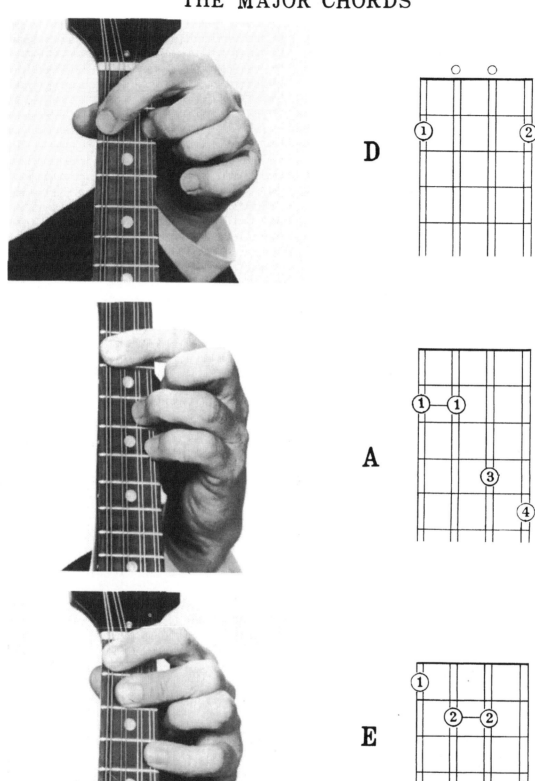

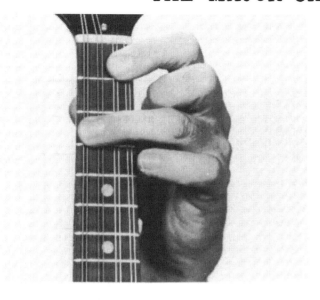

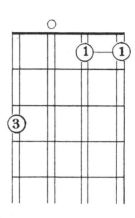

B♭

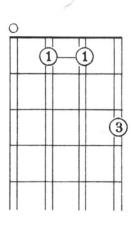

E♭

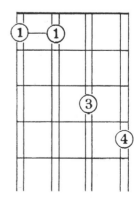

A♭

THE MAJOR CHORDS

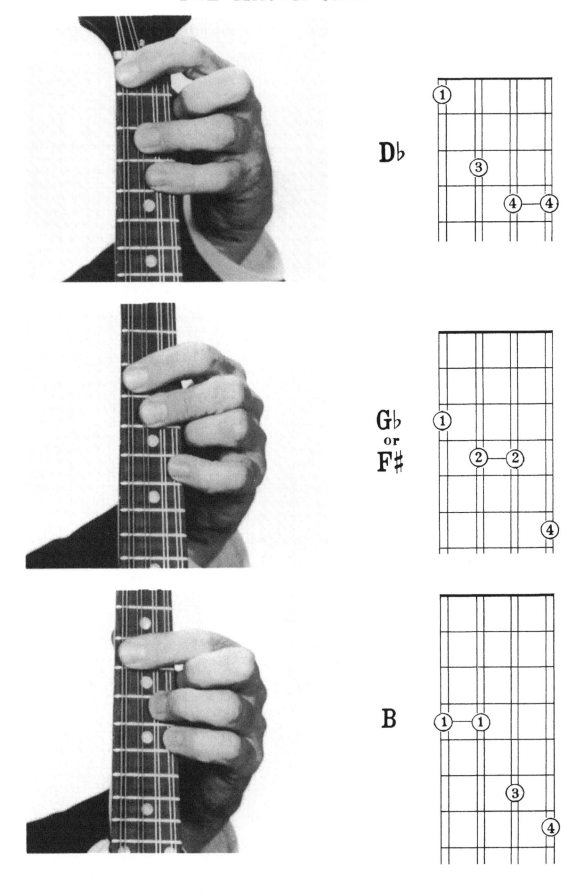

THE MINOR CHORDS
(m = Minor)

Cm

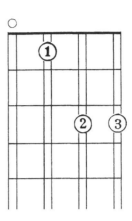

Fm

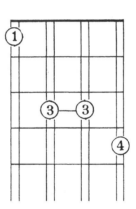

Gm

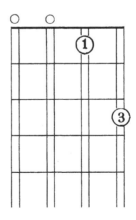

THE MINOR CHORDS

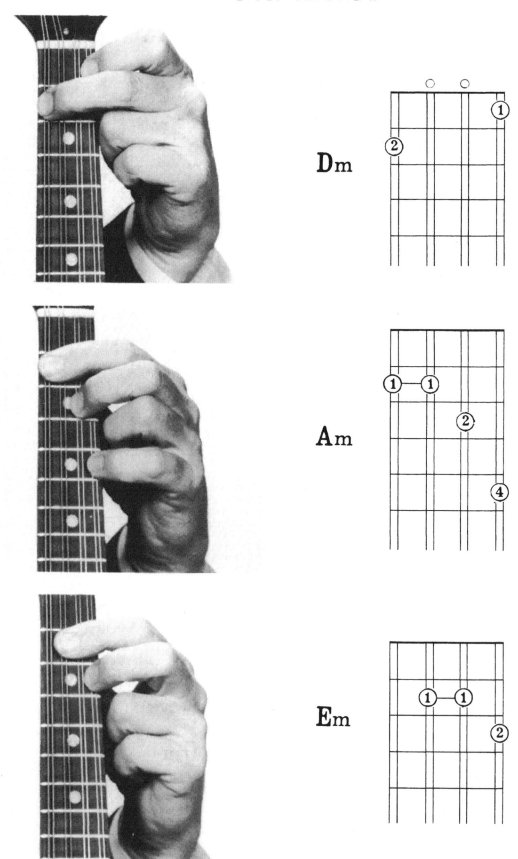

Dm

Am

Em

SEE THE MEL BAY "FUN WITH THE MANDOLIN"

B♭m

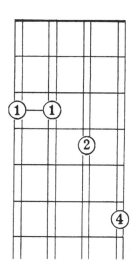

E♭m

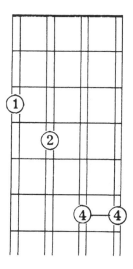

A♭m

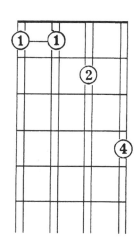

THE MINOR CHORDS

D♭m

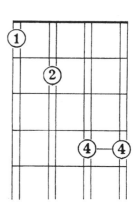

G♭m
or
F♯m

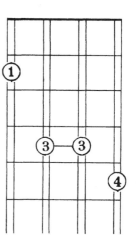

Bm

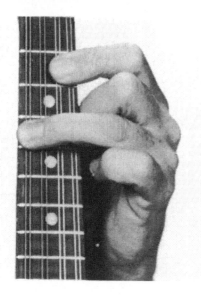

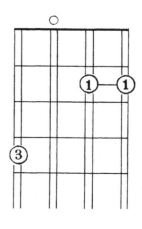

THE SEVENTH CHORDS
(7 = Seventh Chord)

C7

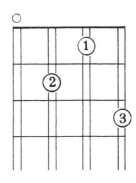

F7

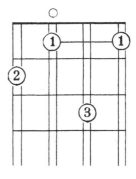

G7

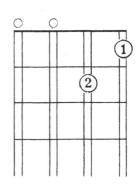

THE SEVENTH CHORDS

D7

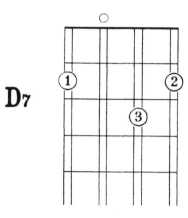

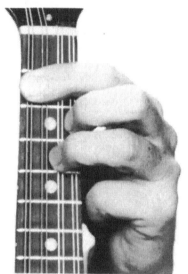

A7

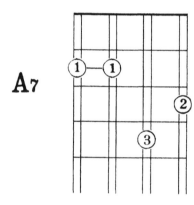

E7

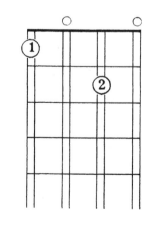

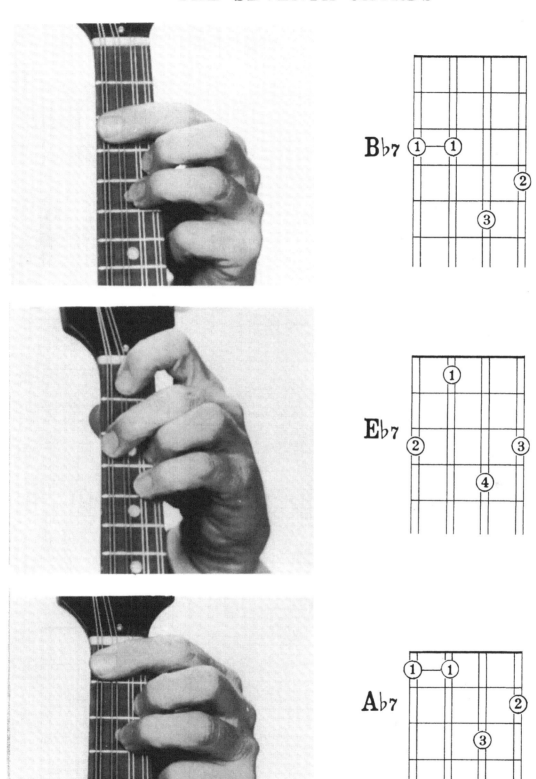

SEE THE MEL BAY "FUN WITH THE MANDOLIN"

THE SEVENTH CHORDS

D♭7

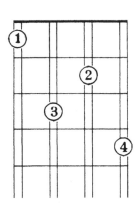

G♭7
or
F♯7

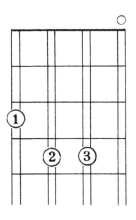

B7

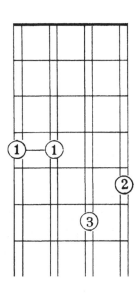

THE DIMINISHED CHORDS

(−) = Diminished)

A♭-
G♯- D- B- F-

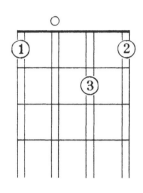

A- E♭- C- F♯-
         G♭-

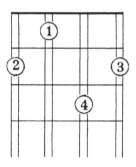

B♭- E- C♯- G-
        D♭-

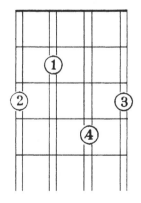

Each Diminished form can represent four different chords.

THE AUGMENTED CHORDS
(+) = Augmented

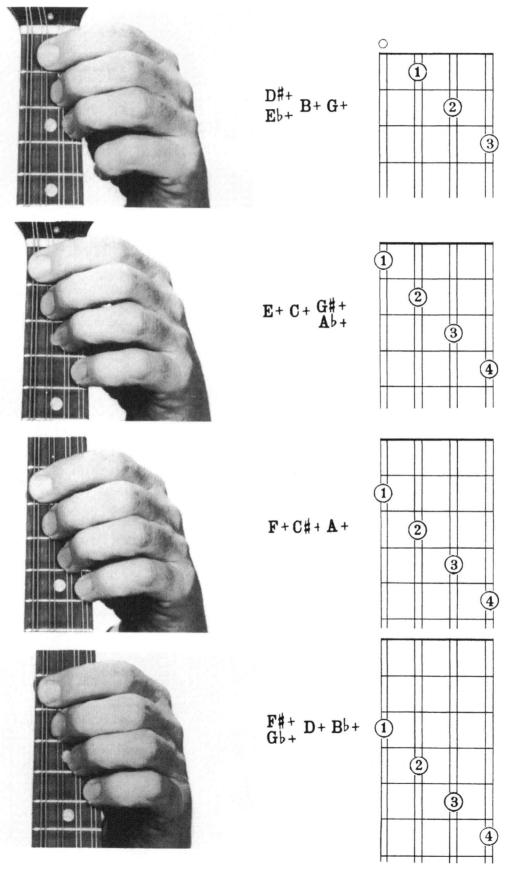

D#+
Eb+ B+ G+

E+ C+ G#+
Ab+

F+ C#+ A+

F#+
Gb+ D+ Bb+

Each form represents three chords.

THE NINTH CHORDS
(9 = Ninth)

C_9

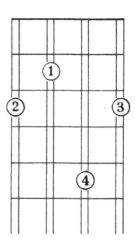

F_9

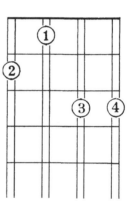

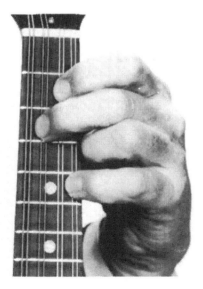

G_9

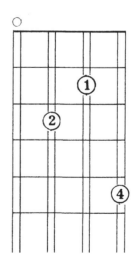

THE NINTH CHORDS

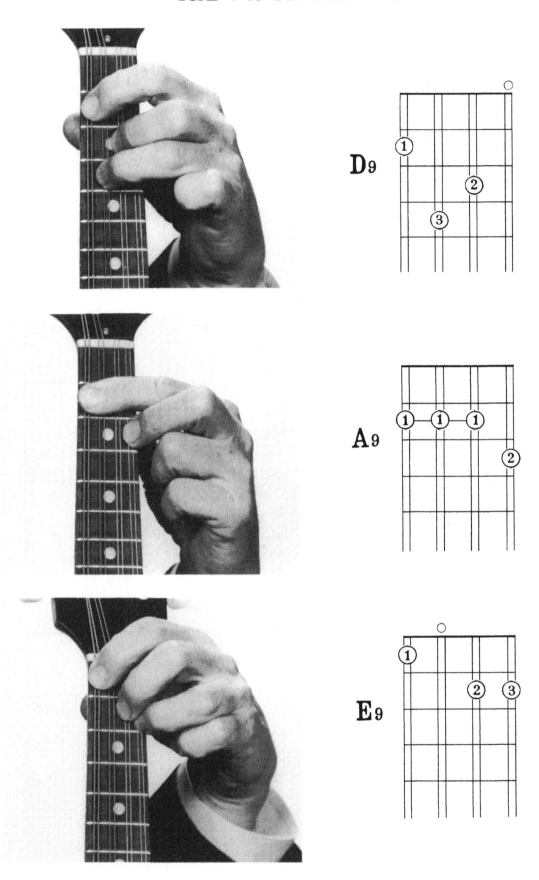

SEE THE MEL BAY "FUN WITH THE MANDOLIN"

THE NINTH CHORDS

B♭9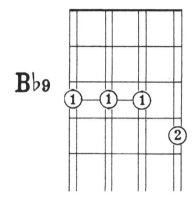

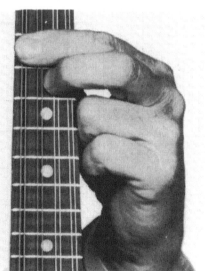

E♭9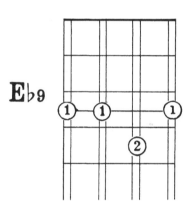

A♭9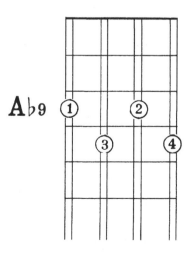

THE NINTH CHORDS

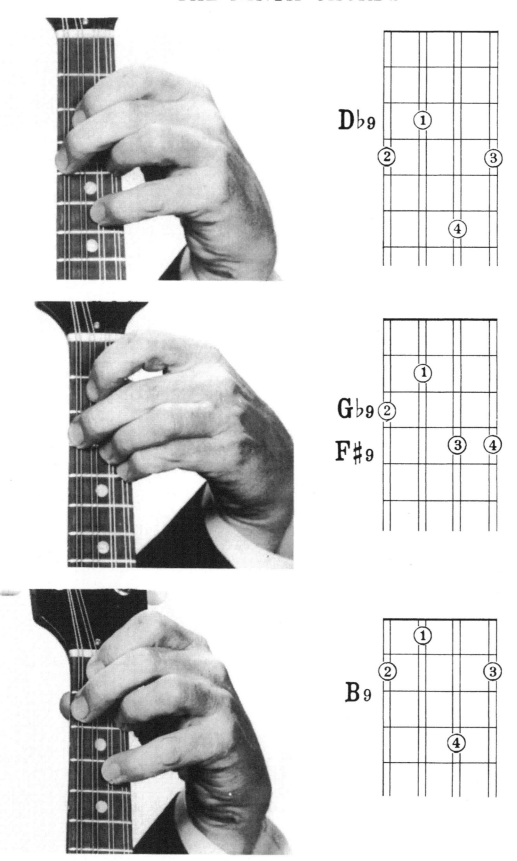

THE MAJOR SEVENTH CHORDS

(ma7 = Major Seventh)

Cma7

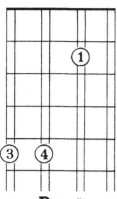

Fma7

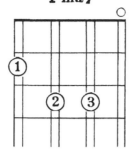

Gma7

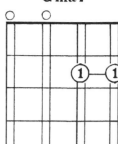

Dma7

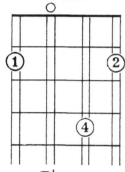

Ama7

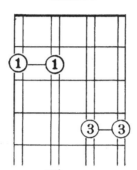

Ema7

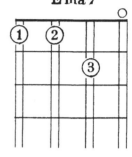

B♭ma7

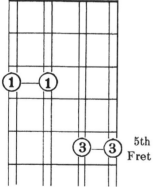

5th Fret

E♭ma7

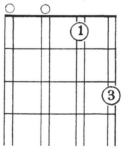

A♭ma7

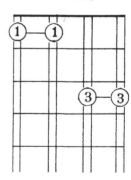

D♭ma7

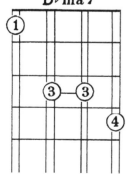

G♭ma7 & F♯ma7

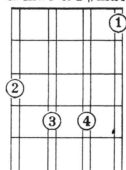

Bma7

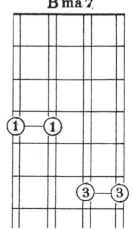

6th Fret

THE MINOR SEVENTH CHORDS
(m7 = Minor Seventh)

Cm7
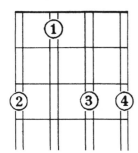

Fm7
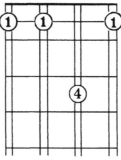

Gm7
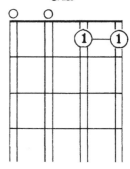

Dm7
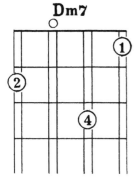

Am7
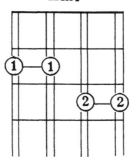

Em7
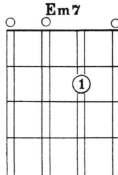

B♭m7
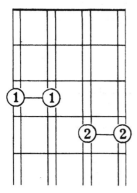

E♭m7
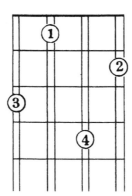

A♭m7
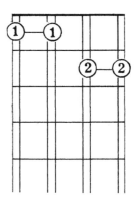

D♭m7
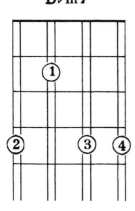

G♭m7 & F#m7
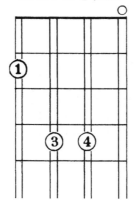

Bm7
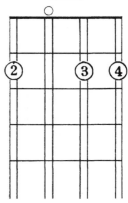

THE SIXTH CHORDS
(6 = Sixth)

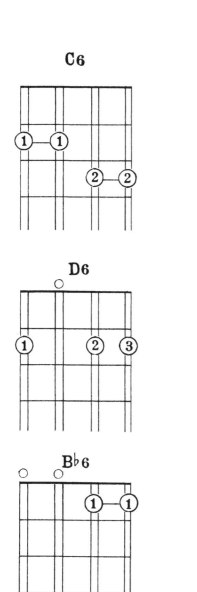

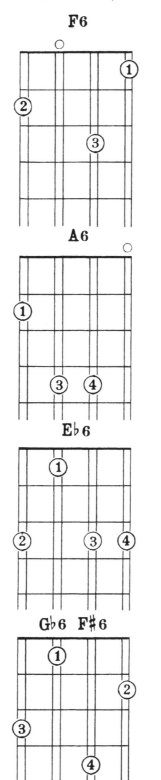

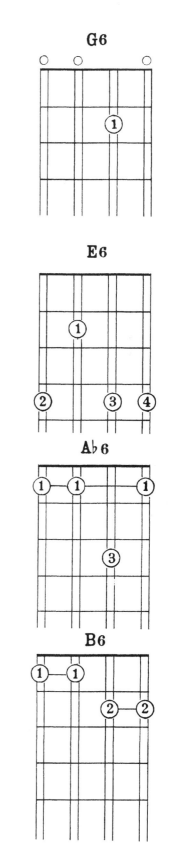

THE MINOR SIXTH CHORDS
(m6 = Minor Sixth)

Cm6
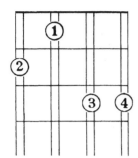

Fm6
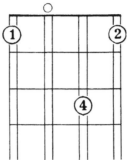

Gm6
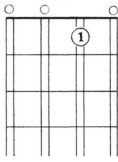

Dm6
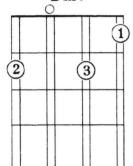

Am6
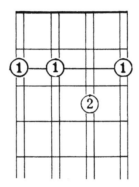

Em6
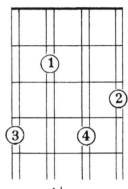

B♭m6
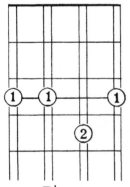

E♭m6
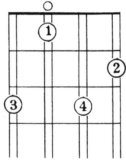

A♭m6
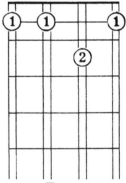

D♭m6
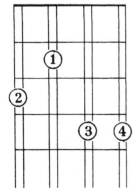

G♭m6 F♯m6
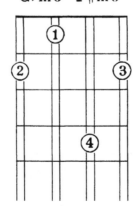

Bm6
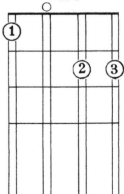

THE SEVENTH AUGMENTED FIFTH
(7 +5)

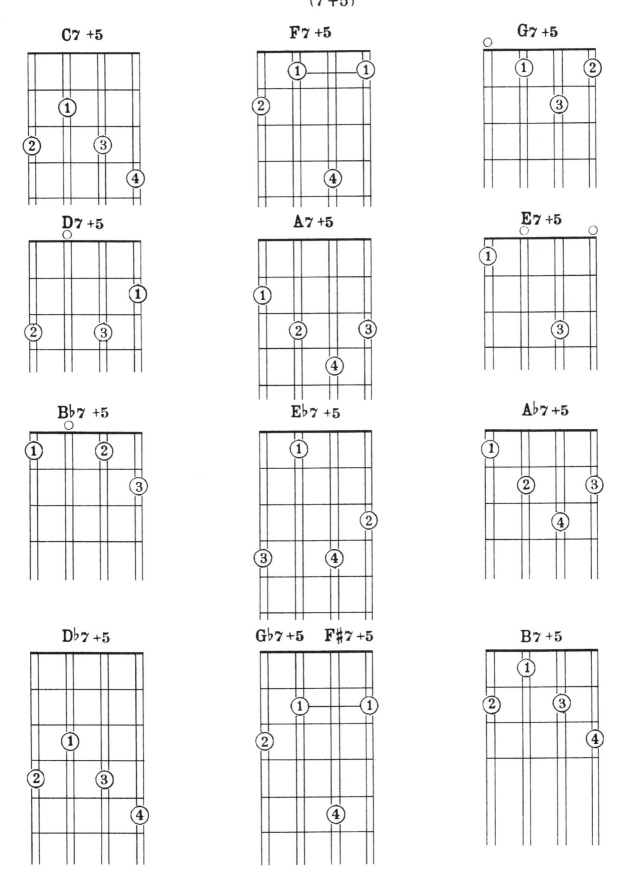

SEE THE MEL BAY "FUN WITH THE MANDOLIN"

THE SEVENTH DIMINISHED FIFTH
(7 −5)

C7 −5

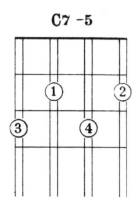

F7 −5

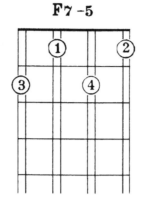

G7 −5

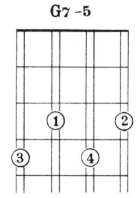

D7 −5

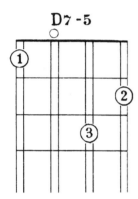

A7 −5

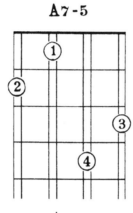

E7 −5

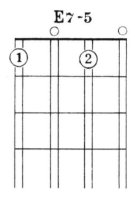

B♭7 −5

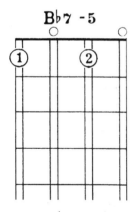

E♭7 −5

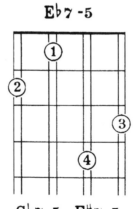

A♭7 −5

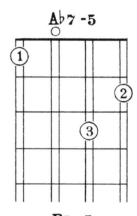

D♭7 −5

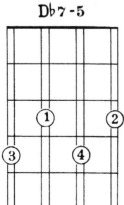

G♭7 −5   F♯7 −5

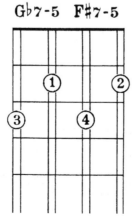

B7 −5

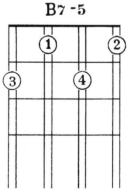

SUMMARY
The Major Chords

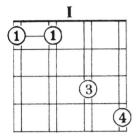

I

Frets	1	2	3	4	5	6	7	8	9	10	11	12
Chords	Ab	A	Bb	B	C	C# Db	D	Eb	E	F	F# Gb	G

III

Frets	1	2	3	4	5	6	7	8	9	10	11	12
Chords	E	F	F# Gb	G	Ab	A	Bb	B	C	C# Db	D	Eb

V

Frets	1	2	3	4	5	6	7	8	9	10	11	12
Chords	C# Db	D	Eb	E	F	F# Gb	G	Ab	A	Bb	B	C

The Minor Chords

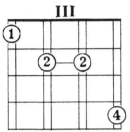

Im

Frets	1	2	3	4	5	6	7	8	9	10	11	12
Chords	Abm	Am	Bbm	Bm	Cm	C#m Dbm	Dm	Ebm	Em	Fm	F#m Gbm	Gm

IIIm

Frets	1	2	3	4	5	6	7	8	9	10	11	12
Chords	Fm	F#m Gbm	Gm	Abm	Am	Bbm	Bm	Cm	C#m Dbm	Dm	Ebm	Em

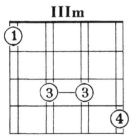

Vm

Frets	1	2	3	4	5	6	7	8	9	10	11	12
Chords	Dbm	Dm	Ebm	Em	Fm	Gbm F#m	Gm	Abm	Am	Bbm	Bm	Cm

THE SEVENTH CHORDS

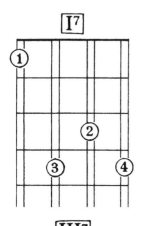

I⁷

Frets	1	2	3	4	5	6	7	8	9	10	11	12
Chords	A♭7	A7	B♭7	B7	C7	D♭7 C♯7	D7	E♭7	E7	F7	G♭7 F♯7	G7

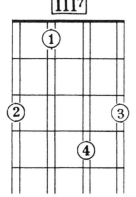

III⁷

Frets	1	2	3	4	5	6	7	8	9	10	11	12
Chords	E♭7	E7	F7	F♯7 G♭7	G7	A♭7	A7	B♭7	B7	C7	C♯7 D♭7	D7

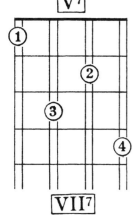

V⁷

Frets	1	2	3	4	5	6	7	8	9	10	11	12
Chords	D♭7	D7	E♭7	E7	F7	G♭7 F♯7	G7	A♭7	A7	B♭7	B7	C7

VII⁷

Frets	1	2	3	4	5	6	7	8	9	10	11	12
Chords	A♭7	A7	B♭7	B7	C7	D♭7 C♯7	D7	E♭7	E7	F7	G♭7 F♯7	G7

THE ROMAN NUMERAL ABOVE THE FORM INDICATES
THE CHORDAL TONE FOUND ON THE FIRST STRING.

SEE THE MEL BAY "FUN WITH THE MANDOLIN"

Printed in Poland
by Amazon Fulfillment
Poland Sp. z o.o., Wrocław